BLOCKADE RUNNERS OF THE CONFEDERACY

Courtesy of the Library of Congress

Powder Monkey on USS *New Hampshire* off Charleston.

Blockade Runners
of the Confederacy

HAMILTON COCHRAN

With a New Introduction by Robert M. Browning Jr.

THE UNIVERSITY OF ALABAMA PRESS
Tuscaloosa

To the memory of my mother, Helen Scudder Cochran

"Gashed with honorable scars,
Low in glory's lap they lie,
Though they fell they fell like stars,
Screaming splendor through the sky."

Introduction to the 2005 Edition
Copyright © 2005
The University of Alabama Press
Tuscaloosa, Alabama 35487-0380
All rights reserved
Manufactured in the United States of America

Typeface: AGaramond

∞

The paper on which this book is printed meets the minimum requirements of
American National Standard for Information Science—Permanence of Paper
for Printed Library Materials, ANSI Z39.48–1984.

Library of Congress Cataloging-in-Publication Data

Cochran, Hamilton, 1898–
  Blockade runners of the Confederacy / Hamilton Cochran ; with a new
introduction by Robert M. Browning Jr.
    p. cm.
"Fire Ant books."
  Previously published: Indianapolis : Bobbs-Merrill, [1958].
  Includes bibliographical references and index.
  ISBN 0-8173-5169-8 (pbk. : alk. paper)
  1. United States—History—Civil War, 1861–1865—Blockades. 2. Confed-
erate States of America. Navy—History. I. Title.
  E600.C6 2005
  973.7'57—dc22   2004016605

Contents

List of Illustrations

Introduction to the 2005 Edition

Robert M. Browning Jr.

O_N 19 A_{PRIL} 1861, less than a week after the surrender of Fort Sumter, President Abraham Lincoln proclaimed his intention to block-ade the Southern states. This proclamation officially gave the navy its first task of the Civil War. Lincoln, however, could not have fully comprehended the magnitude of such an assignment. This presidential decree authorized warships to halt the maritime trade along a coast stretching more than 3,000 miles. With less than fifty commissioned vessels, the naval force was far from capable of effectively performing this duty. The call for a blockade, which created the need for a large navy may have been the wisest of Lincoln's wartime decisions.

In the first months after Lincoln's proclamation, sailing vessels predomi-nantly ran the blockade. But as the Union Navy was able to build and buy more gunboats to watch the coast of the Southern states, vessels powered by wind alone could not successfully elude the burgeoning number of Union warships stationed off the coast. Nevertheless, sailing vessels, particularly fast schooners, continued successfully to run the blockade in small num-bers for the remainder of the war.

As the war unfolded, stopping the steam blockade runners developed into a major challenge for the U.S. Navy. During 1861, when the navy had few ships at sea, virtually any vessel might be used as a blockade runner. But as the navy deployed greater numbers of ships to watch the coast, the blockade runners gradually evolved to meet the challenges posed by the large number of blockading vessels. New, specially designed blockade run-ners were constructed expressively for speed. They were usually built of iron or steel, had extremely narrow beams, rakish designs, and sometimes turtle-back forward decks to help them drive through heavy seas.

The swift blockade runners regularly slipped through the cordon of Union ships. Avoiding detection was singularly the most important characteristic necessary for their success. In many cases these vessels carried only a light pair of lower masts, and the hull was designed to show little above the wa-ter. To make them even harder to spot, they were usually camouflaged with a dull grey coat of paint. The captain kept the ship's boats lowered to the gunwales, and some steamers had telescoping funnels that could be lowered to the deck in order to maintain a low profile. When they approached the shore, these vessels blew their steam off under water, showed no lights, and sometimes muffled their paddle wheels with canvas, all to avoid detection. Under certain stages of the moon and the atmosphere the blockade runners were almost invisible at even 100 yards. They blended so perfectly with their surroundings that on dark nights only their wakes could be seen as they steamed by the Union sentinels. The famed blockade running Captain John Wilkinson boasted that the blockade runners seemed "almost as invisible as Harlequin in the pantomime."

It is easy to imagine the masters of these sleek vessels carefully approaching the coast, probing their way to ensure they would avoid detection. Avoiding the Union ships, though, was not always difficult. The blockaders themselves often served as navigational aids. Most of the large blockaders had lofty masts and rigging that betrayed their positions long before the Yankee lookouts could spot the diminutive blockade runners. The Union officers referred to their vessels as "buoys" and "floating beacons" that warned the blockade runners to steer clear.

The blockade was more complex than just having warships anchored off the coast and watching the major ports. In a larger context, the Union blockade of the South was an attack on its economic infrastructure. This economic warfare was carried further with the capture of coastal towns by the union forces. Small landing parties from naval warships often destroyed the Confederate populace's means of making a living and also disrupted the local economy. Just the presence of the gunboats along the coasts and in the rivers and sounds was usually enough to keep the local populace concerned.

A successful blockade-running trade was essential for the South to sustain itself in the war with the more industrialized and more populous Union. During the four years of conflict, blockade runners brought into the South at least 400,000 small arms from Europe. Historians have estimated that over 300 cargoes of munitions alone reached Confederate ports. The munitions imports virtually sustained the Confederate army during four years of fighting.

Just how much was imported and exported is still being argued. Nevertheless, tremendous amounts of goods came through the blockade and varied in size from straight pins to marine engines. To balance its foreign trade the Confederacy exported mostly cotton, but early in the war did export small quantities of flour and meal, bacon, hams, lard, linseed oil, corn, rice, tallow, and wheat. Cotton continued to be the main export during the war, but large quantities of tobacco and naval stores also found their way to foreign markets.

High profits on the cargoes were the lure for many foreign businessmen to get into the trade. A single round trip might allow profits enough to pay for both cargoes and the vessel. These high returns ensured that the trade continued throughout the war.

The Union blockade was never able to keep all contraband from reaching the Confederacy. Nevertheless, the blockade did severely damage the Confederate war effort. Without a blockade, the Confederacy would have been free to import every object necessary for the continuation of the war, and to export freely cotton to sustain its purchases. Instead the South could import only the most important articles, while shipments containing items such as locomotives, railroad iron, and other equipment and machinery came into the Confederacy in small quantities. The blockade aggravated the monetary system and helped to add to the tremendous rate of inflation, and financial problems developed abroad. Suffice it to say that the Union blockade was an important factor in the destruction of the South's ability to fully wage war, and it prevented the Confederates from establishing a full-scale war economy.

As the blockade became more stringent it kept all but a small number of specialized ships from even attempting to risk capture. The Union blockade isolated the South both politically and diplomatically. It also prevented the Confederates from establishing a full-scale war economy, and by early 1865 the South had expended a great deal of its resources to win the war. The United States Navy's blockade of the Confederacy was a key factor in winning the war.

Currently hundreds of books on the American Civil War are in print. Few of these, however, relate to the naval aspects of the conflict. Most Civil War readers only have a passing knowledge of the blockade or of the numerous naval actions, and few have any appreciation for the Union's combined operations. Yet, the blockade of the Southern states was the war's longest campaign, and arguably the most important and perhaps the most decisive of all the war's campaigns.

Initially, writers began to discuss the blockade shortly after the Civil War ended. Men who ran the blockade—such as John Wilkinson, Thomas Taylor, and Augustus Hobart-Hampden—dominated the early writing. In 1883, scholarship took a huge step when Charles Scribner's Sons published its three volume series, *Navy in the Civil War.* James Russell Soley, a professor at the U.S. Naval Academy, wrote *The Blockade and the Cruisers*—the first significant effort to look at the blockade from the Union perspective. Also in the series was *Gulf and Inland Waters* by Alfred Thayer Mahan and Daniel Ammen's *The Atlantic Coast.* The latter two authors served on the Union blockade.

The next major work came nearly forty years later. In 1925, Francis B. C. Bradlee's *Blockade Running during the Civil War and the Effect of Land and Water Transportation on the Confederacy* looked at the blockade-running companies. But he retold many of the same stories. In 1931, one of the most important works on blockade running appeared. Written by Frank Owsley and entitled *King Cotton Diplomacy: Foreign Relations of the Confederate States of America.* Owsley argued that blockade running was essential to the success of the Confederate war effort.

After World War II the scholarship of the naval blockade and blockade running improved greatly. Historian Marcus Price completed one of the earliest in-depth statistical studies. In a series of articles published in the *American Neptune,* he indicated that in 1861 a blockade runner had a one-in-ten chance of being captured; not more than one in eight in 1862; one in four in 1863; about one in three in 1864; and in 1865 after most ports were closed, about a one-in-two chance. Steam blockade runners made as many as 1,300 attempts to run through the blockade, 1,000 of which succeeded.

The next important work to come along was by Frank Vandiver. In a new departure in the literature, Vandiver's *Confederate Blockade Running through Bermuda, 1861–1865,* studied the trade from the perspective of the operations from Bermuda. A more recent work by Stephen R. Wise made a substantial leap in the scholarship of the field. In his book, *Lifeline of the Confederacy: Blockade Running during the Civil War,* Wise provided a detailed study of the trade, the ships and the overall success of the blockade. Recent literature includes regional studies and in-depth examinations of some of the Union-blockading squadrons. David Surdam has authored the most recent book that scrutinizes the blockade. It is an important work because he assesses the total impact of the blockade by looking at the Confederacy's war economy and the military logistical system of the South.

Hamilton Cochran's *Blockade Runners of the Confederacy* was published nearly fifty years ago, and it fits nicely with all these other studies. Historians and those interested in the Civil War are all familiar with Cochran's book. He was the first author to address in a single source many of the subjects that other historians scrutinized in entire books. He used primary documents to provide a narrative overview of the dashing figures, the spies, the fast ships, and some of the more unusual aspects of the trade. But Cochran also describes how the blockade was conceived and how it affected the local populace. His lively accounts bring both the men and ships that ran the blockade to life. Cochran's book serves as a fundamental starting place for those interested in the fascinating and often dramatic story of blockade runners during the Civil War.

Many are unaware that Hamilton Cochran was a prolific writer and his early experiences shaped his writing career. He was born on 9 September 1898 in Philadelphia, Pennsylvania. His father Joseph, a clergyman, sought to give his son a good education and sent him to Swarthmore Preparatory School. In April 1917, after the United States declared war on Germany, Hamilton, at only eighteen, left school within a week and enlisted in the United States Coast Guard.

After three months of training in New London, Connecticut, at the Coast Guard Academy, located in Fort Trumball, the Service assigned him to the USCGC *Algonquin*. This Coast Guard cutter was one of six warships that the Coast Guard sent to fight in Europe. On 25 September, the *Algonquin* steamed from Boston, towing a minesweeper to Halifax and then sailed for Gibraltar, arriving there on 16 October.

During the war, the *Algonquin* convoyed merchant ships between the English Channel ports and Gibraltar. Hamilton spent fifteen months on this duty. The *Algonquin* participated in twenty-one convoys without losing a single ship. It returned to New London in February 1919. During Cochran's twenty-three months in the Coast Guard, he visited twenty-eight different ports and returned to the states a seasoned tar.

Service to his country had a huge impact on the young Cochran. Within months after stepping off the *Algonquin,* he wrote a couple of documents that related to his wartime experiences. One was entitled "Hunting the Hun with the Coast Guard." Restless for knowledge, Cochran entered the University of Michigan that fall. After only three years of study, he received a Bachelor of Arts degree in journalism.

After college, Cochran could not shake the sea from his veins and sailed on the Red Star and Munson lines in passenger and freight vessels. For seven years he worked for Ronald Press as a salesman and from 1930 until 1932 he served as a vice president of the Diamond Wax Paper Company in Rochester, New York.

In 1932, his life took a turn that would foster his writing for the rest of his life. He accepted a job as the Commissioner of Public Welfare for the government of the Virgin Islands, St. Thomas. While in the islands, he became fascinated by the history of the area and particularly the tales of pirates. Here he was able to gather much of the material he would use for his first and many of his later books.

In 1937, he wrote his first book entitled *These are the Virgin Islands*. It is a historic synthesis of the rich history of the islands. It narrates some of the islands' unique maritime tales and relates the events and the people, which make up the region's rich lore. Between 1935 and 1943, Cochran worked for Standard Oil Company as an advertising executive. During these years his writing career flourished. In 1941 he wrote his first novel entitled *Buccaneer Islands*. It was written for young readers and was published by Thomas Nelson. Later came *Windward Passage*, Bobbs-Merrill (1942) and *Captain Ebony*, Bobbs-Merrill (1943). In writing these books he utilized material he collected while he had worked in the Virgin Islands. In 1944 he landed a job with Curtis Publishing Company as the automotive marketing manager for the *Saturday Evening Post*. Three years later he wrote his fourth novel, *Rogue's Holiday*, published by Bobbs-Merrill.

During World War II, at the age of forty-four, feeling that his country needed him, he again joined the Coast Guard. He served as a temporary reservist in Flotilla 605. This was a volunteer position. He received no pay or allowances, but he did wear a uniform. From April to November 1943, Cochran worked several days each month for the Coast Guard.

By the late 1940s he had traveled extensively throughout the Western Hemisphere. During his life he logged more than 100,000 miles at sea. In 1960, Curtis Publishing Company made Cochran the director of advertising. Two years later he began work for Stanley Publishing Company as a vice president. Cochran retired in 1964 devoting his time to writing and volunteer work with the Philadelphia Maritime Museum.

Cochran also contributed poems to three anthologies and wrote articles for the *Saturday Evening Post, Esquire,* and other magazines. In 1976, a year before he died, his final book, *Pirate Wench: The Voyages and Adventures of Ann O'Shea* was published by R. Hale. In all, he wrote thirteen books during his lifetime. We are fortunate to have Hamilton Cochran's *Blockade Runners of the Confederacy* as a resource. For decades it has served as an indispensable general resource for everyone who is interested in reading about the Civil War blockade.

CHAPTER 1

The Blockade Begins

On April 19, 1861, five days after the evacuation of Fort Sumter, President Lincoln proclaimed a blockade of the six Southern states which had seceded up to that time and which constituted the Confederate States of America: South Carolina, Georgia, Alabama, Florida, Mississippi and Texas. The proclamation declared them to be in a state of insurrection, and stated that in order to protect the "combination of persons, public peace and the lives and property of quiet and orderly citizens pursuing their lawful occupations . . . the President deemed it advisable to set on foot a blockade of the ports within the States aforesaid." For this purpose, "a competent force will be posted so as to prevent the entrance and exit of the vessels from the ports aforesaid.

"If, therefore, with a view to violate such blockades any vessel shall attempt to leave any of said ports, the vessel will be duly warned . . . and if the same vessel shall again attempt to enter or leave the blockaded port, she will be captured and sent to the nearest commercial port, for such proceedings against her and her cargo as may be deemed advisable."

Eight days later, the President issued another decree, extending the blockade to include North Carolina and Virginia. This made the blockade of the South complete—from Cape Henry to the Mexican border, four thousand miles of coast line.

At once a wave of protest surged northward from these two states. What right had the Federal government, they asked, to declare that their coasts and ports were to be blockaded by men-of-war when neither state had seceded? No answer came from Washington. There was a great deal going on at the capital just then. It is more than likely that this act of the President's was

13

uppermost in the minds of the many legislators of Virginia and North Carolina when they severed their connections with the Union within the next month.

Elsewhere in the South, the first reaction to President Lincoln's announcement was anger. It was unjust and unlawful, they declared, and motivated as much by a desire to create hardships for Southern people as to prevent foreign commerce. But after Southern newspaper editors pointed out that it was virtually impossible to enforce such a blockade and that the whole thing was an empty threat, the anger of most Southerners turned to disdain and raucous mirth.

A man from Charleston, writing to a friend in England, in May 1861, remarked, "You have heard, no doubt, Old Abe has blockaded our port. A nice blockade indeed! On the second day, a British ship, the *A and A* ran the gantlet with a snug freight of $30,000. Today two vessels passed safely in, both British, I understand. A captain told me that one of them can carry more cotton than the *A and A* and that she is engaged at five cents a pound, which will give a freight of $35,000 to $40,000. Don't you wish you had a hundred ships for one voyage? You might become your own insurer with impunity."

Eastward, across the Atlantic, the reaction to the blockade was one of surprise and bewilderment. In spite of the bombardment of Fort Sumter, the people of England and the Continent still believed that a peaceful settlement would be found. Scarcely thirty days before the first gun was fired, official word from Washington stated that "the President entertains a full confidence in the speedy restoration of the harmony and the unity of the government." Again, on April 10, another dispatch said that "the President neither looks for nor apprehends any actual and permanent dismemberment of the American Union. . . . He is not disposed to reject a cardinal dogma of the South, namely, that the Federal government cannot reduce the seceding States to obedience by conquest, even though he were disposed to question that proposition. But, in fact, the President willingly accepts it as true."

When news of the proclamation of a blockade reached Europe

her statesmen were puzzled by the very use of the word. It was a novelty, they said, *to see a nation blockade its own ports, since blockade is a recognized agency of war only between independent nations!* Among themselves, they whispered that someone in Washington was either ignorant or stupid, or both.

In the light of subsequent events, most historians agree that the person to whom those terms applied most pointedly was William H. Seward, Secretary of State. Gideon Welles, the bewhiskered and indefatigable Secretary of the Navy, blamed Seward in no uncertain terms. He charged that Seward had placed the United States government in a most embarrassing position in the eyes of the whole world. Welles knew, as anyone with a rudimentary understanding of international law knew, that a nation at war *closes* its insurrectionary ports, but only *blockades* the ports of an *enemy nation*. Welles realized that Seward's blunder was tantamount to recognition of the Confederate States as a belligerent. As a belligerent, the South was entitled to certain established rights under international law. By the same token, foreign nations, who wished to continue trading with Southern ports, were also entitled to their legal rights.

United States Senator Charles Sumner summed up the feelings of many members of Congress when he said in a speech in the Senate, some years later, "Had President Lincoln proclaimed a closing of the rebel ports [instead of a blockade] there could have been no concession [of belligerency] . . . the whole case of England is made to stand on the use of the word 'blockade'. It is this word which, with magical might, opened the gates to all those bountiful supplies by which hostile expeditions were equipped against the United States."

It is not the intention of this book to argue the pros and cons of the blockade as related to international law and politics. Rather it is the "bountiful supplies" and the gallant little steamers and their skippers who brought these cargoes safely through the blockade into Southern ports that form the substance of this volume.

If Secretary Seward was as careless and ignorant as Welles and Sumner and others declared him to be, he also might not have been aware of another vital principle of international law. It states, in essence, that a blockade, to be recognized by foreign powers, *"must be effective."* This was the law laid down by the Treaty of Paris. Since the United States government was a party to that treaty, it was up to Washington to *make it a blockade in fact as well as in word.* To issue a proclamation declaring that the entire coast line of the South was to be blockaded was one thing; to enforce that blockade was quite another. As Secretary of the Navy, it was up to Gideon Welles to carry out the provisions of Lincoln's decree. It was a task that only a man of extraordinary patience, determination and singleness of purpose could be willing to undertake. Welles was such a man.

He was well aware of the tremendous problems involved. In the first place, the distance from Cape Henry to the Mexican border was greater than from New York to Liverpool. There were many inlets and harbors along this great stretch, but few really good ports. In 1861 this was especially true, for only a handful of the coastal cities of the South had satisfactory connections with the interior, by railroad or by navigable rivers for any distance. In studying maps of the South, Welles and his naval aides counted ten ports of utmost importance which would have to be blockaded at once. These were Norfolk; Beaufort, New Bern and Wilmington in North Carolina; Charleston; Savannah; Pensacola; Mobile; New Orleans and Galveston. Of secondary importance were Key West and St. Augustine. If the Federal government could clamp an economic stranglehold on the South by rendering these ports useless to the Confederacy, it would contribute greatly to the over-all strategy of the war.

A less resolute man than Welles might have thrown up his hands at the seemingly hopeless task of creating the vast, properly manned fleet that was so necessary for the job. Welles recognized this, yet he did not falter for one moment. In his annual report for the year 1861 he described the situation: "With so few vessels in commission on our coast, and our crews in distant seas, the department was very indifferently prepared to meet the exigencies that were arising. Every movement was closely watched by the disaffected and threatened to precipitate measures that the country seemed anxious to avoid. Demoralization prevailed among the officers, many of whom, occupying the most responsible positions, betrayed symptoms of that infidelity that has dishonored the service."

These words were written in heat, anger and disillusionment at the alarming number of officers who resigned from the service during the first spring of the war. After the fourth of March, 1861, 259 officers of the Navy resigned their commissions or were dismissed from the service. Many others, who belonged to the states which had already seceded, had previously resigned.

Welles took quite a different view from that of Southern naval men regarding their separation from the service. One of their spokesmen, Captain John Wilkinson, who became one of the most intrepid blockade runners of the Confederacy, wrote that those who resigned their commissions in order to render aid to the South felt this act absolved them from any further obligation to the Federal government; that they had become private citizens and could go their ways without suffering the stigma of ingratitude, disloyalty or treason.

Unfortunately for Welles, the few naval vessels in commission at the time seemed to have been placed in positions at home and abroad so as to be of minimum usefulness to the Secretary in this crisis. As of March 4, the home squadron was made up of twelve vessels. Of these, only four were in Northern ports. Of these four, two were small steamers, the third a sailing store-ship. The fourth had returned from a cruise only a month before and was not in any shape to put to sea. Several of the U.S. war vessels in Southern ports were in charge of officers suspected of Southern sympathies and for a time it was thought they would deliver their ships into the hands of Confederate representatives. Luckily for Welles, he was able to order the ships home without losing any to his enemies.

U.S. men-of-war on foreign stations were as follows: the sailing frigates *Constellation* and *Portsmouth*, twenty-two guns each; the store-ship *Relief*; the armed steamers *Mohican*, *Mystic*, *Sumter* and *San Jacinto*. These seven vessels were all stationed

on the coast of Africa. In addition, there was the steam frigate
Niagara, twenty guns, en route home to Boston from Japan.
Other U.S. men-of-war were scattered about the Mediterranean, along the coast of South America and in the East Indies.
All together, the naval register of that year showed a total
force of only ninety vessels. In addition there were some old
sailing vessels that might have been put into commission. However, those in service had been found so inadequate in com-
parison with steamships, that they were laid up as soon as additional steam vessels could be found. The steam frigates *Wabash,*
Minnesota, Colorado and *Roanoke,* forty guns each, were hastily
refitted in Northern yards and rushed South as a gesture of enforcing the blockade. For months the blockade existed mostly
on paper as far as its effectiveness was concerned. Naval personnel of all ranks and ratings was variously estimated at five thousand to seven thousand men—proportionately as inadequate as
the number of ships.

Another major setback suffered by the Navy Department and
the Northern cause was the loss of the Norfolk Navy Yard to
the Confederates on April 20, 1861. Norfolk was in Virginia;
and Virginia was on the point of seceding. The city seethed
with excitement. Southern sentiment was strong. Many Northern members of Congress tried to persuade Welles to fire most
of the Democratic jobholders at the Norfolk Navy Yard and put
reliable Republicans in their places. But he refused, fearing perhaps that this might add fuel to the already blazing Southern
fire. What troubled him also was the officer personnel at the
Yard. A number of high-ranking officers, including Matthew
Fontaine Maury, a Virginian, Captain G. A. Magruder, of the
Bureau of Ordnance and Hydrography, and Captain Franklin
Buchanan, were believed to be waiting only for the secession of
Virginia before tendering their resignations from the service.
Certain other officers of high rank were old and infirm and considered unreliable in an emergency. In spite of precautionary
measures set in motion by Welles and the Commandant of Nor-
folk Navy Yard, aged Commodore Charles S. McCauley, sys-
tematic sabotage began under the direction of energetic young

officers of Southern sympathies. They blocked the Commodore's attempt to get the splendid steam frigate *Merrimac* out of the yard and to a safer berth by sinking several hulks in the channel. Rather than let the vessel fall into Confederate hands, McCauley scuttled her at the dock. Norfolk mobs ranged the streets shouting, looting and drinking to the fall of Fort Sumter. They yelled repeatedly that Confederate troops were on their way to capture the Yard.

At this time Welles dispatched Commodore Paulding, who was the Department's senior officer, to Norfolk, to give Mc-Cauley a hand. After a quick appraisal of the situation he concluded that the Yard was doomed. So he lost no time in blowing up the warehouses, boat sheds, the dry dock and miscellaneous buildings, dumped all naval guns into the river and left the blazing place to the Confederates.

In no way deterred by this serious loss, Welles plunged ahead to carry out the great task that lay ahead. "I had been told by the President," he wrote in his diary, ". . . that I must take such means as might seem to me necessary in the emergency to maintain the national authority, and that he would share with me or take upon himself the responsibility of such orders as I in my discretion, should issue. When, therefore, the Cabinet officers . . . were assembled . . . I stated the necessity of chartering or purchasing without delay vessels for the naval service—to close the rebel ports, and assert national supremacy. All concurred in my proposition. Orders were, therefore, instanter written to the commandants of the Navy yards at New York, Philadelphia and Boston, to charter or purchase forthwith, twenty steamers, capable of sustaining an armament for naval purposes."

Although Welles issued his orders "instanter," they were not carried out nearly so fast as he wished. The whole area around Washington was in a state of turmoil. The capital city was separated from the Northern states and without mail or telegraph communication. Dissident elements were making hostile demonstrations in the principal streets and the mayor could not, or would not, control them. Federal troops which had been sent to the capital (many of them undisciplined and unorganized) with few competent officers, were delayed and in some cases stopped before they could reach Washington. It was to Paymaster Horatio Bridge, of the Bureau of Provisions and Clothing, that Welles assigned the task of carrying important instructions to the commandants of the Northern navy yards. Conditions were so uncertain and dangerous that Bridge had to take a roundabout route. He had to go by way of Wheeling, West Virginia, via the Ohio Railroad in order to skirt the state of Maryland, which had not yet decided whether to remain with the North or to back the South.

Meanwhile Welles took over a number of river steamers, armed them with small-caliber guns, sent crews aboard and set them to patrolling the Potomac River. It was even considered advisable to move the Naval Academy from Annapolis, since the place was seething with secessionist sentiment. Welles sent a messenger to Captain S. F. Du Pont at Philadelphia with instructions to charter and arm a vessel and send it immediately to Annapolis. One of its main objectives was to keep communications open by water with Washington. Du Pont responded promptly, and a week later contact between the nation's capital and the Northern states had been re-established. Midshipmen from the Academy whose sympathies lay with the South had already resigned and were on their way home. The loyal midshipmen were bundled aboard the historic frigate *Constitution*, which set sail for Newport, Rhode Island.

After the first weeks of confusion following the outbreak of the war, the purchase or charter of vessels for the new Federal Navy went more swiftly. A well-planned program of naval construction was also put into operation, taking into consideration the various types of vessels needed both for the high seas and the inland waters. These consisted of sloops of war, heavily armed, iron-plated screw gunboats, paddle-wheel steamers for use in narrow waters, and the famous ironclads. According to reliable figures, the United States government constructed during the war 126 wooden vessels, having 1,307 guns, and 74 ironclads, mounting 213 guns: a total of 200 vessels mounting 1,520 guns.

What resources did the Secretary of the Navy of the Confederate States of America have with which to counter the measures of vigorous Gideon Welles? Nothing, literally nothing, except men—without ships. Stephen Russell Mallory was primarily a lawyer and a politician with limited experience in naval matters. He grew up in Key West, and quit school at the age of sixteen. Later he became Collector of Customs for Key West and saw active service in the Seminole War. He studied law and was admitted to the bar in 1839. In 1851 he was elected to the United States Senate for six years. He continued to represent his home state until Florida seceded. During most of his service in the Senate he was Chairman of the Naval Affairs Committee. He took an active part in matters pertaining to the defense of his state immediately after Florida separated from the Union and when he was offered the post of Secretary of the Navy by President Jefferson Davis, he promptly accepted.

A revenue cutter or two and a few steamers had fallen into Confederate hands, but these vessels were of negligible value, compared to the immense number of ships that would be needed to fight a successful war on the Atlantic and on the inland waters. Mallory, as the head of the Naval Department, not only had to organize and administer, but also had to build or buy all the vessels he would need, find guns with which to arm them, and bring into being a naval force in a land which was about to be largely cut off from the world by the greatest and most persistent blockade in the history of the world up to that time.

The resources of the Confederate States of America consisted mainly of raw materials. Her factories were few and completely inadequate for war purposes. The timber for Confederate ships still stood on her forest-covered slopes. The iron she needed was buried in the mines. There were neither furnaces nor workshops. Even the hemp required for rope had to be grown and reaped, and there was no ropewalk. The Southern states had never produced enough iron for the uses of their people in time of peace, and now that the war was to multiply the uses of that indispensable metal, the price rose from $25 to $1,500 per ton; neither money nor industry could supply the demands of the navy, the army and the fast-wearing rails and engines of Southern railroads.

In the whole of the South there was not a single rolling mill capable of turning out a 2½-inch iron plate, or a machine shop that could build a complete marine engine. Later on, after Virginia seceded and joined the Confederacy, the Tredegar Iron Works and the Belona Foundry of Richmond became indispensable assets to the Confederate States Navy as well as to the army.

The capture of the Norfolk Navy Yard was a windfall for the South. Most of the guns which had been tossed into the water when the United States Navy evacuated the place were salvaged and some of the machinery and equipment put back to use. The great granite dry dock had been mined, but the explosives failed to function and the dry dock was salvaged intact. Probably the most valuable spoils yielded by the Norfolk Navy Yard were the guns. Altogether there were 1,198 of them, of all sizes including fifty-two 9-inch Dahlgrens. Those that had been spiked were repaired and put to immediate use in Confederate coast defenses.

The steam frigate *Merrimac*, which had been sunk by the Federals along with many other naval vessels when the yard was abandoned, was raised by Flag Officer Forrest and placed in dry dock. Other vessels, including the sloop-of-war *Germantown* and the *Plymouth*, were also successfully salvaged. The hull of the *Merrimac* was found to be uninjured and her engines in repairable condition. It was this vessel, rebuilt as an ironclad and christened the *Virginia*, that played such havoc with the Union vessels at Hampton Roads until defeated by a "Yankee cheesebox on a raft," the courageous *Monitor*. Because of the success of Ericson's radically different man-of-war, a whole flotilla of monitors was later constructed. They took an active and decisive part in many engagements along the Atlantic Coast, particularly at Charleston and Fort Fisher.

In order to find work for the oversupply of Confederate States Navy officers, Mallory sent some of them to shore batteries; others were put to work developing various means of defense or securing supplies, refitting captured vessels, or in one way or another doing everything in their power to assist in the protection of the South.

The many complexities of Mallory's job included the defense of rivers, harbors, bays and inlets from attack by Federal war vessels. This necessitated the erection of forts and shore batteries as well as the use of armed patrol vessels.

As for the blockade, it is quite possible that the harassed Mallory gave it some thought at this time. But he was unable to put into action any plans for circumventing the blockade simply because there was little, if any, blockading actually being done. So he decided to leave this problem to shipowners who had a vital interest in keeping the avenues of trade and communication open with England and the Continent.

Secretary Mallory of the Confederate States Navy was no less anxious to buy and arm ships than Welles. But for Mallory the prospects were far from promising. Nevertheless as early as May 10, 1861, he secured the passage of secret acts of the Confederate Congress authorizing Naval Agent James D. Bulloch to go to England and see what he could pick up there. Even earlier, in March, a naval officer was dispatched to New York to investigate shipping there and find out whether there were any vessels available and, if so, whether they could be converted into men-of-war. Other agents were sent to Philadelphia and Baltimore on the same errands. Apparently the only vessel they could find was the *Caroline* in Philadelphia. Unfortunately for the Confederates, negotiations for her purchase fell through after the riots attending the passage of Massachusetts troops through Baltimore. Other agents in Canada reported that the "Yankees have been here before us and rounded up practically anything that will float."

The impact of the blockade on Southern shipowners was one of caution and uncertainty. Most of them kept their vessels in port. No one knew what was going to happen. Some were fearful that the Federal Navy would immediately send cruisers to intercept shipping at every Southern harbor entrance. Others sneered at the whole affair, declaring that it would be impossible to prevent the free entrance and exit of Southern ships. As for the Southern public, there was universal resentment against the

United States government's policy of attempting to cut off the Confederacy from contact with the outside world and prevent her cotton from going to market.

After the first wave of uncertainty had passed, Southern ship-owners woke up to the fact that the blockade was something of a farce. True, a few cruisers were steaming up and down off Charleston, Savannah and other ports. The nights were dark, the seas wide and Southern pilots thoroughly familiar with all the inlets, bays, sounds, shoals and sand bars. Consequently Southern vessels, as well as those that sailed under foreign flags were soon steaming merrily in and out of Southern ports with small chance of getting caught—unless the captain was dead drunk or the engines stopped.

Once in a while, hard-working Federal vessels caught up with a saucy Southern ship, overhauled and captured her. The first prize captured by the United States Navy on the Southern coast was the *General Parkhill*, a steamer owned by a Charleston firm. She was overtaken by the screw frigate U.S.S. *Niagara* on May 15, 1861. The *General Parkhill* was homeward bound from Liverpool with a valuable cargo of merchandise. A couple of small, armed Confederate steamers tried to protect her on her approach to Charleston Harbor, but scurried back after the *Niagara* fired a couple of shots at them from her bow chasers.

The most notorious blockade runner at this time was the British mail steamer *Theodora*, which left Charleston on October 11. Aboard were Messrs. Mason and Slidell, Confederate States envoys to Great Britain and France. Their departure was a well-kept secret and it was not until November 2 that news of their exit from the Confederate mainland was published in the newspapers.

The *Theodora* eluded Union men-of-war by choosing a dark and stormy night for her flight from Charleston Harbor. On board in addition to the two Confederate envoys were four ladies, the wife and two daughters of Mr. Slidell, and Mrs. Eustis, wife of Slidell's secretary. MacFarland, secretary to Mason, was also aboard. The *Theodora* arrived in Nassau on

October 13 after a rough but uneventful passage. Here a disappointment awaited the Confederate notables. They had expected to proceed to England aboard a certain English steamer, but found to their dismay that she was scheduled to stop at New York en route to Liverpool. So Mason, Slidell and company continued aboard the *Theodora* to Havana. The little steamer gaily entered the harbor not only with the Union Jack flying, but also with the Confederate flag at her masthead. Messrs. Mason and Slidell were welcomed with warmth by the citizenry of Havana. Ceremonies included the presentation of a Confederate flag by a bevy of Cuban ladies to intrepid Commander Lockwood of the *Theodora* for having brought the distinguished visitors safely through the blockade.

Mason and Slidell and their entourage sailed for Europe aboard the steamer *Trent*, while Lockwood conned the *Theodora* back to Charleston. As the *Trent* was steaming through the narrow Bahama Channel she was overhauled by the U.S. frigate *San Jacinto*, commanded by Captain Charles Wilkes. He ordered Mason and Slidell to quit the *Trent* and took them aboard the Federal man-of-war.

As everyone knows, the affair became a *cause célèbre* and was characterized by a Southern writer living in London in these words: "This outrage created the greatest excitement in England, and to prevent a collision between the two governments, the United States gave up the commissioners to the representatives of the British government authorized to receive them. They subsequently arrived safely in England." The Federal government was in a delicate position in her relations with Great Britain. War was frankly discussed as a result. Secretary of State Seward finally bowed before the growls of the British, wrote a smoothly worded letter of explanation and gave up the prisoners. As a Canadian paper remarked, it was "a bitter pill for the fire-eaters to cram down their noisy throats."

The Northern reaction was somewhat different. A newspaper cartoon depicted Mason and Slidell as skunks being plucked out of John Bull's back pockets by a patriotic U.S. naval officer.

Citizens of the North made a hero of Wilkes and felt that the niceties of international law might well be ignored in capturing two such "important and villainous Rebels."

In December, to add to Welles's headaches, work on Federal ships being converted and armed for blockading duty was found to be dragging. So was new construction. Impatient at what he considered unnecessary delays, Welles conceived what he thought to be a quick and easy means of completely bottling up Confederate shipping inside Charleston Harbor, Savannah and elsewhere. The plan entailed loading old wooden vessels with stone and sinking them across the main channels of each harbor. Where could such vessels be obtained? In New England his agents found the answer. The war had gravely crippled the whaling industry. Whalers dared not cruise Southern waters for fear of Rebel raiders. (Seventy were burned by Confederate privateers during the war.) Most of the whaling vessels were tied up in their home ports—crews dispersed. Many of the ships had deteriorated to a point where they were unseaworthy. Here then, was a solution made to order to fit into Welles's plan. After a quick survey of the ports of Mystic, New Bedford, Nantucket, Sag Harbor and Fairhaven, more than two dozen decrepit whalers were located and bought. These venerable vessels were popularly dubbed the Stone Fleet, for no attempt was made at secrecy. The New York papers knew all about it. Said the *Herald*, "There are twenty-five vessels, averaging 335 tons each, and they will be so heavily loaded with stone that, when once sunk, it will be no easy matter to raise them. They will thus become the real blockading fleet, that no storm or fog can interfere with or no small vessel pass by."

On sailing day the skippers of the various whalers got sealed orders which they were not to open until they were well out at sea. The instructions were brief and explicit. Upon reaching their destinations, the captains were to turn over their ships to the commanding officer of the blockading fleet. Officers and crews were to be given passage back to New York by the Navy.

"On the voyage down," read the orders, "it would be well, as far as practicable, to keep in company of your consorts, to exhibit lights by night and sound horns or bells in case of fog near the coast. You will also examine daily the pipe in the quarter of your ship under water, to see that it remains safe." In referring to the condition of each vessel, the orders pointed out that "as she is old and heavily laden [with stone] you will use special care that she sustains no damage from unskilled seamanship or want of prudence and care."

The pipe referred to was of lead and fitted into a hole that had been bored into the bottom of the vessel. The pipe was five inches in diameter and equipped with a valve so that water could be let in at such speed that the vessel would sink in fifteen or twenty minutes. Just in case the vessel did not go under fast enough, the thoughtful Navy Department provided each captain with a set of huge augers to hurry up the job. The basic plan called for the vessels to be sunk broadside to the channel.

When news of the Stone Fleet reached Charleston, Savannah and other Southern ports, there was an outburst of indignation. Southern papers declared that the right to open and close ports of entry was never before understood to carry the right to destroy the natural roadsteads which provided a harbor of refuge from the storms of the coast. It was felt that Seward, as the diplomatic chief of his government, should have sense enough to know that "such barbarism would not be tolerated by enlightened governments." Secretary Welles also came in for a generous share of rebuke for thinking up such a fiendish plan.

The situation was closely watched in Great Britain, especially by the Liverpool Shipowners Association, which felt it necessary to call the matter to the attention of Lord John Russell. He termed the Stone Fleet "a cruel plan which would seem to imply despair of the restoration of the Union, the professed object of the war; for it never could be the wish of the United States government to destroy cities from which their own country was to derive a portion of its riches and prosperity. Such a plan could only be adopted as a measure of revenge, and of irremediable injury against an enemy." France took much the same position. Another international crisis began to brew and might have boiled over except for the fact that the Stone Fleet was a dismal failure.

Whether Welles's chief naval advisors were busy elsewhere at the time the plan was conceived or whether he overrode their technical objections is unknown. In any case the author of the scheme failed to take tides and currents of the harbors into account. These were so powerful that they broke up and destroyed a number of the hulks after they had been sunk. Others, which held together, sank into the ever-shifting sands and acted as jetties, thus scouring the channels deeper. The main result of it all was merely to make the route of blockade runners in and out of port a bit more devious than before.

Although Welles's scheme for a quick and easy way to blockade the South proved to be a dud, his opponents in the Confederate States government were committing far more serious sins of omission and commission. While the United States Navy was working desperately to build up an armada to enforce the blockade, President Davis and his financial advisers made no moves to use their one salable commodity, cotton, to finance their war. These were months of comparative quiet and preparation, during which the Confederacy could have sold, delivered and stored in Europe enough cotton to supply the whole of Europe. In exchange, she could have bought ships and arms and equipment.

The basic reason why nothing was done about these vital matters was that the foreign policy of the Confederacy was composed mostly of delusions. They were glittering to Southern politicians and plausible. That policy, in brief, was this: the North needed cotton; the mills of Lancashire in England were starving for the stuff; France and Europe needed it badly also. Therefore, why not hold cotton off the world market until the need for it reached a critical stage? The result would be a fantastic increase in the price along with a realization on the part of Queen Victoria's government and that of Napoleon Third and others in Europe that it might be very politic officially to recognize the Confederate States of America if Europe expected to continue to clothe their people in cotton fabrics. The Confederate policy deceived its creators for another reason: in the years before 1861, Southern cotton crops had been unusually heavy. The world carry-over was therefore so large that throughout 1861 and 1862 England found herself not only with enough cotton in her warehouses for her own needs, but was actually able to ship some to New England in answer to the pitiful cries of millowners there. Not until late in 1862 did the cotton shortage become acute. All of this had an effect on blockade running. Since the Confederacy was hoarding cotton, her exports consisted chiefly of tobacco, lumber, naval stores and other raw materials. Inbound cargoes included a wide variety of war supplies as well as quantities of civilian goods and luxuries unobtainable from the North. By this time the Confederate treasury was virtually empty of gold, its currency suspected and there was no credit with which to collect and transport cotton for export.

CHAPTER 2

Du Pont Plays Hide and Seek

Because of the promptness and efficiency shown by Captain Samuel F. Du Pont in reopening communications between Washington and other cities along the Atlantic seaboard during the first hectic weeks following Sumter, Gideon Welles brought him to Washington and made him chairman of a strategy board. This board was given the task of studying all aspects of the blockade problem and the geography of the coasts. It was also assigned the job of selecting Southern bases of operation, capturing them and making them into naval supply points. Another member of the board was Captain David Glasgow Farragut. To Commodore Silas Stringham, in whom Welles had the utmost confidence, went the all-important post of Flag Officer of the Atlantic Blockading Squadron. With these key men in position, the energetic Secretary of the Navy pushed forward with his grand scheme for throttling the South by means of a blockade. Much of the time he had to improvise and make do with converted merchantmen, many of which were unsuitable for the work ahead. He had no time to construct special ships. It was urgent, he declared, to put a stop to an already flourishing blockade-running business.

By July the Atlantic Squadron had grown to an impressive fleet of ships which were divided into two divisions. One was to operate south of the North Carolina-South Carolina state line; the other to the north of that line. As set forth by Du Pont's strategy board, the next job was to capture and establish bases for both squadrons. To do this would require the aid of the army, for a number of the principal Southern ports were heavily fortified, especially Charleston and Savannah. It was clearly realized that all of the forts could not be taken by naval action alone. A number of them would have to be attacked and taken by storm by a landing force of infantry.

In casting about for a weak link in Southern coastal defenses, Welles and Du Pont gave careful attention to Port Royal, South Carolina. Its great deep-water bay lay between Savannah and Charleston. If a base of operations could be established there, it would be ideally situated as a coaling, refitting, and supply station; also for conducting blockading operations against both seaports. Once the objective was agreed upon, Welles impressed on Du Pont (whom he made commander of the South Atlantic Squadron) the necessity for secrecy. Without it, there could be no surprise. And without surprise the expedition might well fail. Du Pont carried out his instructions to the letter. He realized, of course, that the extensive preparations necessary for such an expedition would generate interest and curiosity, on the part not only of Northern newspapers and citizens, but also of the scores of Confederate spies who infested Washington as well as the coastal cities. So a number of rumors were released as to the destination of the fleet. Some said that it was headed for St. Helena, South Carolina. Others that it was Fernandina, Florida, or Wilmington or New Bern, North Carolina—anywhere but Port Royal. Afterward the New York *Times* congratulated Welles on being the only executive in Washington who could "keep a secret, under even hydraulic pressure."

Meanwhile, an expedition under Flag Officer Stringham and the blustering General Ben Butler had bombarded and captured forts Clark and Hatteras from their Confederate defenders, most of whom were green troops using hastily mounted shore batteries. Within a little more than twenty-four hours after arrival of the Federals off the forts, the Confederates surrendered. The next day the fleet sailed back north, taking along nearly seven hundred prisoners and leaving strong garrisons to man the captured forts upon which the Confederates had relied to protect strategic Hatteras Inlet.

By the last week of October 1861, Flag Officer Du Pont was ready to move. His men-of-war and transports carrying 12,000 troops were rendezvoused in Chesapeake Bay. The fleet sailed

under sealed orders on October 29. It was a formidable aggre-
gation of vessels—seventeen war ships mounting a total of 175
guns, some of 11-inch caliber. In addition, there were fifty
supply ships and transports. It was the largest armada that had
ever been commanded by an American naval officer up to that
time. The army contingents were under the command of Major
General T. W. Sherman (not to be confused with the more
famous William Tecumseh Sherman).

A severe storm off Hatteras delayed the expedition's southern
progress, but the vessels rode it out and were reinforced by additional ships that had been cruising off Charleston. On November 4 the great fleet pointed in toward the entrance to Port
Royal harbor.

The Confederates had a pitifully small naval force to oppose
the powerful fleet of the Federals. It consisted of only three
armed river steamers under orders from brave and gentlemanly
Commodore Josiah Tattnall. The broad channel leading to the
harbor was protected by Fort Beauregard (eighteen guns) on
one side and Fort Walker (twenty-three guns) on the other.
Each was situated on an island. Bad weather held up the attack
for two days. But on November 7 as the weather cleared, the
long-awaited signals streamed from Du Pont's flagship, the U.S.S.
Wabash. The Union men-of-war formed line of battle and
steamed majestically toward the enemy. With broadsides blazing they headed up the channel, brushing aside Tattnall's puny
steamers. For four hours the big Federal guns poured shot and
shell into Fort Walker, knocking out all but three guns. Early
in the afternoon it was discovered that the Confederate garrison
had evacuated Walker. The fort was easily possessed by a landing party. It had been planned to concentrate the same sort of
destructive fire on Fort Beauregard the next morning, but when
daylight came, Du Pont saw plainly through his telescope that
the place had been abandoned by the enemy during the night.
To all intents and purposes the battle was over. For three days
afterward the fleet steamed slowly up the network of rivers and
inlets, putting ashore armed forces to secure the area. Finally

Port Royal and Beaufort were taken over without expenditure of powder or lives on either side.

Du Pont's victory at Port Royal opened up the inland waters between Charleston and Savannah to the Federal navy, confined Confederate naval operations to these two ports and adjacent coasts, and put teeth into the blockade.

All through the stormy fall and winter of 1861 and well into the spring of 1862, Du Pont was busy maneuvering his vessels along the coast and tightening the blockade of Savannah, Fernandina and other ports at the southern end of his command. He was also trying hard, but not too successfully, to stop up the various exits to the port of Charleston. Northern critics, especially the newspapers, were all too ready to declare that the blockade was ineffective and insufficiently supplied with men and ships.

Nettled, Du Pont wrote to Secretary Welles that "too ready credence" was being given to public functionaries and merchants and newspapers to the "representation of parties interested in making out a case against the government."

Du Pont claimed to have a list of 160 suspected vessels for which he was on the lookout: schooners, sailing vessels and steamers of all types. Of this large number, he declared, few had even run the blockade or attempted to do so. The only vessels that had been successful, he reported, were a few very light craft "and three rebel steamers, with the assistance of local pilots of long experience, with concerted signals from row boats and from shore and under protection of night or dense fogs. . . ."

All of which was quite true. Most of the Confederate and British skippers were still hesitant to match their wits and seamanship against Yankee naval guns. Nevertheless, it would not be long before blockade runners had mastered a successful formula for penetrating the line of Union craft; speed plus low visibility plus darkness and courage equaled success.

Even at that early date, the British and their Southern customers had learned one most important lesson, namely, the folly of attempting to run the blockade in large, slow and deep-draught vessels coming direct from England. A number of these had already been caught and shipowners did not intend to repeat the costly experiment. Du Pont was well informed on this situation, as noted in a dispatch dated April 23, 1862. "The steamers *Gladiator, Talisman, Sidney Hall, Gage, Cambridge, Imperative, Economist, Southwark, Herald, Bahama, Minna, Sedgewick* and others which have left the shores of Great Britain, said to be loaded with arms and munitions of war of all kinds for the rebels, seek shelter in the so-called neutral colonies off our coast [Bermuda and Nassau] and not venturing to approach the blockaded ports, trans-ship their cargoes into small vessels of the lightest draught, provided in a great measure by the merchants of the same colonies who seem ever-ready to assist in the attempt to embarrass the government of the United States." Later on, in this same dispatch, he adds a poignant note: "I beg leave to remind the Department how much the difficulty of maintaining a close blockade has been increased by the introduction of steam." It was those very same light-draught steamers described by the harassed Du Pont which were soon to flit like ghosts in and out of Southern ports in great numbers, feeding the munitions-hungry Confederate armies with most of the wherewithal of war.

A month later, Du Pont again refers to the difficulties of closing Southern ports against "daring and desperate adventurers," and reminded the Department of previous requests for more ships suitable for that arduous duty. Although he claimed that the port of Charleston was the only one on the whole coast where the blockade was being violated, it had been clearly established that at Wilmington, North Carolina, blockade runners were going in and out on regular schedules.

In commenting on the condition of his blockading forces, Du Pont reported that their morale was good; the officers vigilant, and that a spirit of rivalry existed between the ships. Some of the commanding officers with suitable ships were very bold, Du Pont wrote with evident satisfaction. From sunset to sunrise they were personally on watch; the blockading force, variously grouped during the day, changed their stations after nightfall, and were constantly shifted, so as to avoid bearings being taken of them from the harbor. In pursuing blockade runners, Union men-of-war would risk grounding their vessels in order to approach shallow channels and often drew the fire of Confederate shore batteries. Yet most of the Union war vessels were too deep draught to get within a mile of a channel navigable to a light-draught blockade runner. This distance was sufficient for the runner to make a getaway. Another constant worry to the commander of the blockading squadron was the heavy strain on the vessels. They were under way every day and the wear and tear of wind, weather and seas soon began to be evidenced by break-downs of machinery. The necessary repairs were beyond the capacity of the squadron's machine shop. So from time to time it was necessary to detach frigates and gunboats from the squadron, and send them north to New York for repairs. The effectiveness of the blockade was consequently weakened by these absences.

In spite of the enthusiasm of Du Pont's sea dogs, their pursuit of blockade runners more often ended in failure than success. The advantage, of course, was on the side of the faster and lighter steamers which could easily outrun and outmaneuver Union men-of-war. What took place on June 23, 1862, was typical. Between two and three o'clock in the morning the blockading squadron sighted two black shapes approaching Charleston Harbor from the sea. One of them, a screw steamer, was supposed to be the elusive *Hero*, flying British colors. By the time she was discovered she had already slipped through the cordon of Federal vessels and had entered Maffitt's Channel. When daylight enabled her pursuers to see, it was discovered that the *Hero* in her haste to make port had run aground near Moultrie House and close to a battery of four Confederate guns. The guns of Fort Sumter and the battery on Cummings Point were also within range to protect the stranded vessel. Nevertheless the U.S.S. *Seneca* steamed as close as she could without running aground, and fired several shells at the stranded blockade runner. They fell short. The Confederate batteries promptly returned the fire. Being rifled cannon, they had a far greater range than those of

the *Seneca* but overshot their mark and their shells splashed
three or four hundred yards beyond the Federal vessel. Seeing
that further attempts to destroy the blockade runner were impossible, the *Seneca* withdrew. It is not known what happened
to the grounded Britisher, but it is very likely that willing hands
from Charleston quickly relieved her of her cargo and refloated
her on the first high tide. The other steamer, the *Nashville*, a
side-wheeler, failed in an attempt to penetrate the line of Union
war vessels and turned tail and fled out to sea. She was followed
by three Federal cruisers, the *Keystone State, Flag* and *James
Adger*. The *Flag* and *Adger* were slow vessels and soon gave up
the chase. But the *Keystone State* stubbornly held to the pursuit
during the entire day, tossing overboard every spare bit of gear
to lighten the vessel. By evening the *Nashville* was being rapidly
overhauled. It looked as if she was doomed to be captured. Just
then, however, a black rain squall swept down, completely hiding her from her pursuer. This bit of luck enabled the *Nashville*
to make good her escape. The chase had covered three hundred
miles of sea and Du Pont reported to his superiors that of all his
vessels, the *Keystone State* was the only one that was fast enough
to catch swift blockade runners like the *Nashville*. Du Pont
added somewhat sadly, "It is unnecessary for me to state to the
Department how much I regret this occurrance; but having myself visited the Charleston station, and giving personal attention
to the proper placing of the blockade vessels, I am satisfied that
no improvement can be made in this respect, and in justice to the
officers off there, I do not hesitate to say that greater vigilance
could not be exercised."

The estimate of the situation by the commander of the Southern blockading squadron was precise and accurate. An arc of
thirteen miles had to be covered outside the entrance to Charleston Harbor. He had only eight steamers and four sailing vessels
to cover this area. The vigilant guard aboard these vessels knew
from bitter experience that a ship could pass within two cable
lengths on an ordinary dark night without being seen. Du Pont
wrote to Gideon Welles that he should have at least twenty
vessels off Charleston, except that he also had to cover necessary

operations in Stono Inlet and Georgetown, South Carolina. He added the pointed remark that if the Department wished to make the running of the blockade absolutely impossible they would have to send him more steamers.

Other troubles beset the patient Du Pont besides the duties of watching for and pursuing blockade runners. As time went on, his men began to grow restive because they had no chance to go ashore and enjoy liberty. Storms continued to harass his vessels, smash his small boats and damage rudders, propellers and machinery.

When a Union vessel captured a blockade runner it was sometimes discovered that her captain or pilot were old offenders. On July 10, 1862, for example, the steamer *Emilie*, formerly the *William Seabrook* of Charleston, was overhauled and captured. Her captain, D. B. Vincent, was sent to Philadelphia along with the captured vessel. He was identified as having been engaged more than once in running the blockade. He also attained notoriety on one occasion by falsely pretending to be in distress and actually received assistance from the U.S.S. *Roanoke*. With this aid the wily Vincent was able to run safely into Charleston. The supercargo of the *Emilie* was also an old offender. Du Pont recommended to Secretary Welles that both these culprits be imprisoned in Fort Lafayette, adding that he respecfully submitted that the Department "cannot exercise too much vigilance in preventing the return of these men, who, from their local knowledge of this part of the coast, are the most efficient instruments of the rebels in violating the blockade."

On one occasion a British blockade runner, in attempting to evade capture, ran almost directly under the guns of a Union war vessel. On August 4, 1862, the British steamer *Lodona* tried to run into Tybee Channel and from there up the Savannah River past Fort Pulaski; but she was fired on by a Union battery near the Martello Tower on Tybee. One of the shots shattered her cabin. She immediately turned about and headed out to sea and cruised up and down until the following night when she tried to enter Ossebaw Sound. Here she ran almost head on into the U.S. gunboat, *Unadilla*, which promptly captured her.

The *Lodona* turned out to be a new steamer, built early the same year especially for the blockade-running business. Her cargo consisted of brandy, wines, tea, coffee, salt, clothing, boots, drugs, watches, figs, raisins, whisky, starch, soap, tin plates, soda, dry goods, paints, quinine and other medicines. Both her supercargo Purdue, and her captain, Charles E. Luckie, admitted under questioning that they were attempting to run the blockade. Commander Du Pont in his report to the honorable John Cadwalader, United States District Judge in Philadelphia, gives a good description of the vessel, which was typical of blockade runners of the time. He described her as having been built at Kingston-upon-Hull. She had one deck, three masts and was barque-rigged with an elliptical stern. Her hull was of iron and she measured 204 feet in length with a beam of 28 feet and drew 16½ feet of water. Her total tonnage, 687. She was equipped with two powerful engines. The *Lodona* was one of the first blockade runners to reduce her silhouette. When she was captured she had all her yards and topmasts on deck.

An important extra duty of the squadron under Du Pont's command was to conduct raids on enemy-held territory surrounding the various harbors and inlets for the purpose of destroying Confederate batteries and concentrations of troops stationed there to assist blockade runners coming in and out. Many lively skirmishes took place. In most cases the Union Navy was successful in clearing out these nests of Confederate resistance.

On August 2, 1862, an expedition was sent up the Santee River under Commander Prentice with three gunboats to burn a railroad bridge seventy miles from the mouth of the river. In passing Blake's Plantation they were fired upon by artillery, riflemen and cavalry. Commander Prentice shelled and destroyed the mill and dwelling which harbored Confederate troops. He found out later that this place had been used as the headquarters of a regiment stationed there to protect vessels running the blockade through South Santee and Alligator Creek.

Sometimes the boarding of a captured blockade runner was not conducted according to the best traditions of the United States

Navy. In the case of the *Emilie*, mentioned before, the Union prize crew got out of hand. They were so angry at the long chase that the British ensign was hauled down unceremoniously and with some passion. What happened next, according to the official report, was that the officers and crew of the *Emilie* set up round after round of drinks purposely to intoxicate the boarding party. Perhaps the Englishmen hoped to get the Federal sailors so dead drunk that they could recapture their vessel. It is more likely that all hands, seeing the amount of liquor available, fell to with gusto, although the official report tells of officers throwing liquor overboard to keep it out of the hands of their thirsty men.

Spurred on by the liquor, the Union boarding party broke open trunks and boxes and attempted to smuggle their loot ashore. Besides personal belongings, there was a pig, about thirty pounds of ham and a small looking glass. In reporting the incident, honest Du Pont admitted frankly that "I will not conceal from the Department that some irregularities appear to have occurred owing mainly to the inexperience of the officers, particularly in permitting their crews to go into the cabin and saloons of the prize, where the liquor, before referred to, was scattered about."

It is a rare feat for a sailing vessel to capture a steamer, but such an event occurred on October 24, 1862, when the British steamer *Scotia* submitted to the U.S. barque *Restless*, acting volunteer Lieutenant E. Conroy commanding. The sharp eyes of the lookout aboard the *Restless* discovered the *Scotia* standing in toward Bull's Island, South Carolina. Lieutenant Conroy immediately got under way with his vessel and at the same time sent two armed boats to leeward of the steamer. This maneuver forced her to run ashore. The *Restless* then came in close to cut off her escape and kept her from running out if she was able to claw her way off the sandbank before the small boats could reach her.

When the boats got alongside, Conroy recognized the captain, whose name was Libbie, to be an old blockade-running offender. The crew were mostly all drunk and were so troublesome that Conroy ordered them all put into irons. Then he began the task of refloating the grounded vessel. On the morning of the twenty-sixth, after much work, he pulled her off but kept the *Restless* anchored close aboard, within gunshot of the prize, to protect her.

By this time the *Scotia* was using her engines to help get her off the sand bar, for her engineers had sobered up sufficiently to render good assistance. Lieutenant Conroy promised that they would receive pay for their efforts and preferential treatment when they were brought into a Northern port.

Because the Confederate States government was unable to buy or build anything that could honestly be called a navy, they were not at any time strong enough to raise the blockade along the Atlantic Coast. The raids they made for this purpose were merely sudden and courageous dashes into the midst of the blockading fleet. Though often well organized and fearlessly carried out, the raids failed to accomplish anything more important than disabling one or two vessels and increasing the vigilance of the cruisers.

The most effective attack by Confederate naval forces took place off Charleston Harbor on January 31, 1863. Through a thick haze, two Confederate ironclad gunboats, the *Chicora* and *Palmetto State*, both rams, ventured out by the main ship channel. They were not sighted by the Federal squadron and began their attack against the cruisers, *Mercedita* and *Keystone State*. The Northern ships did not have the protection of the heavier men-of-war such as the *Powhatan* and *Canandaigua*, for they were at Port Royal coaling and repairing.

The *Mercedita* was the first Union vessel attacked. As the Confederate ironclad suddenly appeared out of the haze, the *Mercedita* immediately opened fire. But the ironclad was so close aboard and lying so low in the water that the Union vessel's guns could not be brought to bear. A heavy rifle shot from the Confederate entered the starboard side of the *Mercedita*, passed through her condenser and exploded against the port side, blowing a five-foot hole and killing the gunner. The escaping steam scalded a number of men and immobilized the engine. Unable to use his guns and being at the mercy of the enemy who was lying alongside on the starboard quarter, Captain Stellwagon deemed all further resistance hopeless, and he surrendered. The next object of the Confederate attack was the U.S.S. *Keystone State*, Commander Le Roy. A hot engagement followed, and when a shell from the ironclad exploded in the forehold of the *Keystone State*, she was set afire. Commander Le Roy ordered full steam ahead and tried to ram the enemy. Meanwhile her guns were trained and depressed for a plunging fire at the moment of collison. The ship was proceeding at the speed of twelve knots when a shell from the enemy passed through both her boilers and stopped her dead in the water. Altogether the *Keystone State* received ten shells, eight in her hull and two on the quarterdeck. The U.S.S. *Augusta* and U.S.S. *Quaker City* were both fired upon and struck in their hulls. The *Memphis* received damage to her rigging. At the same time the *Keystone State* was taken in tow by the *Memphis*. A lucky shell from the U.S.S. *Housatonic* struck the pilothouse of one of the ironclads and was thought to have done some damage. Having completely disorganized the blockading squadron, the Confederate vessels steamed northward under heavy shell fire and took refuge in the Swash Channel, which was protected by shoals. The *Keystone State* suffered casualties of one-quarter of her crew killed and wounded.

Apparently Admiral Du Pont was not satisfied with the conduct of the *Mercedita* and directed a court of inquiry to examine into the circumstances of her surrender. Strangely enough the *Mercedita* was not seized by the enemy following her surrender. Apparently both the Union and Confederate naval forces believed that she was sinking and neither took her in tow. Later on she was recovered by the Federals, patched up and sent North for repairs.

Admiral Du Pont's failure to subdue Fort Sumter and the other fortifications surrounding Charleston Harbor and his consequent inability to capture the city were a severe disappointment to the Navy Department and the nation as a whole. It also caused a certain amount of uncertainty on the part of European nations as to the success of the Union naval forces.

A great deal of correspondence went back and forth among

Du Pont, Secretary Gideon Welles and the Department. The net result was that on June 3, 1863, Rear Admiral Du Pont was relieved of the command of the South Atlantic Blockading Squadron and was replaced by Rear Admiral Andrew Hull Foote. Du Pont's command had covered a period of twenty-one months afloat. He left his post in a somewhat embittered frame of mind as is evidenced by his last communication to Gideon Welles, dated July 5, 1863. He wrote "I was not prepared for a continuance of that censure from the Department which had characterized the letters to me since the Monitors failed to take Charleston. I can only add now, that to an officer of my temperament, whose sole aim has been to do his whole duty and who has passed through 47 years of service without a word of reproof, these censures of the Navy Department would be keenly felt, if I did not know they were wholly undeserved."

Du Pont retired and died in June 1865. Unfortunately the brave but aging Admiral Foote had never completely recovered from his grueling service on the Western rivers. In New York he became suddenly ill and died within a few days. Gideon Welles, saddened by the loss, reluctantly assigned to Admiral John Dahlgren the responsibility for continuing attacks against Charleston and bottling up all other South Atlantic ports.

CHAPTER 3

Rich Cargoes

From the vantage point of nearly a hundred years, it seems incredible that the Federal government in Washington should have ignored the activities of the Confederate States government in purchasing war supplies in the North before even a single shot was fired at Fort Sumter. Soon after the provisional government was established, in February 1861, President Jefferson Davis instructed Captain Raphael Semmes, who had recently resigned from the United States Navy, to travel to the North and buy supplies. Davis realized that he had better act quickly before the door was slammed. As a result, Semmes was able to purchase important quantities of munitions in New York, Washington and various New England cities and have them shipped into the South.

In April of the same year, Captain Caleb Huse was sent to Europe on a buying mission for the Confederate States government. His particular interest was in the acquisition of ordnance stores and artillery. Shortly thereafter, Major Edward C. Anderson was dispatched to Europe to buy all types of supplies for the Confederate government. The Liverpool firm of Fraser, Trenholm & Co. (whose American branch in Charleston was to do so much for the Confederacy) was contacted and arrangements made for them to conduct commercial transactions for the Confederate States government.

In spite of a shortage of funds and competition from many U.S. agents who were actively buying munitions and war supplies abroad, Anderson and Huse were successful in purchasing satisfactory amounts of quartermaster and medical supplies as well as ordnance and forwarding them through the blockade to the hard-pressed Confederate army.

43

The first of these rich cargoes was shipped direct from England to Savannah aboard the steamer *Bermuda,* which arrived on September 28, 1861. In November, the steamer *Fingal* reached Savannah with a large cargo of naval and military supplies. These included 7,520 Enfield rifles, half of which were rushed to Albert Sidney Johnston's ill-equipped army defending Tennessee. The *Fingal* also brought in 17,000 pounds of cannon powder, a godsend to the Confederate artillery.

It was not long before the owners of large British steamers found that the increasing vigilance of the United States Navy on blockade duty was making it virtually impossible to escape destruction or capture. Thereupon they decided that speedy ships, built especially for the blockading business, were the solution to the problem. As soon as these were ready, a system was set up which remained in force throughout the war: the large British merchant ships carried cargoes from English ports to Bermuda and Nassau where they would be warehoused and transferred to small, fast, light-draught blockade runners which brought them through the Union cordon.

Bermuda and Nassau were strategically located in relation to the South Atlantic Coast. Bermuda was only 674 miles from Wilmington, North Carolina, and was mainly used by vessels running to that port. Since Nassau was closer to the coast of South Carolina and Georgia, it was the main headquarters for vessels running into Charleston (515 miles) and Savannah (500 miles).

All vessels leaving Europe or Bermuda or Nassau for Southern blockaded ports gave neutral ports as their destination on their ships' papers. A blockade runner leaving Bermuda for Wilmington, for example, would give Nassau as her destination. All of John T. Bourne's* manifests, covering scores of different blockade runners, invariably give Nassau as the port of destination. Of course none could be deceived by this pretense of an innocent voyage; and the U.S. courts, looking only at the final destination, condemned captured blockade runners when there was evidence of an ultimate *intention* to break the blockade.

* Agent for the Confederate government in Bermuda.

This decision rested solidly on an old principle of the English prize courts, known as the Doctrine of Continuous Voyage. According to this, the mere touching at an intermediate port of a vessel making an illegal voyage could not break the continuity of the voyage or remove the taint of illegality.

To get around this difficulty (they hoped) British and Confederate merchants and blockade runners thought up a new device. All cargoes would be transshipped at Bermuda or Nassau, either directly from ship to ship, or stored in warehouses and then transferred to the steamer that was to take them through the blockade. But here again the courts stepped in and held that though a transshipment was made, even after landing the cargo and going through a form of sale, the two voyages were parts of one and the same transaction, and the cargo from the outset was liable to condemnation, of both ship and cargo, if the original intention had been to forward the goods to a blockaded port. The Chief Justice of the United States Supreme Court summed up the situation when he said, "The ships are planks of the same bridge, all of the same kind, and necessary for the convenient passage of persons and property from one end to the other."

With these legal rights to support them, U.S. men-of-war roamed the waters between Bermuda, Nassau and the Southern mainland, continuously on the lookout for vessels heading east. It was a ninety-nine to one chance that they would be carrying contraband.

It will be recalled that at the outset of the war the Confederate government purposely refrained from buying and shipping cotton in the hope that its scarcity would induce the European powers officially to recognize the South and give it diplomatic status. But less than a year later President Davis and his advisers woke up to their mistake and scrambled frantically to buy up cotton stocks and ship them in order to finance the vast purchase of war materials being made abroad by Confederate agents. But the actual cotton buying was never properly organized until August 1864 as will be presently explained.

Meanwhile a commercial agent for the Confederate government had been appointed in Bermuda. He was a reputable merchant by the name of John Tory Bourne. Mr. Bourne kept a complete and accurate record of the cargo manifests of the Confederate blockade runners with whom he did business. Fortunately for posterity, copies of these manifests remained virtually complete and in relatively good condition for nearly a century in a grocery store conducted by a descendant, C. S. Bourne. Shortly after the death of C. S. Bourne the letter books of John T. Bourne came to light, thanks to the co-operation of customs officials at Saint George's, Bermuda, and leading citizens of the island.

Not only was Bermuda ideally situated for blockade running but its people were strongly in sympathy with the Southern cause. So much so, in fact, that on at least one occasion the U.S. consul was attacked in his office. On another day he was knocked down in the street by Bermudians who had become enraged at his activities favoring the Federal government. The sentiment in behalf of the Confederacy was further heightened by the rigid restrictions placed by the United States government on traffic between Northern ports and Bermuda and Nassau.

The new trade of blockade running brought with it a big increase in revenues to everyone in Bermuda. Life was gay and easy. The home of Mrs. Norman Walker (wife of the chief Confederate agent) was always open to Southern supporters. Rose Hill, residence of Mr. Bourne, overlooking beautiful Saint George's Harbor, was constantly filled with Confederate agents and Naval officers. Young girls of the islands entertained visiting young Confederate officers with all sorts of balls, dances and festivities. Saint George's had "become not only a harbor of refuge, but a pleasant resting place after the excitement and fatigue of an outward voyage," wrote one of the blockade runners.

Warehouses were crammed with crates marked "merchandise" or "nails" or "combustibles." Bourne's was filled to the ceiling with greatcloth, shoes, blankets, and Confederate government commissary stores awaiting shipment. Saint George's was a boom town in every respect, not only for officers and civilians but for common sailors as well. They filled the streets and overflowed the drinking places. Ladies of light virtue flocked to the town from Atlantic Coast ports, and "Shinbone Alley" boasted scores of bawdy houses and iniquitous dives.

Gamblers and speculators came to Bermuda and Nassau in droves, hoping to make quick and handsome profits—and many of them did. Popular speculations were in cut nails, salt, leather and medicines. During the first six months of the war the entire cut nail supply of the South was in the hands of four or five speculators in Richmond. Prices skyrocketed from $4 to $7 per keg and then to $10. As there was only one source of salt in the entire Confederacy, the price soared in two years from 1 cent per pound to 50 cents. In the early months, a great deal of salt was smuggled into the South from across the border in exchange for cotton.

Another favorite commodity of speculators was "Bermuda Bacon." The plan was simplicity itself. The bacon buyer would visit hog raisers in New York and other near-by states and offer the hog raisers far more a pound for their hams and bacon than the United States government or civilian merchants were offering. So it was very easy to buy up large supplies of pork products. These were salted and shipped out of New York or Philadelphia to Bermuda or Nassau. This was especially true during the first years of the war. No one seemed to wonder why the people of these islands were suddenly taking to eating vast quantities of pork products. Upon arrival in the islands, the hams and bacon were sold at quadruple their cost to agents of the Confederate States Quartermaster Corps, then shipped to hungry soldiers on the firing line.

War supplies of all kinds continued to flow through Bermuda in a seemingly endless stream. In February 1863, the chief of ordnance in Richmond received shipments from the island consisting of 70,980 long Enfield rifles, 9,715 short Enfields, 354 carbine Enfields, 20 small-bore Enfields, 27,000 Austrian rifles, 21,040 British muskets and 2,020 Brunswick rifles. There were also cases, molds, kegs and screwdrivers. Shipments of artillery: 129 guns of various types. An almost interminable list could be enumerated including percussion caps, tools, serge, cartridge bags, lead, copper, shellac, tin plate and steel.

The South was hard put to keep its soldiers supplied with lead bullets and the superintendent of Confederate ordnance laboratories wrote in March 1863 that lead was so scarce that if an unexpected emergency arose they would be unable to supply the demand. "The question of lead supply is nearly if not all together as vital as that of niter and such a demand upon the owners of vessels running the blockade would seem no illegitimate exercise of authority in such a crisis as this." What he referred to was his suggestion that blockade runners should be ordered to bring in a fixed amount of lead as part of each incoming cargo. All too often blockade-running captains who ran into danger of pursuit or capture threw the lead overboard to lighten their ships.

Between September 1862 and September 1863, a great deal had been accomplished by the Confederate government to improve their purchasing facilities abroad and keep open their lines of supply. During this period 113,504 small arms were brought through the blockade, in addition to great quantities of saltpeter, cartridges, flannel, paper for cartridges, leather and hardware. In contrast, only 35,000 arms were manufactured in the various armories of the Confederacy during the same period. Thus blockade running had provided more than three times the number of arms produced by the South itself. The following year, however, when Southern production increased and munitions and arms were flowing from Southern manufacturing plants, blockade running was of immense benefit in augmenting the scanty home supplies of food and clothing. The quartermaster general admitted in a letter to General Lee that his chief reliance on blockade running was to supply shoes, blankets and leather that winter.

One of the main reasons for the inadequate supply of food in the South throughout the war, both for civilians and for the Confederate army, was poor distribution, poor condition of the railroads and downright bad management. The shortage of meat was particularly acute following the fall of Vicksburg and the consequent disruption of communication with the trans-Mississippi department. To fulfill this need, every effort was made to import meat. This was successfully accomplished as shown by the fact that 8,632,000 pounds of meat were imported into the Confederacy between November 1, 1863, and December 8, 1864, all of this on government account along with more than half a million pounds of coffee.

Because the Confederate government neglected to control blockade running with strict rules and regulations, the owners of blockade runners did pretty much as they chose with regard to the cargoes they carried. There were many examples where meat destined for the South was allowed to spoil on the wharves of the islands because blockade-running captains favored less bulky and more profitable cargoes such as medicines, drugs, liquors and silks.

The closest approach to government control of blockade running was in the Ordnance Department of the Confederate States government. Here the Chief of Ordnance, who was charged with the responsibility for importing cannon, shot, shell, lead and saltpeter, operated four fast government-owned blockade runners. They were the *Cornubia, R. E. Lee, Merrimack* and *Phantom*. These efficient, speedy little packets operated with clocklike regularity between the islands and Southern seaports. Up to August 2, 1863, these four ships made more than fifty trips in and out of the blockade without a single loss.

A reorganization of the methods of buying and shipping war supplies was made in March 1864. If such changes had been made a year or more earlier, it is very likely that the success of blockade running and the volume of supplies brought into the Confederacy would have been far greater.

Involved in the reorganization was Lieutenant Colonel Thomas L. Bayne, who was designated to special service under the direction of the Secretary of War. He was put in charge of everything concerning cotton exports and with "supervision, so far as it pertains to the War Department, of the importation of supplies from the Islands, and the provision of cotton to pay for all supplies purchased by the various bureaus of the War Department, the payment for which is to be made in cotton."

Another regulation which should have been put into force a long time before was "an act to prohibit the importation of luxuries, or of articles not necessary or of common use." Heavy penalties were imposed for bringing such unnecessary goods into the Confederacy. A third act which had long been needed placed the export of cotton and tobacco fully in the hands of the government and the separate states of the Confederacy. Heavy fines were set forth for violation. Furthermore, orders were issued which provided that one-half of the inbound cargo space of blockade runners must be devoted to Confederate freight at fixed prices.

"By August, 1864, all cotton buying east of the Mississippi was centralized under the Bureau of Foreign Supplies and the proceeds credited to treasury agents in Europe," according to the records. Now at last cotton was being fully and effectively employed for the purpose which it should have served from the very beginning of the war. It was made to *work* rather than threaten, to provide payment instead of bribing. The good results that came out of this procedure were soon noticeable. It is reasonable to suppose that if the new plan of operation had been instituted two years earlier, the Confederacy might have built up a large number of ships to penetrate the blockade. Thus, shortages of all kinds could have been eliminated. In the opinion of one authority, "blockade running was not one of the Confederacy's blunders. It was perhaps the most successful, large-scale campaign attempted by the South. Its failure was not due to any weakness in its own makeup, but to the collapse of its foundation—the collapse of the Confederacy itself." This opinion is open to some question, however. The Confederate States government never fully realized the importance of blockade running or they would have taken over its regulation as soon as it was in operation. Too much freedom was allowed blockade-running vessels in the selection of their cargoes and their methods of operation.

In scanning the five letter books of John Tory Bourne, a number of significant facts come to life regarding the part which Bermuda commission agents played in the blockade-running business. The following excerpts from his letters will illustrate these facts.

In writing to John Fraser & Co., of Charleston, South Carolina, in March 1862, Mr. Bourne describes the facilities of the port of Saint George's: "The port, as you will observe in the chart [apparently a chart of the Island accompanied his letter] is easy of ingress and egress for steamers and sailing vessels of large class, say drawing twenty feet. Our pilots are very skillful and all natives. The facilities for coaling steamships are greater here than in Madeira; the coal is carried off in lighters; at this port I put the ships alongside the wharf, coaling with barrows which considerably facilitates their movements and in fifteen minutes after the anchor is weighed the ships are at sea. Labour just at this time is high, mainly five shillings per diem, three shillings, six pence and four shillings is the usual rate but there are so many ships arriving here and discharging their cargoes and making repairs that labour is scarce."

Financial transactions between the Confederate States government and English export firms were difficult because there was no bank in Bermuda. Bermuda agents were unable to effect the sale of foreign bank bills on any terms. Large private bills on English banks were difficult to negotiate. English merchants found it best to ship gold uninsured and make necessary disbursements in that manner. Agent Bourne not only had to contend with all sorts of mercantile and financial transactions, but once in a while had to handle a mutiny. In his letter of April 8, 1862, to Fraser, Trenholm, & Co. of Liverpool, he described what happened aboard the company's vessel, the *Herald*, Captain Tate. She arrived in Bermuda on the twenty-fourth of March fifteen days out from Madeira. "On the morning of her arrival it came to my knowledge that the whole crew were in a state of mutiny, the engineer stated to Captain Tate. They learned since arrival that the ship was bound for Charleston, they would not go, and if on their going to sea they found her steered in that direction, they would stop the engines; on my going aboard to look after the delivery of coal I found no discipline and the work progressing very slowly; great dissatisfaction and ill feeling was shown by Captain Tate toward Mr. Mitchel [apparently one of the mutinous crew] which I do not consider Mr. M. deserving of; Captain Tate is totally unfit to be in charge of this property and has *no nerve* to enable him to persevere with Mr. M. to take the ship to her port of destination, this fact became known to the world on the morning of the 28th, when Captain Tate with Mr. Fraser, the first engineer, without ever making reference to anyone on board or to me as agent, went to the Mayor's office and noted a protest (certified copy of which Captain Westendorf will enclose to you) and put himself under the Federal consul, Mr. Allen of this port who advises him (as Captain T. tells me) by no means to let the vessel go out of port until the owners are heard from."

After much hurly-burly and arguments back and forth in which the governor became involved, Captain Tate and his dissatisfied crew were persuaded to quit the ship after being paid several months' wages and fare back to England.

The interest in, and sympathy for, the Southern cause on the part of Mr. Bourne is shown in a letter of June 1862, addressed to John Fraser & Co., of Charleston, in which he says, "I assure you sympathy for the South is now being more widely felt and particularly so when their wishes are put before all Christian men in a truthful light; at this distance we are better able to judge of the progress of the North; they have done nothing; the taking possession of the seaport towns was expected on account of their superior force by sea [a reference to the capture of Port Royal and other Southern ports]. On shore even with the assistance of gunboats they have been defeated and driven back; no confidence can be placed in any of the Northern papers; they invariably claim a victory but their so-called victorious army never pursues, always retires—by that means the world judges of their defeat."

Federal cruisers operating off Bermuda had become such a nuisance that Mr. Bourne suggested in a letter to Fraser, Trenholm & Co., on June 14, 1862, a new plan of operations. "The Federal Cruisers have instructions to intercept all steamers bound to Nassau. I suggested to Messrs. J. & O. Fraser & Co. per *Herald* that they divide their business between that port and this, the U.S. Cruisers can go to Key West, coal and return to the Bahama channel in 48 hours where they can anchor at pleasure but they can not do that in these waters, distance 700 to 800 miles from any coal depot—ocean water outside the reef all round Bermuda, they cannot hold on. Any accident happening to their machinery the dockyard authorities will be very cautious what leniency they give them. Several parties have sent steamers and other vessels to Nassau and I learn that port is full of vessels of all sorts concerned in this trade which makes it appear dangerous. We have not had a visit from any of them." Thus Nassau took its place as the second important transshipping point for war supplies as well as cotton coming in from Southern ports.

Many references have been made to the speed of blockade runners by contemporary writers. Mr. Bourne confirms their fast-steaming qualities by a reference to the steamer *Cornubia*. "The C. is a very fast ship of 18 knots and will be on the wind early next week."

In these early days of blockade running the Confederate States government often neglected to issue the necessary orders permitting the importation of war supplies from vessels awaiting such orders in Bermuda. An example of this was the steamer *Harriet Pinckney*, which lay in harbor at Saint George's from the first of August until late in December loaded with a battery of field artillery and other cargo awaiting orders from Richmond.

By November 1863, the tightening of the Union blockade, especially at Wilmington, was noted by Mr. Bourne in a letter dated the nineteenth to J. Stewart Oxley & Co. of Liverpool. He says in part, "I regret I cannot advise further shipments of cotton, the *Flora* arrived yesterday with cotton from Wilmington and brings the news of five captures out of seven blockade runners, therefore so far as Bermuda is concerned you may not expect to receive over 300 bales in the next three months. Please wind up all sales of cotton in your hands vesting proceeds thereof in 50 coils of Manila rope and the balance in bagging fit for cotton bales and cement, all to be insured and when you have blockade runners from England I will be able to ship more cotton."

The capture of a blockade runner by a Federal cruiser frequently resulted in bags of mail falling into Federal hands. An incident of this sort is reported by John T. Bourne in a letter dated December 2, 1863, and addressed to John Fraser & Co. of Charleston. It reads in part, "I regret to say that the letter bags of the *Cornubia, Ella and Annie,* and *R. E. Lee* have fallen into the hands of the Yankees; how this happened I am unable to say; there were several letters in the *Ella and Annie's* bag for you and the others you received per *Hansa.* The New York *Herald* published some of the correspondence and I enclose the sheet for your perusal; by Messrs. Reid & Co.'s contract the Confederate government seems wishful of passing its business into other hands, by setting aside those mercantile men, who have passed through with them the trying ordeal of the first days of their struggle for independence."

Apparently Mr. Bourne felt that there was a good deal to be desired in the way the Confederate States government conducted its business in connection with blockade running, for he says, "How much better it would be for the government to send their orders for supplies into the hands of Messrs. Fraser, Trenholm & Co. through Mr. Mason or his deputy and dispense with their agents; these agents are no doubt good patriotic and moral men but not brought up to business habits and consider these apparent lucrative bargains beneficial. If the Confederate government is to own two-thirds of five steamers surely it would be better to own the *whole* of *four* and run them on their own account and risk; by this means they would avoid any collision with the jobbing houses and be on a respectable and safer footing. The fewer agents sent from the Confederacy to the Island and Europe the better; this would insure secrecy with men of business and the wants of the Confederacy supplied without the knowledge of the enemy and their friends; from what we read in the papers, I fear all this trouble in England has arisen from parties sent from the Confederate States as lookers-on, and aspiring to power, tell their errand to their new friends, before their work is complete."

In the early spring of 1864, Mr. Bourne gives an interesting sidelight on the repatriation of Confederate prisoners. This letter was directed to John Fraser & Company of Charleston: "As considerable feeling exists in Bermuda about taking into the Confederacy, soldiers who have escaped from Federal prison (and very useful men) in the steamers going in from time to time; will you be kind enough to give me authority to act in such particular cases with any ships in which you may be interested for this purpose. You are aware that these men have only what they stand in on arrival here from Halifax and as circumstances direct two or three of these men may be conveyed across to their corps with little expense to the owners of steamers which would only be their consumption." Apparently this last phrase refers to the fact that the only expense to the owners of the steamers would be the food that these escaped prisoners would consume during the three-day voyage between Bermuda and Charleston.

A little later Mr. Bourne reports what happened to the steamer *Thistle*, which was run ashore "close to the guns of Fort Fisher; her cargo had been thrown overboard. But she was tight and, as soon as the tide and weather would permit the coals were removed and a steam tug sent to her assistance." It is to be presumed that the *Thistle* was successfully salvaged by the Confederates.

During the last two years of the war the steamers which were able to make a successful round trip, due to skillful navigation and a generous measure of good luck, showed handsome profits. On April 16, 1864, Mr. Bourne reported to Mr. B. W. Harte, Esq., of London that "steamer *Minnie*, Captain Gilpin, has made a splendid trip bringing 700 odd bales of cotton and a good lot of tobacco, paying for herself and the *Emily*. There is no news from the coast." It is quite believable that a successful voyage of this kind would net money sufficient to pay for two blockade runners.

That yellow fever often swept through the Islands as well as the mainland is shown by correspondence between Mr. Bourne

and Messrs. Lane Hankey & Co. of London. The letter is dated
May 13, 1864. "The season having so far advanced that the trade
of the steamers to Wilmington being now expected to be principally to Bermuda instead of Nassau, in consequence of the
prevalence there of fever during the summer months which subjects them to quarantine at Wilmington after the 20th, I deem
it would be to the advantage of all parties concerned in the
Lady-of-the-Lake to order her in here and I hope shortly to be
able to wait on you with account sales of her cargo."

In another letter written the same day, Bourne refers to a
"large fire at Wilmington which destroyed upwards of 6000
bales of cotton."

There is a gap of nine months between Mr. Bourne's letter
books No. 3 and No. 4. The latter begins with February 1865,
and he refers to the rumor of an armistice "being concluded between the North and South—I have to request that you will be
kind enough to ask the Secretary of State, whether during such
armistice being happily concluded, if vessels laden with merchandise, such as provisions, dry goods and medicines, will be permitted to pass through the blockade of any port in the Southern
states—and such documents being produced to you satisfactorily
showing that such vessels have nothing contraband of war on
board such as gunpowder, arms, etc." One of the concluding
documents in Bourne's letter book No. 4 is a letter dated at
Saint George's on March 23, 1865, and directed to Gosling
Brothers of Hamilton, Bermuda, in which he states that he has
"the pleasure herewith to enclose your account: current showing balance in my favor of 883 pounds, six shillings, ten pence
which I trust on examination will be found correct—the business
hitherto carried on in our Island is now considered to be at an
end and I am closing up all those transactions connected there-
with. . ."

Another person vitally concerned with supplies for the Confederate army was Major Smith Stansbury, C.S.A. His letter
book has also been preserved and a few excerpts throw an interesting light on the desperate needs of the Confederacy. Writing
from Saint George's, Bermuda, to Major Caleb Huse in England,

Major Stansbury comments on the urgent need for saltpetre "to keep our powder works at Augusta, Georgia in operation."

"The capacity of the mills is to produce 5000 pounds per working diem of ten hours or 10,000 to 12,000 pounds, working day and night, and this could be nearly doubled by certain improvements. The supplies of saltpetre are from first, running the blockade; second the limestone caves of Virginia, Tennessee; and third, the nitre beds—The last will hardly yield anything for a year to come, and the supply from No. 2 is very uncertain. You are doubtless aware that it was the policy of the old U.S. government to accumulate a stock of this material in time of peace and a certain amount of money was annually appropriated for the purpose. At the commencement of the war the supply at the North was quite large, there being two million pounds at Frankfort arsenal alone. The deficiency in the supply of lead has at times been very embarrassing and the importance of having always on hand large supplies of this material cannot be overestimated. We are also in need of percussion caps and it would be well to send over four or five millions as soon as possible."

Inefficiency in arranging for an adequate coal supply at Bermuda for blockade runners often caused costly delays. Major Stansbury refers to this in a letter in July 1863, in which he says that the Confederate steamers *Florida* and *R. E. Lee* had been detained several days "for want of coal, and for which we had been compelled to send to Halifax. Our steamers which run the blockade at Wilmington, require the coincidence of a high tide to cross the bar and of a dark night to evade the blockade. The detention of a single day in the regular trips often involves a further detention of ten or twelve days or greatly increased risk of capture—I earnestly recommend, that 700 tons of Cardiff coal* be dispatched here per month, to meet the perspective wants of our vessels and that a reserve of 2000 tons be accumulated as soon as possible to meet the contingency." Whether Major Caleb Huse, in London, met this request is unknown, but frequent references to Cardiff coal in the records would indicate that he did. Some of the purchases made for the Confederate

* Anthracite.

army in England and Europe turned out to be bad bargains. Major Stansbury refers to 60,000 Austrian muskets "which judging from the samples I have seen are also condemed arms and to us utterly worthless. I am afraid that the cargo of the *Miriam* consists of a number or similar amount of trash." Later on he revised his opinion after examining the shipment more thoroughly.

As the fortunes of the Confederacy waned, the thirst of certain political gentlemen in Richmond waxed greater, for we find a letter of August 5, 1863, referring to 300 cases of brandy at thirty-five shillings a case and 547 gallons of brandy at sixteen shillings per gallon. "These will be forwarded to Wilmington as soon as the transportation can be spared."

As the volume of war supplies leaving Bermuda got larger, the paper work increased proportionately. Major Stansbury was working with a very small staff, for he writes to Colonel J. Gorgas, Chief of the Ordnance Bureau, in August of 1863, begging for the three clerks "asked for in my letter of the 30th ultimo. The business cannot be conducted here with anything like system without a corps of at least half-a-dozen first class clerks between Major Walker and myself. At present Major Walker has one and one-fourth and I have one—the mere duplication of writing in my own office could hardly be performed by a racehorse clerk working twelve hours a day—the three men asked for are worth more than any dozen that could be engaged here and with the additional advantage that they are of tried fidelity."

Warehouse space was in great demand for the storage of war materials as well as civilian goods. In his correspondence, Major Stansbury refers to four warehouses besides Bourne's rented by the Confederate States government: Penno's, Musson's, Doctor Hunter's and Mrs. Todd's. Attached to each warehouse was a wharf. One of the difficulties was that only one steamer could occupy a wharf at a time. "Only four vessels whether public or private can be discharged or loaded at the same time for the reason that a custom house officer is required for each vessel and there are only four custom house officers. Several detentions have

occurred from this cause since I have been upon the Island."
Loading or discharging vessels was not an easy matter. "Gang-
ways have to be rigged and unrigged and this with their poor
appliances is generally the work of a day—but the loss of a day,
most frequently involves the loss of a moon*—so that even if a
second wharf were vacant, as a general rule a vessel cannot be
loaded partly from one storehouse and partly from another.
Neither can the stores be transported from one storehouse to
another as there are no carts or drays. I do not think we could
depend upon hiring half a dozen for a single day in Saint
George's. We cannot open boxes of arms and clean and oil them
and so forth or do any work of the kind—no room—no work-
men—no tools—no conveniences—this is not a city or a town but
a village."

The cost of living in Bermuda was estimated by Major Stansbury as "fully 25% of that above New York. Without going
into a statement of the cost of provisions and clothing, the cost
of very indifferent board, with the most slender accommodations
is about $1.50 a day." While this might seem very reasonable by
today's standards, it was considered exorbitant in 1863. By the
end of December 1863, prices for everything in Bermuda had
gone up greatly. A resident writing to a friend in London said:
"I must say the expense of living in Bermuda is higher now than
I ever knew, properties which commanded little or no rent last
winter, have gone up to fabulous prices and these prices are only
paid by the strangers and non-colonists." In a letter to a firm in
Nassau, Bourne notes that freight rates had risen to $150—$200
a ton.

An examination of the cargo manifests of the blockade runners
plying between Bermuda and the Confederate States gives an
interesting picture of the type and quantity of supplies being
run through to Southern ports both for military and civilian use.
Among the civilian articles of merchandise there were cigars,
soap, pepper, coffee, whisky, bonnet frames, sherry wine, hams,

* Blockade runners dared not operate during moonlight nights for fear
of being detected.

cheeses, dry goods, bay rum, wearing apparel, brandy, boots and shoes, candles, tea, preserved meats and wire frames for hoop skirts.

Bermuda collapsed nearly three months before Appomattox. The second battle of Fort Fisher and the occupation of Wilmington by Union troops had slammed and locked the Confederacy's last exit to the outside world. Some of the Bermuda-based runners went to Havana hoping that they could run cargoes from there to Galveston, but before they got fairly established the war was over.

In Bermuda today one can occasionally hear an exciting tale of blockade running, told by descendants of Bermudians who lived during those wild days. One of the oldest families on the Island is the Darrell family. At Mount Wyndham, the beautiful residence of the present generation of Darrells, there is an interesting if somewhat tragic relic of the Confederacy. During the latter stages of the war, the Richmond government sent instructions to England for the making of the Great Seal of the Confederacy. In due time the seal and its huge press arrived in Bermuda. A Bermudian blockade runner was chosen to carry the seal and the press through the blockade. Three times the fast little steamer tried to penetrate the tight cordon stretched across both mouths of the Cape Fear, and three times she turned back, unable to slip through. So, to this day, the Great Seal of the Confederacy and its press remain at Mount Wyndham, cherished relics of a bygone era.

Like Bermuda, Nassau was awakened from centuries of somnolence by the advent of blockade running. Depopulated and abandoned by the Spaniards early in the seventeenth century, the British a few years later established themselves as owners of the archipelago. One time the haunt of pirates, New Providence Island, the capital and the outer islands had, until the outbreak of the war, depended on sponging, fishing, turtling and wrecking for a precarious livelihood.

Blockade running changed all that. Gold poured into the dusty island's lap in a sudden and bewildering stream. The town teemed with turmoil and life. Everyone down to the humblest black had a job. Everyone ate regularly. Important British and Southern firms established agencies on New Providence and almost every day, at the height of the trade, steamers managed by these firms left Nassau Harbor to try their luck at evading Federal war vessels off the Carolina coast or arrived from there loaded to the gunwales with cotton.

The islands that formed the Bahama chain had definite strategic value for vessels wishing to enter blockaded ports. Those little spots of land extended some hundreds of miles in the direction of the Southern mainland, providing extra protection from Federal cruisers, since the waters immediately adjacent to the Bahamas were under British authority.

In his memoirs, Captain Wilkinson gives a graphic picture of the waterfront at Nassau during this period: "Cotton, cotton, everywhere! Blockade runners discharging it into lighters; tier upon tier of it, piled high upon the wharves, and merchant vessels, chiefly under the British flag, loading with it. Here and there in the crowded harbor might be seen a low, long, rakish looking lead-colored steamer with short masts and a convex forecastle deck extending nearly as far aft as the waist, and placed there to enable her to be forced *through* and not *over* a heavy head sea. These were the genuine blockade runners, built for speed; and some of them survived all the desperate hazards of the war."

When one studies the crisp and graceful lines of these little steamers, one can see in them the inspiration for what later developed into the modern destroyer. In fact, the earliest destroyers or torpedo-boat destroyers, as they were called, had the same type of convex forecastles and raked stacks and masts as described by Captain Wilkinson.

At the time of his visit to Nassau, the place was in the midst of an epidemic of yellow fever. Wilkinson humorously describes the visit to his ship of a mulatto undertaker who came on board to take the measure for coffins of two passengers who had died en route. This visit, Wilkinson says, "did not leave us in a very cheerful state of mind, although the undertaker was in fine spirits, in anticipation of a brisk demand for his stock in trade.

"Presenting each one of us with his card, he politely expressed the hope that we would give him our custom, if we needed anything in his line. Fortunately we had no occasion for his services. Just before leaving the ship he was invited to take a glass of brandy and water. Holding the glass in his hands which were yet stained with coffin paint, he drank to our death, a toast to which Dyer, my Wilmington pilot, responded, 'You shouldn't bury me, you d——d rascal, if I did die!' "

The first vessel to bring cotton to Nassau arrived there in December 1861, with 144 bales. Between that time and the close of the war 397 vessels entered Nassau from Southern ports, and 588 sailed from Nassau for Southern ports. Of the clearances 432 were ostensibly for Saint John, New Brunswick, and of that number only thirty-two flew the Confederate flag. This indicates the extent to which British shipowners were involved in the trade.

An obscure travel book called *The Atlantic Islands*, published in 1878, gives a colorful description of Nassau during the height of the blockade-running business: "During the Confederate years the little town actually swarmed with Southern refugees, the captains and crews of blockade-runners, cotton brokers, rum-sellers, Jews and Gentiles of high and low degree, coining money and squandering it as if they owned the secret of transmutation of metals. They played toss-penny on the verandahs of the Royal Victoria Hotel with gold eagles! The shops were packed to the ceilings; the streets were crowded with bales, boxes and barrels—cotton coming in, Confederate uniforms and pills of lead and quinine to pepper patriots and patients, going out. Semmes and his bold boys twisted their mustaches at every corner, danced involuntary reels and hornpipes from groggery to groggery. They were also often seen on the waxed floors of Government House, where they were always sure of a cordial reception, along with other guests from the *Banshee*, and *Alabama*—bully chappies who brandished their revolvers in the faces of Union men, whose lives were too uncertain to insure thereabouts in those rollicking days."

A spicy little paper called *Young Punch*, edited by a witty

Confederate in Nassau, under the sobriquet of "The Can't Get Away Club," gives a glimpse of the state of things then existing and shows that there was some real fun connected with blockade running. A rather grim joke was played at the expense of the rebels via Nassau. A large invoice of prayer books was brought from England and reshipped to Charleston, with the express understanding that they were suited to the devotional wants of the Confederacy. Quite a number had been distributed before it was discovered that the prayers for the President and Congress of the United States had not been altered! "It is a fact that some of the goods smuggled into the Confederacy by way of Nassau were from Northern ports, as for example, shiploads of pistols brought from Boston in barrels of lard."

A blockade runner steaming into the harbor of Nassau or Bermuda was a memorable sight. At a distance she had an odd, brown, squarish appearance unlike any vessel ever seen. On closer approach the reason was easily discernible: the vessel's decks were crammed with bales of cotton. Every square inch of space was taken up with the stuff, each bale compressed to half its original size by steam presses at Southern ports. The upper deck was piled with two or three tiers of bales. The pilothouse and engine-room hatches were protected from shot and shell by bulwarks of baled cotton. Cargoes varied from 600 to 800 bales, depending on the capacity of the vessel. One large steamer was known to have staggered into Nassau with 1,200 bales.

In the latter two years of the war, the profits resulting from the export of cotton through the blockade were enough to make any opportunist drool. Cotton which could be bought anywhere in the South for 6 cents a pound brought from 56 cents to 66 cents a pound, laid down in England, realizing a gross profit of from 50 cents to 60 cents. A steamer with an average capacity of 800 bales often earned $420,000 on a successful round trip. It was a common saying among the blockade-running fraternity that a shipowner could shrug off the loss of his vessel after two safe round trips through the blockade.

In casting up his accounts after the loss of the *Banshee*, supercargo Tom Taylor wrote that "Some idea of the vast profits accruing from blockade running at this time (1863-1864) can be gathered from the fact that notwithstanding the total loss of the *Banshee* by capture, she earned sufficient on the eight successful round trips which she made, to pay her shareholders 700% on their investment." On a cargo of meat and provisions sold to the Commissary General in Richmond in the fall of 1864, Taylor chalked up a net profit of 350 per cent. He received $27,000 for the foodstuffs, having paid only $6,000 in Nassau.

Where there were shortages of civilian items in the South (and that meant practically everything) profits soared for those who were willing to risk death and destruction through the blockade. On one occasion a captain arrived in Wilmington with his cabin crammed with boxes of shoe thread. One Southern speculator promptly bought up the entire lot, paying $3.00 a pound. The captain cleared $8,000 in a matter of minutes.

The pay of the officers, pilots and crew of blockade runners was in keeping with the risks involved and the high earning power of the ships they manned. Below are listed the rates of pay aboard a first-class vessel when the business was at its height, based on a report of the master of the famous *Don*. The figures shown are for a single round trip from Nassau to Wilmington. Since the round trip could be made in ten days at the most, assuming there were no delays in the turnaround, it would seem that these seagoing sailormen had plenty of cash to toss around the grop shops and brothels:

Captain	$5,000
Pilot	3,750
Chief Engineer	2,500
Chief Officer	1,250
Crew and firemen	250

These sums were paid the men in British gold or U.S. currency. In addition to their regular pay, officers were permitted to stow away little cargoes of their own and so make a private speculation on each trip. If a captain wanted to make a handsome gift

Blockade runner at St. Georges, Bermuda.

Unloading cotton at Nassau.

to a friend in Bermuda or Nassau, he would present him with a cotton bale, most likely brought over in the captain's cabin. A number of skippers who were fortunate enough to make frequent safe trips over a six months' period piled up so much money that they were able to retire at the end of that time.

At both ends of the blockade-running line the merchants and shipowners who correctly evaluated the shrinking fortunes of the Confederacy got out ahead of time with comfortable fortunes, for they had steadily converted their Confederate currency into sound U.S. dollars or British gold. Patriotic Southerners and speculators less observant of the hastening end of the Confederacy, found themselves staring at bales of Confederate paper money with the grim thought that it would make a pretty poor bonfire.

Nassau fared worse than Bermuda from the backwash of peace. A year-and-a-half after the fall of Richmond the century's worst hurricane struck the Island. The ocean rolled completely over Hog Island into the harbor in surges so enormous that the crest was on a level with the gallery of the lighthouse, sixty feet above the sea. Houses and forests went down before the wind like reeds. In twenty-four hours the city was like a town sacked and burned by the enemy, and a large part of the wealth accumulated during the Civil War was gone with the wind.

CHAPTER 4

Tom Taylor, Supercargo

AT THE outbreak of the war, a young Englishman, Thomas E. Taylor, was working as an assistant in the office of a firm of Liverpool merchants,* trading chiefly with India and the United States. Like most red-blooded young men, he longed to get out from behind his desk and take part in the fighting. But he could not afford to give up his job, so he kept on working on the firm's account books and correspondence. Meanwhile he followed the war news closely, and like many of fellow countrymen, was incensed at the *Trent* affair.

"There is no doubt that we are prepared to make any sacrifice to resent this outrage," he wrote at the time to an American friend in South Carolina. "Feeling runs very deep here and we await for the answer to our demands for redress. The Federal government is apparently the spoiled child of diplomacy. Her omission of international courtesy, combined with the extravagances of her press, confirm to many of us Englishmen an inchoate partisanship for the South."

Although Taylor did not realize it when he wrote those words, his chance to demonstrate that partisanship was close at hand. Early in 1862, one of the partners in his firm called him into private session and announced that he and several other merchants had bought a steamer and proposed to have a try at running the blockade.

"Would you care to go with her as supercargo?" asked the partner.

* Although nowhere in his narrative does Taylor mention the name of his company, it is thought to be Edward Laurence & Co. This opinion is based on letters written by John T. Bourne, Commercial Agent for the Confederate government at Bermuda.

"By all means," Taylor answered, "if I am not too young." (He was 21.)

"No, it's a young man's job" was the reply.

So began the blockade-running career of Thomas E. Taylor. Many years after the war, he set down his adventure: a narrative of exciting escapes, of coolness and resource in moments of acute danger, of well-calculated risks, boldly accepted and expertly carried out, of losses from fire and shot and shell, and of enormous profits piled up in a matter of days.

Taylor was more than a mere supercargo. He was what would be called in today's parlance an operations officer, for he did not act as a seagoing clerk or direct the movements of his fleet of blockade-running steamers from a desk ashore. He went along and saw them through the Federal squadrons guarding Southern ports. He was a *super* supercargo, who believed in traveling aboard his steamers, and keeping an observant and critical eye on the captain, pilot and crew. That this policy paid off in successful runs through the blockade and handsome profits was apparent.

Although Tom Taylor's sympathies were ardently on the side of the South, his main motive (as well as that of other British merchants and shipowners) was to take advantage of the fantastic amounts of money to be made—and quickly—through blockade running. Only a few Southern blockade runners like Maffitt and Wilkinson (both Confederate naval officers) and a handful of Southern firms were motivated by genuine patriotism. The rest were in the business to make fortunes.

The vessel bought by Taylor's firm was called the *Despatch*. In those early days of blockade running it was thought that almost any kind of vessel would do, since in England the newspapers had given the impression that the blockade was a huge joke as far as its enforcement by the United States Navy was concerned. The *Despatch* proved quite unfit for the trade. She left England loaded down, as deep as she would float, with a cargo of ponderous cases of war materials as well as light goods. Her deck was piled rail high with coal so that she could steam to Nassau without calling at an intermediate port. She had barely one foot of freeboard to her credit. A storm damaged the boilers of the *Despatch* a few hundred miles southwest of Ireland and she was forced to put in to Queenstown for repairs. Later, off the Azores, the ancient vessel came near foundering in a gale, but managed to limp into Nassau.

The bustle and excitement of this port, so recently transformed from the sleepy haunt of sponge fishermen into a thriving center of blockade running, found young Taylor anxious to prepare at once for a run. His supplies were ready. Also awaiting him was the barque *Astoria*, thoughtfully sent out from England to act as his storeship and afterward to carry home the cotton he expected to get out from a Southern port. But certain grim facts put a brake on Taylor's eagerness to weigh anchor. When the seasoned blockade-running captains looked over the *Despatch*, they shook their heads. She wouldn't do. She was much too slow to show her heels to the fast Federal cruisers lately assigned to blockading duty. Moreover, she drew too much water to get over the bars at Charleston or Wilmington. Although young and inexperienced and terribly impatient to make fast money for his employers, Tom Taylor accepted the advice of the experts. "It was a bitter pill to swallow," he wrote. After consulting with the local agent of his firm, he decided to sell the cargo of the *Despatch* on the spot, and "get both vessels home to the best advantage."

For some undisclosed reason (probably because little cotton was coming in at the time) Tom was unable to get freight for either of the vessels direct to England. So he sent the barque to New York in search of cargo and made a contract for the *Despatch* to tow a disabled steamer to the same port on the "no cure no pay" principle; he himself took a fast packet to New York.

On arrival there he was greeted with bad news. Both vessels were in quarantine with yellow fever aboard; also, the *Despatch* had dropped her tow off Port Royal in a gale of wind and came on without her. "This was a pretty mess for a youngster to be in," he commented in his memoirs, "in a strange city like New York, where everything connected with Nassau was looked upon with suspicion, and the fear of yellow fever was rampant."

After innumerable quarantine difficulties and not before several sailors had died, both vessels were given "pratique." But Taylor's troubles were far from finished. His steamer was immediately seized to satisfy a $30,000 suit by the owners of the vessel the *Despatch* had tried to tow. They demanded this sum as damages for letting their vessel go. Soon a U.S. marshal came aboard and secured the necessary papers. Taylor was at his wits' end about what to do to save his ship. "As I had no means for providing the required security, the captain and I formed a rather mad scheme to rescue the *Despatch* from the Marshal's clutches." Gone completely was Taylor's caution. No one but a young and desperate man would even have considered such a plan seriously. But Taylor and his skipper not only considered it, but went right ahead to carry it out. The plot was simple: the captain of the *Despatch* was to get her under way quietly, taking the marshal's officer with him, while Taylor remained ashore to lull suspicion. Early one misty morning the *Despatch* stole away from her anchorage and headed down the bay. But her movements had been watched by sharp eyes aboard a revenue cutter which signaled the forts guarding the Narrows. They immediately opened fire and there was no other choice but to return or be sunk.

"Of course all this made my position worse," Taylor recalled years afterward, "but to make a long story short, a kind friend, a prominent New York banker, went bail for me, and the *Despatch* was released and loaded for home. Finally I compromised the case for about $2000. The barque I sent on to St. John and, following her myself by steamer, I chartered her to carry home a cargo of timber." So ended Tom Taylor's first and unsuccessful attempt at blockade running.

His expenses and troubles in New York apparently did not hurt his standing with his firm, for they soon put him in charge of a steamer that was destined to become famous among the blockade-running fraternity and infamous to the United States Navy. Her name was the *Banshee*, later known as *Banshee No. 1*. She had been building at Liverpool while Taylor was overseas and had been especially designed as a blockade runner. Taylor referred to her as a landmark of marine architecture, for as far as he could find out, she was the first *steel* ship ever laid down. She was a two-funneled paddle steamer of 217 tons net register, with the graceful lines of a yacht, 214 feet over-all, 20 foot beam. Since she drew only eight feet of water, she could easily negotiate the bars off Charleston and the Cape Fear as well as slide over the mudbanks in front of Galveston. Taylor described her masts as "mere poles without yards, and with the best possible rigging. In order to attain greater speed in a seaway she was built with a turtle-back deck forward.

"She had an anticipated sea speed of eleven knots, with a coal consumption of thirty tons a day. Her crew, which included three engineers and twelve firemen, consisted of thirty-six hands all told."

The *Banshee* and other similar steamers in process of construction were thought to incorporate all the lessons learned by the British in their attempts to pierce the blockade during the first two years of the war. The new ships were fast for their day, strong but lightly built, shallow draught and with low silhouette. Taylor remarks that they were expected to develop a buoyancy beyond anything that had yet been seen and U.S. naval officers eagerly waited to catch sight of them.

Early in 1863 the *Banshee* steamed down the Mersey on her maiden voyage across the Atlantic. On the bridge was Tom Taylor, supercargo extraordinary, proud to represent his firm aboard the first steel vessel to make the westward passage. All too soon the *Banshee* showed signs of weakness. First of all, her speed was less than her builders claimed. Secondly, her boilers had been built so low (to protect them from shot and shell) that they did not have enough steam space. Worst of all was the thickness of her plates which varied between ⅛ and 3/16 of an inch. This structural misjudgment caused her decks to "leak like a sieve," as Taylor expressed it. It took three weeks at Queenstown to strengthen her plates and do what little could be done to her boilers and machinery.

"When at last we were able to put out again, it was only to be driven back off the Fastnet," Tom Taylor wrote in describing the voyage. There was a heavy southwesterly gale and it swept the *Banshee* clean from stem to stern of everything on deck, filled her fore stokehold with brine and forced the little steamer back to Ireland once more. After more repairs she again ventured out on the winter sea. This time luck was with her and she steamed into Madeira without a mishap. After a few days of refreshment there she followed the track of sailing vessels southwest to the Bahamas, keeping a strict watch for Federal cruisers. By this time the United States Navy had extended the scope of its blockade enforcement activities far beyond the neighborhood of Southern ports. Taylor has a lot to say about this:

At this time a good deal of bad blood was caused by the way in which the Northerners in their efforts to enforce a blockade were extending the doctrine of the operations permissible to belligerents. But there is no doubt now [this was written in 1896] that they were perfectly right. True, the proposition that a belligerent might seize a neutral ship for an attempted break of the blockade, thousands of miles away from the blockaded coast, was one that would have been condemned by the old school of international lawyers as nothing less than monstrous and none more energetically than the great publicists who have so richly adorned the American bench.

So far were such doctrines from being recognized, that it was generally held that a vessel making a long ocean voyage might even call at a blockaded port to inquire if the blockade was still existent and, no matter how suspicious her intentions, she was entitled to a warning before being captured. But it must be remembered that those were the days of sailing ships, which might have been without any news of passing events for months. No blockade of any importance had yet been subjected to the new conditions of steam navigation, and it was unreasonable to expect that the blockaders would hold themselves bound by rules which never contemplated the existing state of things. If the Americans (Northerners, that is) were stretching the theory of blockade, it was only because we (British) were extending its practice. It was not to be argued that, if we were building a whole fleet of steamers for the express purpose of defying their cruisers, they were not justified in trying to intercept them at any point they chose. From the very outset, the voyages of those vessels proved them to be guilty, and the most barefaced advocate could hardly have maintained without shame that they were protected by their ostensibly neutral destination, when that destination was a notorious nest of offense like Nassau.

Still the new methods were none the less galling to the susceptibilities of British merchants, who of all men claimed to go and come on the high seas as they pleased, and every day those engaged in the service became more pronounced in their Southern sympathies, and louder in their denunciation of the Northerners' high-handed ways.

Taylor goes on to say that as the Federals grew bolder, stronger and more exasperated, they stretched their patrolling activities further and further across the Atlantic. A few weeks after the *Banshee* left Madeira, a Federal man-of-war showed up off Funchal Bay and started cruising back and forth, waiting for one of the British vessels to venture out. It was claimed that the moment a British runner put to sea, the Federal vessel would open fire on her as mercilessly as if she had been coming out of Charleston or Wilmington, instead of from a neutral port. It had now become a fixed attitude on the part of the U.S. naval vessels that every ship bound for Bermuda or Nassau was guilty of an *intention* to break the blockade. "So they seized any ship they had a mind to," Taylor relates, "on the chance of getting her condemned in the United States courts."

After Commander Wilkes's action in removing Mason and Slidell from the *Trent* and the resultant protests from Her Majesty's Government, American cruisers kept at a more respectful distance from Bermuda and Nassau and were more cautious about overhauling and capturing British vessels on the high seas. At any rate, the *Banshee* ran into Nassau unscathed by shot and shell. Her arrival created a sensation, for she was the first steel vessel to enter that port.

Taylor immediately set about preparing for the *Banshee's* maiden run through the Yankee gantlet. By this time it had been established by bloody experience that no steamer could hope to get through except on a moonless night. Invisibility,

speed, knowledge of the coast and grim determination, Taylor
knew, were the ingredients of success. Consequently, the *Banshee* was altered to make her difficult to detect on a black night.
Everything aloft was taken down except her two lower masts.
A small crosstrees was fitted on the foremast to accommodate
a lookout. The boats were lowered to the gunwales and the
vessel painted a dull gray. The precise shade was so nicely ascertained by experience, Taylor states in his narrative, that a properly dressed blockade runner on a dark night was absolutely
indiscernible at a cable's length.* Some captains even insisted
on their crews wearing gray clothing at night, declaring that
one black figure on bridge or deck was enough to betray an
otherwise invisible vessel.

The *Banshee's* new look completely satisfied Taylor, and so
did the crew. His captain was J. W. Steele, rated by the blockade-running fraternity as one of the best in the business: daring,
cool-headed, resourceful and quick to act in an emergency. His
first command had been an unlucky one—the *Tubal Cain*, which
was pursued and captured on her maiden trip. Steele spent a
short time in a Yankee prison and emerged wiser and more cautious. As far as is known, he was never caught again.

The chief engineer, Erskine, was a veteran at the game, having served with distinction aboard the famous Confederate
cruiser *Oreto* (*Florida*) during her successful run into Savannah
through a barrage of gunfire from the Federal blockading squadron. The skipper of the *Oreto* was the famous Captain J. N.
Maffitt, of whom we will hear a good deal later on. Erskine,
Taylor recalled, was "capable of fearlessly risking everything
and straining the last pound [of steam] when word came, in one
of those rousing forms of expression with which old Steele was
wont to notify down the engine room tube, that the critical
moment had come."

The pilot, Tom Burroughs, a Wilmington man, also turned
out to be a jewel. He knew the Carolina coast like the palm of
his hand and was credited with being able to smell a cruiser long

---

* A very early example of marine camouflage.

before he could see her. Taylor was well aware that many a fine blockade runner had been captured, sunk or driven ashore, due to the ignorance or cowardice of the pilot. Really good ones were rare and costly because of the great risks. If captured they could expect to sit out the war in a Federal jail for they were never exchanged.*

Choosing a time when the moon was right, the little *Banshee* stole out of Nassau on her first attempt to pierce the blockade. In her hold was an assorted cargo of contraband of war: rifles, bayonets, gunpowder, coils of lead for bullets, boots and cloth for uniforms. Her destination—Wilmington, North Carolina. Because of the three divisions of cruisers guarding the approach to the Cape Fear River, not to mention the Federal men-of-war patrolling the Gulf Stream, those aboard the *Banshee* knew they would never be safe from danger or from a single hour of anxiety until their vessel came under the protective guns of Fort Fisher.

On her run to Ireland, the *Banshee's* speed had proved most disappointing; not more than nine or ten knots could be made under ordinary conditions. Taylor decided not to run any avoidable risks. He kept to this policy throughout his career as a blockade runner and to it he attributes the success of his steamers. "Others who took greater chances," he says, "almost invariably came to grief."

From the first faint streaks of dawn until total darkness settled down, a lookout was posted on the foremast crosstrees. To keep his eye sharp, he was awarded a dollar for every sail sighted. But if it was seen first from the deck, his pay was docked five dollars.

For the first two days the *Banshee* steamed steadily northwestward, sheltered by the numerous Bahamian isles. Several vessels thought to be hostile were sighted and the *Banshee* altered course to avoid them; but they did not pursue.

At noon of the third day, the ship's position was taken and Steele and Taylor calculated that there was barely enough time to arrive at Fort Fisher by daybreak of the following morning. At this point Tom Taylor's narrative reveals the tenseness he

---

* This was not the case early in the war, when they were released and promptly returned to their trade.

experienced during the next ten hours: "Now the real excitement began, and nothing I have ever experienced can compare with it. Hunting, pig sticking, big-game shooting, polo—I have done a little of each—all have their thrilling moments, but none can approach 'running the blockade:' and perhaps my readers can sympathize with my enthusiasm when they consider the dangers we encountered, after three days of constant anxiety and little sleep, in threading our way through a swarm of blockaders and the accuracy required to hit in the nick of time the mouth of a river only half a mile wide, without lights and with a coastline so low and featureless, that as a rule the first indication we had of its nearness was the dim white line of the surf."

There were different plans for getting in, for the *Banshee* could choose between New Inlet to the north of Smith's Island, protected by Fort Fisher, or Old Inlet to the South, guarded by Fort Caswell. Taylor, Steele and the pilot agreed to take the favorite route which was to run some fifteen or twenty miles north of the Cape Fear in order to round the northernmost of the blockaders, instead of dashing right through the inner line of Federal warships. This method enabled the *Banshee* to creep South toward New Inlet close to the surf (the water was deep close to the shore) until the river mouth was reached.

On through the darkness went the little *Banshee*. There was no moon, but the night was dangerously clear and calm. Not a light showed anywhere. Smoking on deck was strictly forbidden. The engine-room hatchways were screened with tarpaulins, much to the discomfort of the coal heavers who had to work in temperatures like Tophet. Even the binnacle was covered and in order to see the dimly lighted compass, the wheelsman had to peer through a conical aperture carried almost up to his eyes. The ship was as silent as a ghost, except for the steady pulse of the engines and the beat of the paddle floats which sounded distressingly loud.

The crew crouched behind the bulwarks, expecting any moment to see the flash of a Yankee gun and hear the roar of its explosion. On the bridge, Taylor, Steele and Burroughs peered intently into the blackness ahead. Presently the pilot moved close to Steel and whispered, "Better cast the lead, Captain, we're getting close."

Taylor's description of what followed is quite vivid: "A muttered order down the engine-room tube was Steele's reply. The *Banshee* slowed and then stopped. It was an anxious moment while a dim figure stole to the forechains to cast the lead. We waited tensely, for there is always a danger of steam blowing off when engines are unexpectedly stopped, and that would have been enough to betray our presence for miles around. In a minute or two came back the report, 'Sixteen fathoms—sandy bottom with black specks.'

" 'We are not as far in as I thought, Captain,' said Burroughs, 'and we're too far to the southward. Port two points and go a little farther.' "

An hour later another sounding was taken and Burroughs was satisfied that it was now safe to head for the shore.

"Starboard and go ahead easy," he ordered.

Taylor's own words best describe what happened next: "As we crept in not a sound was heard but that of the regular beat of the paddle floats still dangerously loud in spite of our snail's pace. Suddenly Burroughs gripped my arm. 'There's one of them, Mr. Taylor,' he whispered, 'on the starboard bow.'

"In vain I strained my eyes to where he pointed, not a thing could I see; but presently I heard Steele say beneath his breath, 'All right, Burroughs, I see her. Starboard a little, steady!'

"A moment later I could make out a long low object on our starboard side, lying perfectly still. Would she see us? That was the question; but no, though we passed within a hundred yards of her we were not discovered, and I breathed again. Not very long after we dropped her, Burroughs whispered, 'Steamer on the port bow!'

"Yes, another cruiser was close to us.

" 'Hard aport,' said Steele, and round she swung, bringing our friend upon our beam. Still unobserved, we crept quietly on, when all at once a third cruiser shaped herself out of the gloom right ahead and steering slowly across our bow.

" 'Stop her,' said Steele . . . and as we lay like dead, our enemy went on and disappeared in the darkness. It was clear that there was a false reckoning somewhere and that instead of rounding the head of the blockading line, we were passing through the very center of it. However, Burroughs was now of the opinion that we must be inside the squadron and advocated making the land . . . still we could not tell where we were, and, as time was getting on alarmingly near dawn, the only thing to do was to creep down along the surf as close in and as fast as we dared. It was a great relief when we suddenly heard Burroughs say, 'It's all right, I see the Big Hill!'*

"The Big Hill was a hillock about as high as a full grown oak tree, but it was the most prominent feature for miles on that dreary coast, and served to tell us exactly how far we were from Fort Fisher, and fortunate it was for us we were so near. Daylight was already breaking, and before we were opposite the fort we could make out six or seven gunboats, which steamed rapidly toward us and angrily opened fire. Their shots were soon dropping close around us: an unpleasant sensation when you know you have several tons of gunpowder under your feet. To make matters worse, the North Breaker Shoal now compelled us to haul off the shore and steam further out. It began to look ugly for us, when all at once there was a flash from the shore followed by a sound that came like music to our ears—that of a shell whining over our heads. It was Fort Fisher, wide awake and warning the gunboats to keep their distance. With a parting broadside they steamed sulkily out of range, and in half-an-hour we were safely over the bar.

"A boat put off from the fort and then—well, it was the day of champagne cocktails, not whiskies and sodas—and one did not run a blockade every day. For my part I was mighty proud of

* The Big Hill referred to by Tom Taylor was commonly called the Mound and contained a battery of long-range guns. In the early part of the war a dim light was kept burning atop the Mound as a guide to blockade runners. But, since it also helped the Federal cruisers to ascertain their position, it was permanently extinguished.

my first attempt and my baptism of fire. Blockade running seemed the pleasantest and most exhilarating of pastimes. I did not know what a very serious business it could be."

Tom Taylor was not only a shrewd businessman and blockade runner, but he also knew how to build goodwill by entertaining the people best calculated to help him in his ventures.

No sooner had he arrived at Wilmington than he held open house aboard the *Banshee* and "friends flocked to her." One reason was that by the time Taylor arrived, Wilmington was already sadly pinched and war worn. There was little to eat and drink there, both as to quantity and quality. Subsequently, Taylor remarks that the *Banshee* "soon attained great popularity and it was really a sight when our luncheon bell rang to see guests, invited and uninvited, turn up from all quarters." This did not disturb the genial and generous supercargo in the slightest, especially, we surmise, since his ship had earned a small fortune by her successful breach of the blockade. "We made them all welcome," he relates, "and when our little cabin was filled we generally had our overflow meeting on deck."

Taylor really enjoyed those numerous guests. "What a pleasure it was to see them eat and drink! They who had been accustomed to live on corn bread and bacon, and to drink nothing but water, appreciated our delicacies; our bottled beer, good brandy, and, on great occasions, our champagne, warmed their hearts toward us."

All of which paid off handsomely in one way or another. "If any special favor were asked," Taylor wrote with satisfaction, "it was always granted, if possible, to the *Banshee*, and if any push had to be made, there was always someone to make it."

One immediate result of Taylor's open house was that the *Banshee* was loaded with tobacco and cotton in jig-time for her return voyage to Nassau. He was somewhat alarmed at the immense load the frail steamer carried—"piled like a hay wagon in three tiers on deck. . . . The reckless loading, to which high profits and the prerequisites allowed officers led, is to a landsman inconceivable." The prerequisites were a certain amount of space aboard the vessel reserved for cotton or other cargo which an officer could buy and transport on his own account for his own profit. Although Taylor implies that he himself had a personal financial interest in each blockading voyage, he does not reveal how much money he made.

On the voyage out, Steele and Taylor decided on an impudent course (which he calls a cardinal virtue of blockade running) which brought the *Banshee* close by the Admiral's flagship the *Minnesota*, which was out to sea and well clear of the first cordon of cruisers. This strategy was hatched with the aid of information on the fleet's movements supplied by Colonel Lamb at Fort Fisher. It was in the small area surrounding the flagship that the *Banshee* found the hole and slipped through, since the other ships were patrolling further off. Luckily escaping from the two other lines of cruisers, the *Banshee* steamed proudly into Nassau with a heavy list to starboard which Taylor does not explain, but was probably due to the shifting of her deckload of cotton bales and hogsheads of tobacco.

"So ended my first attempt, a triumphant success," Taylor writes exultantly. "Besides the inward freight of £50 ($250) a ton on the war material [taken into Wilmington] I had earned by the tobacco ballast alone £7000 ($35,000) the freight for which had also paid at the rate of £70 ($350) a ton. But this was a fleabite compared to the profit on the five hundred odd bales of cotton we had on board, which was at least £50 ($250) a bale.

"No wonder I took kindly to my new calling, and no wonder I at once set to work to get the *Banshee* reloaded for another run before the moonless nights were over."

Tom Taylor made a total of seven round trips through the blockade—all of them charged with excitement and danger—and all of them successful. Although he attributes the success of the gallant little craft to the ability of officers and crew, combined with a refusal to take unnecessary risks, a great deal of the credit should go to Taylor himself. He was the sort of man who believed in seeing things through *in person* and always was on the spot when danger and disaster threatened. He was indefatigable—

climbing to the crosstrees to ease the *Banshee* through shoal waters; making split-second decisions; working closely with his captain and pilot to hatch new ways of fooling the Yankees.

"It seems nothing short of a miracle," he observes modestly, "that, ill-constructed and ill-engined as she was, she [*Banshee*] so long escaped the numerous dangers to which she was exposed."

On her second run to Wilmington, she came within an ace of ending her career because of an unexpected accident. The *Banshee* had managed to evade the blockade and was heading in for the mouth of the Cape Fear River when all hands were startled by a tearing and rending of wood. Splinters from the port paddle box flew in all directions. Steele ordered the engines stopped at once. A hasty examination revealed that one of the steel paddle floats had split and the broken part had violently flailed the paddle box on every turn of the wheel. The only thing that could be done was to risk enemy attack and try to unscrew the damaged float. A sail was placed round the paddle box and two of the engineers were lowered down and started to work. Soon after, a Federal cruiser hove into sight and those aboard the *Banshee* were sure that they had been discovered. Nevertheless, in the darkness, the man-of-war passed her by a scant hundred yards and huffed off to southward. In another half hour the damaged paddle was repaired and the *Banshee* made the safety of the Cape Fear River after a lively peppering from inshore gunboats.

By the time the *Banshee* had made four trips she had become notorious among officers and men of the blockading squadron as one of the cleverest and most evasive of the blockade runners. What infuriated them most was that she was a comparatively slow steamer and many of the Yankee cruisers could out-distance her in a chase.

It had been Tom Taylor's practice to make his run to New Inlet from the north, parallel to the beach, since this course enabled him to slip by the Federal cruisers at the extreme end of the line. Meanwhile the United States Navy decided to stop up this hole by assigning a lighter-draught vessel to guard this extremity.

It was a very dark night when the *Banshee* made her fifth try with a valuable cargo for Wilmington. She fetched the land about twelve miles above Fort Fisher and was creeping quietly down as usual when all at once they spied a cruiser on their port bow, moving slowly, about a thousand yards from shore. The immediate question in the minds of Taylor, Steele and Burroughs was whether to go inside or outside the enemy. If they went outside, they felt certain she would see them and would close them into the very jaws of the fleet. A quick decision by Taylor caused the *Banshee* to keep on her course parallel to the beach, keeping *inside* of the Federal cruiser. They hoped that the *Banshee's* slim silhouette against the dark background of the shore would be unobserved. Just when they thought they had glided by, a hoarse shout escaped across the water, "Stop that steamer or I will sink you!"

"Hell's fire, we haven't time," Captain Steele growled to Taylor, then turned and shouted down the engine-room tube to Erskine to "pile on the coals and give her every ounce of steam!"

As the *Banshee* shot ahead the cruiser opened fire and steered close to her prey. She was the new, fast U.S.S. *Niphon*, nemesis of blockade runners. The tense trio on the *Banshee's* bridge were so close that they heard the skirl of a bos'n's pipe and the high-pitched call, "Boarders away!"

Shouts and curses hurtled across the narrow, black ribbon of water as the two vessels steamed bow to stern along the dim, white rim of the surf. Shell after shell screamed across the decks of the fleeing *Banshee*. Suddenly her foremast seemed to explode in a shower of splinters and fell drunkenly to port as one of the *Niphon's* shots found its target. The *Banshee's* carpenter quickly cut away the spar. A few seconds later another shell ripped through the steamer's thin skin and exploded in the bunkers.

Erskine, his face black from coal dust and his dungarees smudged with grease, drove his coal heavers like the devil himself. His bloodshot eyes were fastened on the steam gauge and he grinned as the needle crept to full pressure and beyond. Gradually the *Banshee* began to pull away from her pursuer. In a last desperate effort to capture her prize, the *Niphon* primed her bow chasers with grape and canister, spewing the deadly charges across the *Banshee's* decks.

"It was a miracle that no one was killed," Taylor records in his memoirs, "but the crew were all lying flat on the deck, except the steersman; and at one time I fear he did the same, for as pilot Burroughs suddenly cried, 'My God, Mr. Taylor, look there!' I saw our boat heading right into the surf, so, jumping from the bridge, I ran aft and found the helmsman on his stomach. I rushed at the wheel and got two or three spokes out of it, which hauled her head off the land, but it was a close shave."

Two miles further on another cruiser tried to intercept, but was soon left behind. A little later a large side-wheeler gunboat tried desperately to ram the *Banshee*, missing her by only a few yards. After that she was unmolested and arrived in the shelter of Fort Fisher to be "warmly congratulated by Colonel Lamb, who thought from the violent cannonading that she must certainly have been sunk." Always generous with praise for others, Taylor ends the episode with the remark that "Not more than one man out of a hundred would have brought a boat through as Steele did that night—the other ninety-nine would have run her ashore."

After discharging her cargo in Wilmington and stepping a new foremast and repairing damage to bulwarks and engine room, the *Banshee* was again ready for sea. But she was not destined to sail that day or for many thereafter. This time she came close to disaster, not from Federal cruisers, but from fire. No one knew how it started, but it spread quickly through the deckload of cotton. The flames made such headway that Taylor was certain the little vessel would be a total loss. Not so Captain Steele. He immediately sprang into action: got the steam hose working, breasted the *Banshee* off from the wharf and let go the anchor in midstream. This brought her head to the tide and her stern to the wind, the fire being all forward.

The maneuver was aided by Captain Halpin of the blockade runner *Eugenie* who, in knocking out the cotter pin which held the chain cable, had his clothes catch fire. "It was a sight to see him take a header into the river," Taylor wrote [and we can almost hear his chuckle], "causing the water to hiss again."

Damage to the *Banshee* was far less than expected. The deck cargo and turtleback forward were destroyed and the decks, bulwarks and new foremast charred. After taking on fresh cotton bales and not bothering to stop for repairs, the *Banshee* steamed out into the ocean, dodged the cordon of cruisers and arrived without incident in Nassau, where "they were astonished to see the plight we were in, thinking we had had a fire at sea."

In an earlier part of his book, Tom Taylor made the remark that storms and high seas were virtually as dangerous to the lightly built blockade runners as enemy men-of-war. So it need hardly be remarked that when wind and waves *plus* a Federal cruiser conspired together there were even greater hazards. This was the situation faced by the *Banshee* on her sixth voyage. She was headed for Nassau and had skipped through the blockading squadron when Erskine, who happened to be on deck taking a breather, called Taylor's attention to a large side-wheeler cruiser, with all her square sails set, about four miles astern and coming up "hand over fist." He was astonished that the lookout had not reported the enemy and the man "turned out to be an American whom we had shipped in Nassau, on a previous trip, and about whom both Steele and I had our private suspicions."

But this was no time for disciplinary action, Taylor realized. Daylight was practically on top of them. Erskine ducked below and started the stokers piling on fuel like mad. Soon great billows of smoke spouted from the *Banshee's* twin stacks and she began to move faster through the choppy seas.

The Federal man-of-war (which they later found out was the U.S.S. *James Adger**) quickly began to overhaul the *Banshee*. She got so close that Taylor and his mates could "see the officers in uniform as they stood on the bridge; each one, doubtless, counting his share of the prize money to which he would soon become entitled."

---

* Subsequently sent to cruise in search of the Confederate raider *Alabama*.

Steele ordered the helm put over and brought his steamer into the wind. This forced the *James Adger* to follow suit with the added necessity of taking in her sails. Then began a dingdong race right into the wind's eye. Although the *Banshee* gained a valuable lead by this maneuver, the heavy seas slowed her down badly and she was taking a terrible beating from the waves.

Taylor was sure the jig was up, for the bigger, heavier (2,000 tons) *James Adger* was creeping up again. So he hastily divided sixty gold sovereigns ($300) he had in his possession into three parts: one for Captain Steele, one for Murray-Aynsley,* his friend who was aboard as a passenger, and one for himself. He did so, he told them, so they would not be penniless when captured.

Relentlessly the Federal cruiser shortened the distance between herself and her quarry. In desperation Taylor ordered the deck cargo jettisoned. Soon the blockade runner's wake was more than mere foam, for she left a bobbing trail of cotton bales, worth $400 each. It was a heartbreaking sight for Tom Taylor and he notes sadly, ". . . my little private venture of ten bales of Sea Island cotton had to go first, a dead loss of $4000 or more!"

In clearing out the bales, a stowaway was discovered, a runaway slave who had been standing wedged between two bales for at least forty-eight hours. It remained a mystery how he smuggled himself aboard and how he managed to remain in his hiding place when the ship was fumigated, just before leaving port. "He received an ovation on our landing him at Nassau," Taylor records, "though his freedom cost us (the company) $4000 on our return to Wilmington, this being what he was valued at."

Relieved of her deck cargo, the laboring *Banshee* began to gain in the race. At times she was almost submerged by the green seas that swept her fore and aft.

Just as they thought that danger was receding, a new crisis

---

* Murray-Aynsley was a young British lieutenant on leave from Her Majesty's Navy and at this time the captain of a blockade runner. Years later he retired from the navy with an Admiral's rank.

arose. Due to the enormous strain put upon the engine's bearings, they began to overheat. Erskine declared that it was absolutely necessary to stop for a short time. Steele and Taylor, realizing that the engineer knew what he was talking about, reluctantly agreed. The very brief halt enabled Erskine and his crew to loosen the bearings and by using all the salad oil from the ship's stores, they got the bearings into working order again.

On and on went the grim chase, for the *James Adger* seemed determined to hang on to the very shores of Nassau. In all, the race lasted for fifteen hours—"The longest I ever spent," Taylor remarks. Finally when darkness came, the persistent Yankee turned about and headed back to the fleet.

Although the enemy had vanished, another problem presented itself almost immediately. The chase had forced the *Banshee* to alter her course and steam toward Bermuda for 150 miles. The coal bunkers were almost empty. The logical thing to do in this case was to continue on to Bermuda. But it was imperative for Taylor to land at Nassau because he was expecting two steamers out from England. So he gave orders to alter course for Nassau, hoping the coal would hold out. But it did not. At the end of the third day the last lump of coal had been consumed and they kept the boilers going with wood: first the mainmast, then the bulwarks, then the deck cabin and finally cotton soaked in turpentine.

There was barely enough steam pressure to enable the *Banshee* to limp into one of the northeast Bahama keys, sixty miles from Nassau. They had been anchored for scarcely two hours when a Federal cruiser steamed slowly by, eying them greedily. But she did not dare make a move in their direction for they were safe in British waters.

Bad luck continued to follow Tom Taylor. He chartered a native sloop to take himself and Murray-Aynsley to Nassau. But a near hurricane overtook them and the Negro crew were so terrified they nearly let the craft go on the rocks near Abaco Light. It was only after Taylor and his naval friend produced their revolvers and made threats and bribes that they got the crew to work the ship again.

On arrival in Nassau, Taylor bought coal and sent the sloop back with it to the *Banshee* "utterly wearied out," Taylor records, "having no sleep to speak of for a week, and having lived in our sea boots since we made our first start from Wilmington. My feet were so swollen that the boots had to be cut off." Anxiety and exhaustion combined to rob Taylor of sleep even after he was safe at Nassau although a few nights later he notes that he did go sound asleep with the aid of a sleeping draught.

The *Banshee's* pursuit by the U.S.S. *James Adger* is one of the most notable incidents connected with blockade running during the Civil War. The question inevitably arises as to why the *James Adger* did not open fire since she was running so close and well within cannon shot for such a comparatively long time. Taylor attributes it to the fact that the *James Adger* had no bow chasers. Who was responsible for this gross neglect no one knows. Also it was said that the Federal cruiser was so certain of eventually capturing the *Banshee* the captain did not think it worthwhile to yaw and fire a broadside. In justice to him it must be kept in mind that an extremely heavy sea was running with consequent danger of the cannon breaking loose from their lashings.

Thus ended the last round trip for the intrepid little *Banshee*. It must have been Tom Taylor's luck and good management that enabled her to escape the blockaders for so long, for she was captured on her next voyage. Steele was at her helm as usual and Taylor does not explain how she was caught. Nor does he make clear why Steele remained in a Northern jail for only a few weeks. The United States government would not ordinarily let the captain of a notorious blockade runner off so easily. Perhaps Steele succeeded in hiding his identity or bribed someone. In any event, when he regained his freedom he was overjoyed to learn that he was to command another company steamer, built especially for him and christened *Banshee No. 2*.

The designers and builders of *Banshee No. 2* had profited greatly by the mistakes incorporated into *Banshee No. 1*. The former was, in Taylor's opinion, the queen of them all, the best and most reliable of any blockade runner he ever manipulated.

The new *Banshee* was 252 feet long, with a beam of 31 feet, depth 11 feet. Her registered tonnage was 439, and her crew consisted of 53 hands in all. Her maximum speed was 15½ knots, unusually fast for those days.

After being captured, *Banshee No. 1* was converted into a gunboat by the Federals, but Taylor says she proved anything but a success, "being much too tender." Her engines were cranky and on one occasion those in charge found it impossible to stop her and she ran into a jetty at the Navy Yard in Washington. Was this the ineptness of the engineers or (as I like to think) the gallant little craft's way of getting back at her captors?

The remarkable success of *Banshee No. 1* under Tom Taylor's management encouraged the principals of his company to make further investments and to put more of their funds into blockade running. They formed a joint stock company with a large capital and built steamer after steamer and sent them out for Taylor to manage. The number of firms owning only one or two ships decreased in favor of large companies. Blockade running was becoming big business. The shrewd English operators realized that the greater the number of vessels the less the risk of loss. "Even if half the fleet of a company were captured, the profits earned by the other half would more than counterbalance the loss entailed by failure," Taylor records.

Along with the expansion of the fleet went an increase in Taylor's responsibilities and worries. He was now dealing in big quantities of war materials, a great volume of cotton and naval stores and consequently vast sums of money. In spite of hard work and harassments, Taylor enjoyed his work. He was young and making money. The excitement and danger and the challenge of the unexpected made each day an adventure in itself.

Several of Taylor's new steamers had short and unfortunate careers. One of these was the *Tristram Shandy*. On her first voyage to Wilmington she was chased by a Federal cruiser and her captain felt impelled to throw the entire cargo overside in order to give his vessel more speed. After her return to Nassau she was reloaded and sent out again, fortunately making port safely. But on her run eastward her funnels flamed so badly (due to their peculiar construction) that a gunboat trailed the *Shandy* all night. By dawn the enemy was only three miles astern. The captain must have transferred his terror down the engine-room speaking tube, for the engineer put on steam so suddenly that one of the valve spindles was wrenched off and she lay dead in the water. The exultant gunboat made an easy capture—and a rich one. The *Tristram Shandy* carried $50,000 in specie belonging to the Confederate government, in addition to a fortune in cotton.

When the news reached Taylor in Nassau, it was the third loss for his company that day: another had also been captured and the third run ashore and burned. "A heavy bill of misfortune for one day!" Taylor remarked.

Probably the strangest piece of cargo ever carried in one of Taylor's vessels—and one which nearly caused him the loss of the steamer and his own confinement in a Northern prison—was a horse. A representative of the Confederate government stationed in Egypt had shipped a valuable Arabian thoroughbred to Nassau as a gift for President Jefferson Davis. The Confederate agent asked Taylor to take the animal through the blockade on his next trip. Taylor consented and put the horse aboard the *Banshee No. 2*. Everything went well on the inbound trip. When they ran through the blockaders the night was very still, with hardly a breath of wind. The *Banshee No. 2* was making fast time toward New Inlet when suddenly the horse, no doubt smelling land, let out a loud neigh. Instantly several seamen threw their jackets over its head. But too late, the neigh had been heard by a cruiser steaming close by and she and two of her consorts immediately opened fire. Fortunately the *Banshee No. 2* showed them a fast pair of heels and Taylor's friend Colonel Lamb at Fort Fisher lobbed enough shells at the warships to force them to give up the chase.

On arrival at Wilmington the health officer insisted on putting the steamer in quarantine because of the prevalence of yellow fever at Nassau.

Always a quick thinker, Taylor expostulated. "If we have

to go to quarantine, the horse will surely die, for we have no more food for it. And I don't think that President Davis would be pleased."

Unwilling to take on such a responsibility, the health officer telegraphed to Richmond for instructions. He was told to have the *Banshee* proceed to the Market Street wharf, land the horse and return to quarantine.

The *Banshee* had scarcely made fast when nearly half the crew jumped ashore and disappeared. After reporting this to General Whiting, Taylor remarked, "It's no use our going back to quarantine now, General. My men are all over the place and you either have the infection or not." He then advised the General to telegraph the news to Richmond. The answer came back, "*Banshee* must discharge and load as quickly as possible and proceed to sea; lend all assistance."

As a result, *Banshee No. 2* discharged her war supplies, loaded cotton and was on her way down river in a matter of only three days. She passed a fleet of steamers at the quarantine ground, "whose crews were gnashing their teeth," as Taylor expressed it. "On the return voyage the same vessels were still in quarantine." Thanks to the horse and Taylor's nimble wit, he was able to make a round trip that would otherwise have been impossible, and thus made the owners of the *Banshee* some $100,000 to $150,000 extra.

It is difficult to understand why British merchants, with so many thousands of pounds invested in war cargoes and cotton, would accept the poor workmanship characteristic of many of the steamers especially built for the blockade-running trade. The *Will-o'-the-Wisp*, owned by Taylor's firm was a case in point. She was, according to his account, "built in the Clyde, was a much larger and faster boat than the *Banshee No. 1*, but shamefully put together and most fragile." It is quite possible that the time element had great bearing on the construction of blockade runners. No one knew how long the war would last. Big profits could be made in a matter of weeks. So, time was of the essence. To get the ship in the water and headed for America as fast as possible seemed to be the chief aim. Poor workmanship was responsible for the loss of a number of Taylor's steamers, not to mention the added headaches for him.

By the time the *Will-o'-the-Wisp* arrived in Nassau from England on her maiden voyage, she was leaking so badly the skipper did not dare stop his engines, since they had to be kept going in order to work the pumps. He brought her into the harbor and beached her, then later made necessary repairs in the slipway.

The *Will-o'-the-Wisp* was commanded by Captain Capper, second only to Steele in ability and character, according to Taylor's judgment. After a rough run to the Carolina coast, the steamer (on orders from Taylor who was aboard) audaciously passed between two blockaders who belatedly opened fire and steamed toward each other from either side of the *Will-o'-the-Wisp* so as to intercept her at a given point before she could get on the land side of them.

After having her flagstaff shot away and another shell lodged in her forehold, the steamer managed to scurry within range of Fort Fisher's guns.

"It seemed a miracle that the double fire did not completely sink us," Taylor commented in his memoirs. "It certainly required all one's nerve to stand upon the paddle box, looking, without flinching, almost into the muzzles of the guns which were firing at us. [At one point each of the cruisers was only a hundred and fifty yards from Taylor's vessel.] And proud we were of our crew, not a man of whom showed the white feather." All during that voyage the *Will-o'-the-Wisp* had leaked badly.

One of the remarkable things about the blockade was the immense amount of powder and shot expended in attempting to enforce it. Every eyewitness report of contact between cruisers and blockade runners is filled with descriptions of heavy firing, the air seemingly alive with shot and shell. Whether the frequent failure of U.S. gunners to hit their targets was due to extremely poor marksmanship combined with inaccurate ordnance is a moot point. The fact remains, however, that for every blockade runner struck by a shell there were dozens who got by unscathed.

On her way down the Cape Fear River the *Will-o'-the-Wisp's* leaks got worse and she was purposely run aground and the leaks patched up. But not for long. The water began rising in the hold at an alarming rate while the steamer was dodging Union shells after crossing the New Inlet bar. It crept over the stokehole plates and then, at the worst possible moment, the donkey pumps refused to work, for they had been clogged with river mud. Four of the eight furnaces had been extinguished and the firemen were working up to their waists in water. Things looked hopeless. Captain Capper stood grimly at the wheel. Taylor was on lookout duty at the masthead. All others were at the hand pumps, some even bailing. The wind had risen until it was blowing almost a gale. Even Capper lost hope and said repeatedly, "The beggar's going, the beggar's going."

Taylor refused to believe it and proceeded in characteristic fashion to make his belief come true. He ordered the deck cargo of cotton bales to be dumped—and the good effect soon became visible. The water began to recede so that the men in the engine room could relight the fires. Fortunately, meanwhile, the pursuing cruiser became lost in a fog bank. Nevertheless the struggle between the steamer and Davy Jones went on for sixty hours until at last they staggered into Nassau and beached the sievelike steamer.

Tom Taylor was not only a shrewd businessman, but he was also well acquainted with "doctoring" a ship in order to sell her, much the same way that an unscrupulous used-car dealer will doctor an old car to get rid of it. Taylor believed in the principle of *caveat emptor*, as he reveals in his narrative of how he sold the *Will-o'-the-Wisp*.

"As I found her a constant source of delay, I decided to sell her. After having her cobbled up with plenty of putty and paint, I was fortunate enough to open negotiation with some Jews with a view to her purchase. Having settled all preliminaries we arranged for a trial trip, and after a very sumptuous lunch I proceeded to run her over a measured mile for the benefit of the would-be purchasers. I need scarcely mention that we subjected her machinery to the utmost strain, bottling up steam to a pres-

sure of which our present Board of Trade . . . would express
strong [dis]approval . . . with the satisfactory result that she
logged 17½ knots.* The Jews were delighted, so was I; and the
bargain was clinched. I fear, however, that their joy was short-
lived; a few weeks afterward when attempting to steam into
Galveston she was run ashore and destroyed by the Federals."

Far more satisfactory was the *Wild Darrell*, another new
steamer sent out to Tom Taylor. She had the slim beauty of a
yacht, yet was strongly built, a perfect seaboat and remarkably
well-engined. Taylor went with her on her first voyage. She
got through the blockading squadron successfully by way of
Old Inlet and Fort Caswell, although she nearly came to disaster
when her pilot lost his reckoning and put them ashore on the
bar. Fortunately the flood tide was rising fast and they refloated,
bumping over stem first in a most inglorious fashion.

The pilot turned out to be mediocre, but thanks to Taylor's
management the *Wild Darrell* made good her eastbound voyage.

On her second trip (Taylor was not aboard) the fine new
steamer was run ashore north of Fort Fisher and with a $20,000
cotton cargo became a total loss.

Commented Taylor bitterly: "He [the Captain] said he ran
her ashore to avoid capture—to my mind a futile excuse for any
blockade running captain to make. 'Twere far better to be sunk
by shot and escape in the boats if possible. I am quite certain
that if Steele had commanded her on that trip she would never
have been put ashore, and the chances are she would have come
through all right."

Two other new steamers sent out to Taylor at this time were
the *Stormy Petrel* and the *Wild River*. Both were well made
and fast. The *Stormy Petrel* had bad luck—she got safely into
the anchorage behind Fort Fisher only to rip open her bottom
on the fluke of a submerged anchor. In spite of strenuous efforts
to save her, she became a total wreck. The *Wild River* was more

---

* As far as the author can determine, this is close to the fastest speed
ever recorded by a blockade runner and remarkably fast for steamers of
that period.

successful. She made five round trips through the blockade and survived the war. Later she was sold in South America.

It is not known what star Tom Taylor was born under, but it must have been an amazingly lucky one. Shells whizzed past him harmlessly. He survived fires, strandings, leaky vessels, breakdowns, yellow fever and many other hazards. Yet it remained for the steamer *Night Hawk* to bring him as close to death as anything he ever experienced during his career as a blockade runner.

Taylor judged the *Night Hawk* to be one of the finest boats his company ever owned. He described her as a side-wheeler of some 600 gross tons, rigged as a fore and aft schooner, with two funnels, 220 feet in length, 21½ foot beam and 11 feet in depth. She was ideally suited for the work of blockade running, for she was stanchly built, fast and light in draught so as to get over the bar easily at New Inlet. Most important of all, she was well able to withstand the pounding of the seas during gales and dirty weather.

The *Night Hawk* left Hamilton, Bermuda, on her initial run, with considerable misgivings on the part of Tom Taylor. The captain was an entirely new hand and practically all of the crew were green at the work of blockade running. To make matters worse, the pilot, who hailed from Wilmington, seemed very nervous and lacking in confidence. Taylor's feeling about the man was promptly confirmed when the *Night Hawk* ran aground on one of the coral reefs outside the harbor and hung there until they managed to refloat her at high tide.

"What would I not have given for our trusty Tom Burroughs," Taylor noted in his memoirs. "However, we had to make the best of it, as, owing to the demand, the supply of competent pilots was not nearly sufficient, and towards the close of the blockade the so-called pilots were no more than boatmen or men who had been trading in and out of Wilmington and Charleston in coasters." Certainly the record bears out Taylor's statement.

In spite of the bad start the voyage to the Carolina coast was uneventful, with remarkably few vessels of any sort sighted. Soon after midnight there was a brief brush with a patrolling cruiser. The Federals let loose a broadside which arrived a bit too late to blow off the *Night Hawk's* stern. When she had steamed at full speed within striking distance of Wilmington, probably about one o'clock in the morning, the pilot announced that they should go through the blockaders off Old Inlet by Fort Caswell.

Taylor skeptically questioned him about his intimate knowledge of this passage, only to discover that the pilot knew very little about it. On the other hand, Taylor himself had come to know New Inlet almost as intimately as Tom Burroughs himself. So he decided to conn the *Night Hawk* through the Federal cruisers there. Moreover, he would "have the advantage of our good friend Lamb to protect us." As they swept swiftly past most of the fleet and were approaching the bar, heavily fired on, they fell afoul of two Northern launches which were patrolling practically on the bar itself.

"Unfortunately," records Taylor, "it was dead low water, and although I pressed the pilot to give our boat a turn around, keeping under way, and to wait a while until the tide made, he was demoralized by the firing we had gone through and the nearness of the launches, which were constantly throwing up rockets. . . ." So the jittery pilot insisted on trying to force the *Night Hawk* over the bar which, at low water, was just about eleven feet down, the same measurement as the steamer's draught. The inevitable happened, of course. The vessel dug her bow into the bar and without the strong flood tide quickly broached to. They kept the engines going hoping to drive her across, but it was no use. The breakers were foaming across the bar, so Taylor ordered the engines stopped.

Then the Federal launches closed in for the attack. Aboard the *Night Hawk* there was shouting, confusion and absolute absence of discipline. The pilot and the signalman rushed for the dinghy, let go the falls, jumped in and rowed off into the darkness. The captain left his post on the bridge and disappeared. Meanwhile the crews of the two launches, now close aboard, let go a volley of musketry, then made fast to the *Night Hawk* and swarmed aboard.

Taylor was slightly wounded by a minié ball but he had more important things on his mind just then—the dispatches, which should have been thrown overboard minutes ago. He had hidden them in the starboard lifeboat and now rushed there to do the job. They had been weighted with a lead weight, attached to a lanyard. Desperately he yanked at the line, trying to break it. But it was too strong. So he shouted for a knife. A fireman thrust one into his hand and he cut the line and pitched the bag overboard, just as the Federal bluejackets jumped aboard.

Evidently this was the boat crew's first boarding party, for Taylor notes that they were "terribly excited" and "acted more like maniacs than sane men, firing their revolvers and cutting right and left with their cutlasses, every bit as though they were fighting their way aboard an enemy man-of-war.

"I stood in front of the man [he meant the crew] on the poop and said that we surrendered, but all the reply I received from the lieutenant commanding was, 'Oh you surrender, do you?' accompanied by a string of the choicest Yankee oaths and sundry reflections upon my parentage; whereupon he fired his revolver twice point blank at me not two yards distant; it was a miracle he did not kill me, as I heard the bullets whiz past my head. This roused my wrath and I expostulated in the strongest terms upon his firing on unarmed men; then he cooled down, giving me into the charge of two of his men, one of whom speedily possessed himself of my binoculars. Fortunately, as I had no guard to my watch, they didn't discover it, and I have it still."

The page in Taylor's book which relates this exciting incident has on its margin a notation in pencil. The handwriting appears to be that of an elderly man and reads "probably not true" opposite the sentence which tells of the point blank attempt on Taylor's life. It seems incredible that even a rank amateur could miss at a distance of less than six feet! With due allowance for excitement which can always affect one's aim it is, as Taylor says, a miracle that at least one bullet did not find its mark. A less charitable attitude would be that Taylor embroidered the incident to include this hairbreadth escape so as to add one more lucky escape to his already replete roster. It could be argued that a man who was capable of patching up a worn-out and imperfect steamer with putty and paint in order to sell her might also be capable of some slight exaggerations in recounting his adventures in blockade running.

In any case, he was in a tight spot. The *Night Hawk* was now in possession of Federal naval forces and had officially surrendered to them. It had been the hope of the Northern lieutenant to maneuver the steamer off the bar and take his prize out to the flagship. But they now realized that she was hard and fast; also that at any minute the all-watchful Colonel Lamb might open up on them with grape or canister. So they decided to abandon their prize and ordered the *Night Hawk's* officers and men into the boats (the cowardly captain had meanwhile been discovered hiding behind a lifeboat).

"When all our hands were in the boats, the Yankees set the *Night Hawk* afire and she soon began to blaze merrily," Taylor remarked wryly. "At this moment one of our firemen, an Irishmen, sang out, 'Begorra, we shall all be in the air in a minute, the ship is full of gunpowder!'"

Thus panicked, the Northern sailors made a rush for their launches, shouting to their officers to come along or they would be left behind.

All this time Taylor had been held between two husky sailors. But when they heard about the imminent explosion "they dropped me like a hot potato, and away they rowed as fast as they could, taking all of our crew, with the exception of the second officer, one of the engineers, four seamen and myself, as prisoners."

The statement about the gunpowder was a lie, fortunately for Taylor and the few who remained with him. They were thankful for escaping being made prisoners, but they still faced plenty of trouble. There was only one small boat left aboard, and that was half stove in. The shore and safety were three hundred yards away and in between was angry surf. There was also the danger that the Federals, finding out that there was no powder aboard, would return and make sure of the destruction of the

Captain John Newland Maffitt, C.S.N.

from PICTORIAL and HISTORICAL NEW HANOVER COUNTY,
by William Lord deRosset

The Cruiser *Florida* commanded by Captain Maffitt.

From RUNNING THE BLOCKADE *by Thomas E. Taylor*

Will-o'-the-Wisp's dash for Wilmington.

ship. There was no use trying to put out the fire, although Taylor offered the men $250 apiece to stand by him and persevere. They refused with plenty of curses and began to lower the damaged boat saying that they would leave Taylor to burn with the ship if he didn't jump in.

The trip through the dangerous surf was a harrowing experience for the supercargo, and to liven things up still further the blockaders "immediately opened fire when they knew their own men had left the *Night Hawk* and that she was burning; and Lamb's great shells hurtling over our heads, and those from the blockading fleet bursting all around us, formed a weird picture."

In spite of the boiling surf and shell fire, Taylor and his men reached shore safely. Taylor himself remembers how cold, wet and exhausted he was. But he had hardly tramped up the beach when he was welcomed by Colonel Lamb's orderly and escorted to the fort where his wound was dressed and he was given dry clothing and a stiff tot of hot brandy.

Tom Taylor figured that the *Night Hawk* could not be saved and mentally wrote her off as a total loss. Not so Colonel Lamb! He called for volunteers from his garrison and sent off three boatloads of them. They fought the fire stubbornly. After Taylor left the surgeon, he saw that the fire had lessened. Ignoring his wound he went aboard his vessel and was there when the fire was finally put out.

"But what a wreck she was!" Nevertheless he resolved to salvage her if possible, especially since she had bumped over the bar with the rising tide and now lay on the main beach which was more accessible and sheltered.

With the assistance of about three hundred Negroes, supplied by the company's agent in Wilmington, together with engineers and the pulling power of *Banshee No. 2* (having conveniently run in through the blockade that night) things began to look up. Gradually they began to haul off the stranded *Night Hawk* a little with each tide. At the end of several back-breaking days she finally was floated and proceeded up to Wilmington under her own steam. All during this time they were harassed by enemy shell fire by day and attempted attacks by small boats during the night. "Lamb, however, put a stop to the . . . annoyance by lending us a couple of companies to defend us, and one night when our enemies rowed close up with the intention of boarding us, they were glad to sheer off with the loss of a lieutenant and several men."

It cost a huge sum to repair and prepare the *Night Hawk* for sea, but the immense potential profits in running out a full cargo of cotton spurred Tom Taylor on. He hired a reliable skipper, loaded the *Night Hawk* to the gunwales with cotton bales and ran out through the blockade unscathed . . . "which made her pay, notwithstanding all her bad, bad luck and the amount spent on her."

Tom Taylor caught the fever and ague and nearly died as a result of his harrowing six-day labor salvaging the *Night Hawk*. He had gone without a change of clothing and was wet the entire time.

Here we will take our leave of the brave, resourceful, shrewd and successful Tom Taylor, super-supercargo. He continued his blockade-running career until after the second and successful attack on Fort Fisher by the Union fleet. Meanwhile he had shifted his operations to Havana; running steamers into Galveston. But these ventures showed little profit and he decided to return to Nassau and from there take a ship for home.

Taylor was without doubt the most successful British blockade runner of them all. He made a total of twenty-eight round trips through the various Union squadrons guarding Southern ports. He himself believes this to be a record, especially, he says, "considering the narrow squeaks I had and that I only came to grief once, in the *Night Hawk*." [And he salvaged her!] He adds, "I had a great deal to be thankful for."

After a long rest in England during which he was able to recover completely from the aftereffects of yellow fever and ague, he was rewarded with a partnership in his firm and sent to their branch in Bombay.

CHAPTER 5

Runners of the Gantlet

THE INTREPID CAPTAIN WILKINSON

Spring came early in 1861, and on this April evening in Norfolk the breeze was fragrant with the perfume of roses. Just outside the Navy Yard gate Lieutenant John Wilkinson paused and turned sharply around as he heard the familiar boom of the sunset gun. Glancing up, he saw Old Glory slowly descending from the flagpole of the Administration Building. Involuntarily his hand went up in salute, then jerked abruptly down and became a clenched fist, for he had just resigned his commission in the United States Navy. He would never salute the Stars and Stripes again, he told himself fiercely. From now on that flag was, to him, the ensign of the enemy. He picked up his portmanteau and hurried in the direction of the depot.

After a visit with his family in Virginia, Lieutenant Wilkinson went to Richmond and offered his services to Secretary of the Navy Mallory. They were accepted and Wilkinson eagerly looked forward to being afloat and ready to attack Federal men-of-war within a matter of weeks. Instead, he was assigned to the prosaic task of helping erect naval batteries and train their crews at several points along the James River. Thus, undramatically, began the career of Lieutenant (afterward Captain) John Wilkinson, second only to Captain John Newland Maffitt, as the most daring blockade runner of the Confederacy.

In the battle of New Orleans, we find Wilkinson as executive officer of the Confederate man-of-war *Louisiana* carrying the flag of Commodore Mitchell. He was captured, sent North and for several months was confined in Fort Warren at Boston. He was exchanged in August of 1862 and, after a brief stay at his home, he was called to Richmond for special blockade-running duty. Wilkinson's instructions came directly from the Secretary of War. He ordered Wilkinson to go to England and buy a steamer suitable for running the blockade. Ample funds were provided to purchase the vessel, load her with arms, ammunition and other supplies and bring her into a Confederate port as quickly as possible.

Wilkinson and his novice staff of officers sailed from Wilmington, North Carolina, for Nassau on August 12 aboard the famous blockade runner *Kate* commanded by skillful Captain T. J. Lockwood. This side-wheeler was neither handsome nor fast, having a speed of only nine knots. But she managed to have a long and useful career and earned many hundreds of thousands of dollars for her owners. In those early days of blockade running, the Union fleet off Wilmington maintained masthead lights and thus revealed to the *Kate* their exact location so she was easily able to run past them in the darkness.

Two cases of yellow fever occurred on board during the voyage to Nassau, both proving fatal. One of the patients, Wilkinson recalls, was "brought on deck and placed on a couch under the deck awning. As he had taken no nourishment for two or three days, our good Captain directed that a bowl of soup should be prepared for him. The sick man sat up when the steaming bowl was presented to him, seized it with both hands, drained it to the bottom and fell back dead."

After coming to anchor in Nassau harbor, Captain Lockwood was brought a message telling him of the death of his wife and child from yellow fever. He had left them at Nassau in good health only a week before.

Arriving in England, Captain Wilkinson found that the steamer *Giraffe* had already been spotted by Major Ficklin, C.S.A., as a potential blockade runner. Wilkinson went to Glasgow to outfit her. She was Clyde-built, a side-wheel iron steamer which had formerly plied between Glasgow and Belfast as a passenger packet. He found her to be strongly built and reputed to be very fast, although he later discovered to his disappointment that the best she could do was thirteen and a half knots.

Wilkinson judged the vessel to be adequate for the purpose in hand and decided to buy her for the Confederate government. But on returning to London he was disconcerted to find that she had been sold only a few days before to a British company about to enter the blockade-running business. The firm's name was Alexander Collie & Company. This company was destined to become one of the biggest and most successful of the many British firms engaged in shipping merchandise into the South.

At first Alexander Collie refused to part with the vessel at any price but his objections disappeared when Wilkinson told him that he held a commission in the Confederate States Navy and had been sent abroad to buy a steamer for his government.

"He instantly agreed to transfer possession," wrote Wilkinson in his book, *Narrative of a Blockade Runner*, "for the amount paid by him 32,000 pounds [$160,000] stipulating, however, that the steamer should not be sold during the war to private parties without the consent of the company represented by him, who were to have first preference of her!"

As soon as the deal was settled, Wilkinson set to work to convert the *Giraffe* into a blockade runner. He dismantled her handsome salon and cabins and built bulkheads to separate the officer's and crew's quarters from the cargo space. Meanwhile arms, clothing and munitions were bought through Collie & Company for shipment to the Confederate government.

On week ends during these preparations, Wilkinson explored London and saw a good deal of J. M. Mason, one of the commissioners of the Confederate government, who, at that time, was "living very quietly . . . and was a frequent guest among the nobility and gentry in the English capital." He looked "the equal of any peer in the land," Wilkinson noted, "for he was of a noble presence; and he possessed that rare taste of adapting himself to almost any company in which he might be thrown."

At this time, the autumn of 1862, the credit of the Confederate government was good, both in England and on the Continent. The best firms in England, especially, were eager and ready to furnish supplies. To Wilkinson it seemed wholly practical to ship into Southern ports the plates, machinery and other elements necessary for the construction of small vessels-of-war. Some British firms even went so far as to design such vessels and make models of them. "All of which were afterwards duly submitted to the incompetent Secretary of the Confederate States Navy," Wilkinson recorded bitterly. ". . . but it resulted in nothing. A considerable amount of government funds was lavished abroad upon the building of vessels which could by no possibility be got to sea under the Confederate flag while the war lasted."

Wilkinson must have done a fast job of refitting the *Giraffe*, for she was laden and ready for sea just thirty days after he landed. There were a number of passengers booked aboard the steamer: twenty-six Scottish lithographers who had been engaged by the Confederate Treasury Department, presumably to design and print paper money; also several young Southerners who were returning home to fight under the Bonnie Blue Flag.

After an uneventful voyage by way of Madeira and San Juan, Porto Rico, they approached "that haven of blockade runners, El Dorado of adventurers, and paradise of wreckers and darkies— filthy Nassau," to quote Wilkinson's salty description.

In commenting on the high wages paid to captains, pilots, officers and crewmen of blockade runners, Wilkinson points out a fact that may hitherto have escaped notice. He says that although the subordinate officers and all members of the *crew* of a *government-owned* blockade runner received wages equal to those aboard privately owned steamers, the *captain* and *pilot*, being members of the Confederate States armed services, *received the same pay as others in their respective grades*: so Wilkinson had to be content with his regular pay.

At Nassau a number of the *Giraffe's* original crew were paid off and others shipped to replace them. On December 26, 1862, the little steamer was ready to try her luck against the sharp-eyed Yankee cruisers. Wilkinson had with him two pilots, one from Charleston and one from Wilmington, since his decision as to which port he would try for would depend on wind, weather and the location of the blockading squadron.

The course taken by the *Giraffe* was strange compared to that of most blockade runners. It was probably because blockade running was in its early stages and no set course or concise plan had been worked out for slipping past the lines of cruisers guarding key ports. The *Giraffe* sighted land near Charleston bar on the twenty-eighth but the pilot was afraid to take them any closer. So Wilkinson decided to head for Wilmington. The weather was clear and the sea smooth. Not a sail or wisp of smoke marred the clear-cut horizon. The *Giraffe* steamed so close to the coast that she could exchange signals with Confederate pickets on the beach.

Later on, about three o'clock in the afternoon,* a cruiser was sighted to the northeast, and the *Giraffe* turned her bow away from the enemy and got up more steam, easily preserving her distance.

Wilkinson put in force certain precautionary regulations much the same as used on the *Banshee*: (1) All lights were doused. Anyone who showed a light upon nearing the blockading fleet was liable to death on the spot. (2) Reliable leadsmen were stationed in the port and starboard chains to permit the correct soundings to be taken. (3) The quartermaster took the wheel. (4) A hood was fitted over the binnacle. (5) The fireroom hatch was covered with a tarpaulin.

By ten o'clock that night the *Giraffe* successfully slipped past the first ship of the inside blockading line which was strung out five miles east of the Old Inlet entrance to the Cape Fear River. It seemed to those aboard the *Giraffe* that at the speed being made they would pass through with ease. Just then they all got a jolt—"a shock that threw nearly everyone on board off his feet," Wilkinson recalled, and the steamer ground to a stop, hard and fast on a shoal. It looked as if the *Giraffe* would quickly be made a prize, for the nearest Federal cruiser was only a short distance away. The place where Wilkinson's steamer had grounded was called "The Lump"—a small, sandy submerged knoll a couple of miles outside the bar, with deep water on both

---

* At this time the blockade was rather loosely enforced and runners could often get through in daylight. A year later this would have been impossible.

sides. It was impossible to locate this obstruction because there were no landmarks or bearings which would enable a vessel to steer clear of it. "Many a ton of valuable freight has been launched overboard there," Wilkinson wrote of this spot, "and, indeed all the approaches to Wilmington are paved as thickly with valuables as a certain place is said to be with good intentions."

In this crisis Wilkinson acted promptly and efficiently. He had the two quarter boats lowered, and sent them ashore loaded with the Scotch lithographers and their gear. Then he sent another boat with forty-six persons ashore with a kedge anchor in an effort to enable the *Giraffe* to haul herself off the "Lump." Great care had to be taken not to make the slightest noise or show a glimmer of light for fear the cruiser anchored near by would become suspicious and steam over to investigate. After an hour's frantic work, aided by the rising tide, the *Giraffe* was refloated and a few revolutions of her paddle wheels brought her into deep water. Soon they steamed out of danger and within range of the protecting guns of Fort Caswell.

During this part of the voyage a jittery lookout kept reporting imaginary ships, breakers, and finally a rock. The pilot, losing his patience, exclaimed, "God Almighty, man, there isn't a rock as big as my hat along the coast of the whole damned state of North Carolina!" This remark brought a laugh from all hands and broke the tension. A little later the *Giraffe* passed safely over the bar and anchored off Smithville.

A few days after her arrival in Wilmington the *Giraffe* was formally turned over to the Confederate States government and rechristened the *R. E. Lee.* From then on she flaunted the Stars and Bars.

Wilkinson made several round trips between Wilmington and Nassau during the winter of 1862-1863 without being caught. In March 1863 he shifted his run to Bermuda. He notes in his memoirs the friendly relations that existed between the British naval officers attached to the Royal Dockyard at Saint George's and the officers of Confederate blockade runners and men-of-war.

During the latter part of the same month, the *R. E. Lee* encountered danger not only from Union naval fire, but also from a sudden thunderstorm. From Wilkinson's reminiscences and a letter written by First Officer R. E. Blackford, it is possible to reconstruct the harrowing adventure. It was barely dusk and the smoldering saltworks along the North Carolina coast had been sighted for a short time only when Wilkinson called attention to a mass of dark clouds rapidly forming on the northeast horizon.

"I don't like the look of that sky," he remarked to Blackford. "Those clouds are making up too fast. We're in for a blow."

The mate remarked that he hoped the *Lee* would make her turning point (where she would alter course southward parallel to the coast) before the dirty weather struck. Wilkinson replied by ordering the engines stopped and a leadsman sent into the forechains. Quickly the leadsman took his station on the small platform near the bow. He carefully coiled the sounding line, at the end of which was a heavy lead plummet, and paid out enough line to allow the lead to swing freely. Then he made a long cast. After hauling in his line the leadsman reported the depth to be ten fathoms with a sand and mud bottom (by use of tallow on the lead to which a sample of the bottom adhered). From this report Wilkinson knew that the *Lee* was just about where he reckoned, off Masonboro Inlet.

He then ordered the engine in motion again and sent the mate forward to watch for tide rips that would further confirm their position. He also posted a lookout in the crosstrees. The mate groped his way to the bow and braced himself against the windlass. The wind was cold and clawed at his clothing. Northward the cloud mass had expanded to cover half the sky, darker than the darkness of the night. Blackford peered anxiously into the murk, straining for a glimpse of the churning water that poured into the sea on the bosom of the flood tide. For a moment he thought he saw a patch of dirty gray. Then it disappeared as a cascade of upflung spray dashed against his face.

From aloft came a cry, "White water dead ahead!" On a shout from Wilkinson, Blackford sprinted for the bridge and took the wheel. By now the tumbled area of the tide rips was scarcely a hundred yards away. Far beyond and fairly visible was the shadowy shoreline, broken by the mouth of the inlet. Southward stretched an irregular white ribbon that marked the outer reaches of the surf. The mate no longer watched the compass. His eyes were on the choppy margin of the rips, waiting for an order he knew would come at any moment.

Now at last the *Lee* had reached the turning point, marked by those tumbled tide rips; now she could swing South, hoping to steal unobserved past the Union cruisers.

"Hard aport!" Wilkinson shouted.

Instantly the mate spun the spokes. The *R. E. Lee* heeled sharply in a smother of foam, paddle wheels thrashing. Her nose dipped into the brine, then lifted to toss the water aside. Through the engine-room grating Blackford could hear shouts and curses and the noise of coal shovels sliding across the iron deck as the vessel heeled and the "black gang" lost their footing below. The mate spun the wheel in the opposite direction to bring the rudder amidships on the new course. With a lurch the little steamer righted herself and plunged on. Now she was racing south under full speed, parallel to the beach, and the great land swells caught her on the beam, making her labor and roll.

"The motion was sickening," Blackford wrote. "All hands had to cling to the rails and stanchions to keep from sliding into the scuppers. Yet they laughed and joked and were happy because they felt they were almost safe, skirting the beach where no Yankee dared follow and with barely enough water below the keel. They knew we would be under the guns of Fort Fisher within the hour.

"Then, suddenly, from astern came a rumble and a crash that sounded as if giant trees were being torn apart. It was thunder—the storm had caught up with us at last. Then came the rain, in sheets, driving across the bridge and rattling against the pilot house. The wind shrieked like a thousand harpies."

The *R. E. Lee* began to pitch and roll even more violently and her foredeck was a welter of wild water that surged against her superstructure and cascaded off her flanks. Again came the crash of thunder, followed by a faint show of lightning.

"If there wasn't such a heavy sea running," Wilkinson shouted above the wind to Blackford at the wheel, "I'd be worried about the lightning giving us away. But it won't, I'm certain. The Yankees always haul way offshore in heavy weather. We ought to sight Fisher before long."

At last came the welcome cry and Blackford wrote exultantly: "Safe—safe at last—or so I thought!

"A rain squall blotted out all sight of land but Captain Wilkinson did not slacken speed, for the water was deeper here and the swells less severe. Just then there was a tremendous peal of thunder, followed instantly by a flash of lightning. In the brief glare I saw two long, black shapes, about a thousand yards distant and directly in our path. There was no need to ask Captain Wilkinson what they were: Federal cruisers riding uneasily at anchor, one on each side of the entrance to New Inlet."

Wilkinson acted quickly. He ordered the engines stopped and the steamer lost headway and began to roll in the troughs of the waves. "For a full minute Captain Wilkinson said nothing," Blackford recalled in his letter. "And it irritated me as I mistakenly took his silence to indicate indecision. At last the captain said gruffly to the mate that he did not think the enemy had seen us since if they had, they would have pulled up their anchors and gotten moving."

The cruisers loomed closer now, their hulks and spars faintly outlined against the watery sky. Suddenly a train of sparks rose from the starboard cruiser, followed by a blinding glare. It was a calcium rocket called a Drummond light and it etched in bold relief the two steam frigates and their rows of guns. The rocket not only provided illumination to aid in locating blockade runners, but it also served as a signal to other vessels of the squadron. The Drummond light was immediately followed by two more rockets thrown in the direction of the *R. E. Lee*.

"These signals were probably selected each day for the ensuing night," Wilkinson states in his memoirs, "as they appeared to

be constantly changed, but the rockets were invariably sent up."
The resourceful Wilkinson was prepared and was not to be out-
done. He had ordered a lot of identical rockets from New York,
(apparently shipped to him at Nassau or Bermuda). So now he
sent up two rockets of his own at right angles to his true course.
This so confused the frigates and the other vessels that the *R. E.
Lee* was able to steam between the two guard vessels before they
were properly under way.

"Nevertheless," wrote Blackford, "the nearest vessel fired her
bow chaser at us at almost point blank range. I heard the scream
of the shell as it passed over the pilot house. Fortunately it did
no harm and we were able to escape to the shelter of Fort Fisher
without any damage. After crossing the bar, we anchored for
the night in the river and then steamed up to Wilmington, thankful for our providential escape and grateful for the expert and
courageous handling of the *Lee* by Captain Wilkinson."

On one of his later runs into the same port, Wilkinson brought
in from Bermuda twelve chests of costly China tea which had
been taken from a homeward-bound Indiaman belonging to a
New York company. This vessel had been captured by the
famous Confederate commerce raider *Florida*, under command
of Captain John N. Maffitt.

On an eastbound voyage that began on August 13, 1863, Captain Wilkinson used a device to escape capture which was extensively and successfully employed by the navies of Great Britain,
Germany and the United States during World Wars I and II—
the smoke screen.

Aboard the *Lee* on this voyage was ex-Senator Gwin and his
daughter Lucy; also a Southern physician and his wife. The
R. E. Lee passed safely through the blockading fleet off New
Inlet bar, with only a few badly aimed shots fired at her. By
daylight the steamer had made an offing of some thirty miles
from the coast. Captain Wilkinson had been able to buy only
a small quantity of Welsh coal (anthracite which gave off very
little smoke). It was soon exhausted and he had to rely on North
Carolina coal, "of very inferior quality, and which smoked ter-

ribly. The change of fuel was made soon after daylight and it was not long before the lookout at the masthead called out, 'Sail ho!'

"Where away?" Captain Wilkinson shouted.

"Right astern, sir, and in chase," came the reply.

Wilkinson climbed the mast and joined the lookout. In the clear light he could see the topsails of a large steam frigate. It was common practice for those United States Navy vessels which had steam and sail to use both in giving chase if the wind was favorable. In a good stiff breeze the sails would add one or two, or even three knots to the frigate's speed, sometimes just enough to enable her to overhaul her prey.

Wilkinson stayed aloft for half an hour and by the time he returned to the deck the topgallant sails of the enemy were showing above the horizon. She was identified as the U.S.S. *Iroquois*. At the speed she was making, Wilkinson reckoned that she would be alongside the *R. E. Lee* by midday. So he ordered the entire deck cargo of cotton bales thrown overboard. Soon they were bobbing in a long line astern. At the same time the engineer was ordered to make more steam. He protested that it was impossible because the wretched coal was full of slate and dirt. Meanwhile the *Iroquois* was booming along with every stitch of canvas set. From her stack streamed a long ribbon of smoke.

Wilkinson was steering a course east by south at the time and he saw that if he held to it he would surely be overtaken. On the other hand, he was well aware that if he could maneuver his steamer so as to take the wind out of the frigate's sails, the man-of-war's advantage would be neutralized. He could do this either by bringing the *Lee's* head gradually into the wind, or edge away to bring the wind aft. The first plan would have been the best, except that it would have meant running toward the land and into more trouble. So he began to edge away. In two or three hours, those aboard the *Lee* had the satisfaction of seeing their pursuer being forced to clew up and furl her sails.

Nevertheless, the *Iroquois* was gaining. Wilkinson then resorted to a desperate measure. He ordered the chief engineer to saturate cotton in turpentine and feed it to the fires. There were thirty or forty barrels of turpentine aboard, and of course, plenty of cotton from the holds.

"The result exceeded our expectations," Wilkinson wrote afterwards. "The chief engineer, an excitable little Frenchman from Charleston, very soon made his appearance on the bridge, his eyes sparkling with triumph, and reported a full head of steam. Curious to know the effect upon our speed, I directed him to wait a moment until the log was hove. I threw it myself: nine and one half knots!

" 'Let her go now, sir,' I said.

"Five minutes afterwards I hove the log again: thirteen and a quarter!' "

The increased speed enabled the *Lee* to hold her own against the frigate, but she was dangerously near. The *Iroquois* was plowing majestically along with a "white bone in her teeth," and the worried people aboard the *Lee* could distinctly see her black-muzzled guns. At this point Wilkinson began to have visions of another incarceration in jail at Fort Warren.

To make matters worse, he suddenly remembered that he had aboard a large amount of gold that was being shipped abroad by the Confederate government. What a handsome bonus that would be to the prize money for officers and men on the *Iroquois!* Rather than risk that, Wilkinson had the kegs of gold coins brought up on deck and one of them opened so that he would be ready to distribute the gold among the passengers, officers and crew rather than have it grabbed by the eager Yankees.

"Miss Lucy Gwin," Wilkinson recalled, "who preserved her presence of mind throughout the trying scenes of the day, called me aside and suggested that she should fill a purse for me, and keep it about her person, until the prize crew had taken possession, and all danger of personal search was over, when she would make an opportunity to give it to me; and I have no doubt she would have accomplished her intention if occasion had required."

Apparently both Captain Wilkinson and Miss Lucy were confident that she would not be searched and it is very likely that she would not. Gallantry toward women was practiced by men of both sides in those long-ago days when respect for human beings was an inherent characteristic. There were exceptions, of course, but in general it was unthinkable to lay violent hands on a gentle-woman.

On went the race, all afternoon, with very little change in the relative positions of the two vessels. Then, at about six o'clock, the *Lee's* engineer came to the bridge with bad news. The burned cotton had choked the flues and the steam was running down. Wilkinson told him to do his best to keep up speed until darkness would help them give the Yankees the slip.

He then stationed two of his most reliable officers on each paddle box and told them to watch the *Iroquois* through their glasses and report to him the moment the frigate could no longer be seen on account of the gathering gloom. At the same time he ordered the chief engineer to make as black a smoke as possible and to stand by to cut off the smoke instantly by closing the dampers. Not long after, both officers called out at the same moment, "We have lost sight of her." During this time a dense volume of smoke had been pouring from the *Lee's* twin stacks and streaming astern where it hung low over the water. "Close the dampers!" Wilkinson called down the engine-room speaking tube. At the same moment he ordered the helmsman to spin the wheel hard to starboard. This changed the steamer's course and brought her on a new course at right angles to her old one. Protected by her self-made smoke screen, the little *Lee* shook off the *Iroquois*. Wilkinson was so confident that he was out of danger that he retired to his stateroom an hour afterward, with, as he says, "a comfortable sense of security."

The heat generated by the turpentine-soaked cotton had been so intense that the very planks on the bridge had been scorching hot and Wilkinson recorded that his feet were nearly blistered. So when he got to his cabin he took off his shoes and socks and stuck his bare feet out of the porthole to cool them.

"While in this position," he relates, "Missy Lucy Gwin came along the deck in company with her father. Tapping my foot with her hand she said, 'Ah, Captain, I see we are all safe and I congratulate you !' "

After another round trip through the blockade, Wilkinson was ordered to Richmond and put in charge of an expedition that was to be sent north secretly to try and release Confederate prisoners at Johnson's Island in Sandusky Harbor on Lake Erie. He and his party sailed to Halifax aboard his old vessel, the *Lee*. From there they made their way overland to Montreal. Before any action could be taken to free the prisoners, the secret leaked out and the prison garrison was strengthened: so the expedition had to be abandoned. The party returned to Halifax and from there back to the South by way of Bermuda.

In the meantime the *Lee*, which had brought a full cargo of cotton to Halifax, had started south with a load of war supplies. She was, of course, in charge of another captain and pilot. By the time the steamer sighted land near New Inlet, both captain and pilot seem to have suffered an acute attack of jitters, for neither was willing to take the responsibility for conning the vessel through the blockaders. So they turned the *Lee* around and went out to sea again. What she did out there all night is unknown. Probably she lay to. When the morning light revealed her to the prowling cruisers, they gave chase and made her an easy prize. The capture took place twenty miles offshore in the deep bay between Masonboro Inlet and Cape Lookout Shoals.

Wilkinson attributes the loss of the *Lee* to "culpable mismanagement" and records his keen regret at the loss of his gallant little steamer. His stanch old helmsman, who had been aboard at the time of the capture, served a short jail term in New York. He was released by claiming British citizenship. Somehow he got to Halifax and met Wilkinson on his return from the Johnson Island expedition. In recounting the story of the *Lee's* capture, the helmsman said, with tears in his eyes, "She would have gone in by herself, sir, if they'd only let her alone. . . ."

The *R. E. Lee* deserves a place among the top ten blockade runners for the number of successful voyages and valuable cargoes carried in and out. She ran the gantlet twenty-one times while under Wilkinson's command, carried 7,000 bales of cotton to Nassau, Bermuda and Halifax (worth at the time $2,000,000 in gold) and brought into the Confederacy an immense amount of sorely needed war supplies.

After the abortive expedition to Johnson's Island, Captain Wilkinson returned to Bermuda. Here he was offered command of the new blockade runner *Whisper*, a light but speedy craft, built especially for the trade. He notes that she was a capital sea boat, but could not be compared with the "solidly built, magnificent *Lee*." How it was possible for a commissioned officer of the Confederate States Navy to take command of a privately owned steamer so promptly and easily is not made clear. Apparently the arrangement was sanctioned by the Confederate naval authorities at Saint George's.

On the night that the *Whisper* was to sail, and Captain Wilkinson was dining with the company agent, Mr. Campbell, a caller was announced who wished to see Campbell on urgent business. It turned out that he wanted to ship a box of medicine through the blockade. It was not very large, he said. Campbell, knowing that the *Whisper* was already heavily laden, put the matter up to Wilkinson. He agreed to take the box and put it in his own cabin. The freight which Campbell quoted the man, and which he accepted, was £500 sterling or $2,500 in U.S. currency. Wilkinson was astonished at the fantastic price. In recounting the incident, he did not specify the contents of the box. Yet if it had contained fifty pounds of morphine or quinine (each selling in the South at that time at $100 per ounce) the shipment would have been worth $80,000. From that standpoint the freight was not so excessive as it might have appeared.

Wilkinson himself received a premium of $2,500 for commanding the *Whisper* on this trip. He comments: "As the *Whisper* belonged to a private company, I accepted the bonus without scruple."

On the inbound voyage to Wilmington, a veritable flotilla of blockade runners, six in all, set sail within twenty-four hours of each other. They immediately ran into a strong northeaster with a heavy overcast, which prevented taking sights of sun or stars. They had to navigate by dead reckoning until reaching

the easily identified Gulf Stream early on the third day. Here
they met another hazard, fog. When cold wind from the northwest met the warm waters of the Gulf Stream it created such
dense vapor that visibility was cut to zero. "At such times,"
comments Wilkinson, "the skill and perseverence of the navigator would be taxed to the limit . . . an error of a few miles
in the calculation would probably prove fatal." It did—to five
of the six steamers. All of them, except the *Whisper*, were run
ashore. Several managed to salvage parts of their cargoes with
the aid of Confederate soldiers and sailors on the beach. Others
of the group fell intact into eager Federal hands.

Meanwhile Wilkinson was lucky enough to catch a glimpse
of the sun and ascertain his position, which he found to be about
fifty miles off the Western Bar (Old Inlet) guarded by Fort
Caswell. The gale had pummeled the *Whisper* badly. All but
one of her boats had been swept from their davits and her pilothouse stove in by a great sea. Since most steamers like the *Whisper* were rigged to carry fore-and-aft sails, it was common practice to set some canvas in heavy weather to steady the vessel.
Fearing that the *Whisper* would be badly strained by the rough
waves, Wilkinson brought the steamer into the wind and set and
reefed his mainsail. She rode the rollers like a seagull—close to
the edge of the fog bank in case an enemy appeared. After many
anxious hours the daylight faded into night and before midnight
the vessel had passed safely through the Union fleet and come
to anchor off Smithville.

Another special assignment given Captain Wilkinson during
the latter part of the war was the re-establishment of lights along
the approaches to the Cape Fear River. At the beginning of
hostilities, nearly all the lights along the Southern coast had been
extinguished and the machinery and apparatus removed to places
of safety.

Wilkinson first replaced the light on Smith's Island and then
erected a structure for a light on the Mound at Fort Fisher. At
this time so many blockade runners had been driven ashore or
captured, due to the increasing vigilance and number of ships
of the blockading squadron, the Confederate naval authorities

felt that fixed lights at certain points along the shore, together with the erection of range lights, would be of great assistance to the pilots of the steamers running in and out of both entrances to the Cape Fear River. Captain Wilkinson was also in charge of detailing pilots and signal officers to the various vessels. To assure an unfailing supply of fuel for the lights, each blockade runner was required by law to bring in a barrel of sperm oil on each trip.

In September 1864 Secretary Mallory decided on a program of reprisals against Northern shipping, particularly the coasting trade and fisheries. For this purpose he selected a double-screw steamer called the *Chicamauga*, which had been converted into what Wilkinson terms "a so-called man-of-war." He was ordered to command. The vessel's armament consisted of a twelve-pound rifled gun forward, a sixty-four pounder amidships and a thirty-two pounder aft, all on pivots. She was more strongly built than most blockade runners, but Wilkinson considered her unfit for a cruiser because of her limited fuel capacity and total absence of sailing qualities. Although rigged as a schooner, she had very short masts and could carry such a small amount of sail that she could barely make about three knots under full sail. Consequently about the only use that could be made of her canvas was to steady her in a gale.

On October 29 the *Chicamauga* put to sea, eluded the blockading fleet and headed north. From then on she pursued a career of fire and destruction in the shipping lanes off the Delaware capes, Sandy Hook and as far up the coast as Montauk Point at the tip end of Long Island. Her victims were mostly schooners, barques and clipper ships, carrying various cargoes including lumber, sugar, molasses and vegetables. Most of the vessels were burned. One, the *Shooting Star*, a handsome clipper, was an awesome sight. Wilkinson says in his narrative: "The burning ship was visible for many miles after we left her; and it was a strange, wild spectacle, that flaming beacon in the rough sea."

When he had accumulated a number of passengers from the destroyed ships, Wilkinson bundled them all aboard the barque *Albion Lincoln*, after receiving a solemn promise from her master to shape his course directly for Fortress Monroe. Instead, he headed straight for New York to spread the alarm. "I hope his conscience has since reproached him for violating his oath, though given to a 'rebel,' " Wilkinson remarks.

It had been his intention to round Montauk Point and enter Long Island Sound where he planned to wreak havoc among coastwise shipping. But a northeast gale buffeted the *Chicamauga* badly; this, combined with a dangerously short fuel supply, determined him to turn about and head for Bermuda.

"The governor of the island gave me a vast deal of trouble . . . lending a willing ear to the representation of the American Consul." At first the governor refused to let the cruiser enter the harbor at all, but after a twenty-four-hour delay, finally permitted her to come inside. But the governor forbade Wilkinson to coal ship except for barely enough to take the *Chicamauga* to the nearest Confederate port. Wilkinson attributes the governor's attitude partly to the questionable antecedents of the vessel and her title, but more importantly to the fact that "the fortunes of the Confederacy were now waning; and His Excellency wished perhaps—and may have received instructions—to keep on good terms with the winning side. . . ."

The cruise of the *Chicamauga* came to a speedy end soon afterward. The crew had never been a good one, having been made up of waifs, strays and skulkers from the army. Rather than return to the austerity of the Southern states, many of these men deserted in Bermuda just before the cruiser sailed for Wilmington on November 15, 1864. She fetched land in very thick weather on the night of the eighteenth. They could dimly see breakers very close ahead, but it was impossible to make out a single landmark because of the fog. In this crisis Wilkinson demonstrated his remarkable knowledge of that part of the coast near the mouth of the Cape Fear. To orient himself, he sent off a boat with one of the pilots to move in close and look for landmarks. An hour later the boat returned to the *Chicamauga*. The pilot reported that he had pulled in close to the surf, but could not recognize anything on shore.

"Did you see any wrecks on the beach?" Wilkinson asked him.

"Yes sir," he replied. "I saw three."

"How were they lying?" Wilkinson said.

"Two of them were broadside on the beach. The other was bows on, about a cable's length to the north of the others."

"Good!" exclaimed Wilkinson. "I know exactly where we are."

He felt sure that he was near Masonboro Inlet, since he had spotted those selfsame wrecks at the time he had re-established lights and signal stations along that part of the coast.

When daylight came, the *Chicamauga* ran boldly for New Inlet and, after an exchange of shots with several Federal cruisers at long range, was soon within the comfortable protection of the guns of Fort Fisher.

Captain Wilkinson had been encouraged to believe that he could prevail upon the Confederate naval authorities to fit out a better ship than the *Chicamauga* as a commerce raider; a steamer with propellers that could be disconnected when under sail, proper spars for carrying a large spread of canvas and comfortable quarters for officers and crew. Unfortunately, other serious matters were occupying the attention of Richmond. The Confederate armies were in a bad way. Sherman had already marched virtually unopposed from Atlanta to the sea and was now heading northwest. Even Wilmington was being threatened by a great sea and land force intent on killing blockade running once and for all. Food for the famished Confederate soldiers was urgently needed.

In this crisis Wilkinson was chosen to run a steamer to Bermuda and bring back a load of provisions with all possible speed. Since it was practically certain that the cranky governor of Bermuda would never permit the *Chicamauga*, in her new role as a blockade runner, to discharge a cotton cargo, much less load food for the Confederate army, another ex-commerce raider, the *Tallahassee*, was selected. Her navy crew and all guns were removed and she was appropriately rechristened *Chameleon*. All necessary papers were prepared so that there would be no delays through red tape from the British authorities which might affect her entrance to, or exit from, Bermuda.

The *Chameleon* left Wilmington on the day after Christmas

1864 in the midst of panic and confusion generated by the first, and unsuccessful, attack on Fort Fisher by a powerful Federal army and navy expedition. With the sounds of terrific bombardment echoing across the water, Wilkinson adroitly bypassed the blockading squadron and brought the *Chameleon* into Saint George's harbor in the teeth of a stiff northeast gale. His hope for a speedy turnaround was dashed, for the governor again proved balky and it was five days before the *Chameleon* was allowed to discharge her cotton cargo. More delays followed in loading the foodstuffs and it was not until January 19 that the anxious and frustrated captain at last saw Bermuda sink below the eastern horizon.

On arriving at New Inlet bar, Wilkinson's signalman reported that he could get no reply to his signals, although many lights began to appear through the drizzle. Wilkinson could not know, of course, that Fort Fisher had been attacked for a second time, reduced to rubble and captured. The flickering lights seen from the bridge of the *Chameleon* were the campfires of the victorious Federal infantry.

The skipper of the steamer thought he had made an error in his reckoning, so he headed the *Chameleon* out to sea again at full speed. Out of sight of land he laid low until the next day which he spent cruising up and down fifty miles off the coast. At nightfall he planned to head for shore again. As darkness settled, he shaped his course for Mound Light. Presently he saw familiar range lights and he crossed the bar at New Inlet without any interference and without the slightest suspicion that anything was wrong. This was perfectly possible, because, according to his own statement, it would occasionally happen that a steamer could cross the bar without even seeing an enemy cruiser. What occurred next is best described in gallant Wilkinson's own words:

"We were under the guns of Fort Fisher . . . close to the fleet of U.S. vessels, which had crossed the bar after the fall of the fort, when I directed my signal officer to communicate with the shore station. His signal was promptly acknowledged, but turning to me he said, 'No Confederate signal officer there, sir; he cannot reply to me.' " (Evidently he meant that whoever was signaling from shore did not know the secret code of blockade runners.) Now thoroughly disturbed, Wilkinson instantly ordered the steamer put about and her bow was scarcely pointed seaward when two light cruisers detached themselves from the other Union vessels and steamed full speed in pursuit.

Wilkinson attributes his hairsbreadth escape to the *Chameleon's* twin screws, which "enabled our steamer to turn as if on a pivot in the narrow channel between the bar and the rip." The *Chameleon* kept on running eastward until she reached Nassau. Here Wilkinson learned the details of the fall of Fort Fisher. It was clear to him that since both entrances to the Cape Fear were under Federal control (Fort Caswell guarding Old Inlet had surrendered) it was a matter of days perhaps before Wilmington itself would be occupied. With a pang he realized that the last port open to blockade running had been effectively sealed by the Federals.

Nevertheless, Wilkinson did not give up hope of landing his provisions on Southern soil. He relates that "Charleston was now the only harbor on the Atlantic coast at all accessible, and that must evidently soon fall [it was evacuated February 17]; but a cargo might be landed there before that inevitable catastrophe, and fully appreciating the exigency, I determined to make the effort."

The *Chameleon* had scarcely passed Abaco Light in the Bahamas when she was sighted and pursued by the large, fast paddle-wheel cruiser U.S.S. *Vanderbilt.* "I was afraid that the *Chameleon* had at last found her match," Wilkinson wrote afterward. From then on there was a long, thrilling game of hare-and-hound in which both steam and sail were used to their fullest. Wilkinson's stanch old quartermaster, McLean, stood grimly at the wheel. "He had nerves of steel and would have steered the vessel without flinching against a line of battleships, if so ordered."

The *Chameleon* had one advantage over the *Vanderbilt.* She carried fore-and-aft sails, while the Federal cruiser was square rigged. Splendid seaman that he was, Wilkinson hauled his sheets flat aft so as to sail as close to the wind as possible. He later declared that he certainly would have been overhauled but for this favorable fact. The *Vanderbilt* gradually began to drop to leeward and by midnight was forced to furl her sails.

Yet the *Vanderbilt* stuck stubbornly to the chase, although losing distance as time went on. Just as Wilkinson began to breathe easier, his engineer reported that the engine's bearings had become overheated by the killing pace and it was absolutely imperative to stop and let them cool. Like Tom Taylor in a similar dilemma, Wilkinson knew that he had no alternative but to do so. Especially when he looked down into the hold and "saw the clouds of vapor rising from the overheated journals, as a stream of water was being poured upon them."

Captain Wilkinson had implicit confidence in Shroeder, his engineer, and it had been justly earned; he was a calm man with great presence of mind, and knew his engines thoroughly. Following Wilkinson's order to stop, the steamer "lay like a log upon the water, and the cruiser was rapidly lessening the distance between us, and the suspense was almost intolerable. Our fate was hanging by a thread; but in ten minutes the journals had been cooled off, the bearings eased and the *Chameleon* again sprang ahead with renewed speed . . . and continued her course toward Charleston."

Fate and the Federals again prevented Wilkinson from reaching his objective. On arriving off Charleston he discovered that the blockading squadron had been heavily reinforced by all the light cruisers that had guarded the Cape Fear before the fall of Fort Fisher. Now he knew that the situation was hopeless. It would be suicide to try and run in the cargo of food. With a heavy heart he ordered his vessel turned about and once more headed for Nassau.

Shortly after arrival came more bad news. Charleston had been evacuated and Sherman was storming through Georgia and into South Carolina. The last thin thread of communication between Confederate blockade runners and their government had been snapped.

After talking over the situation with Mr. Heyliger, the Confederate agent in Nassau, it was decided to unload the provisions and sail the *Chameleon* to England. On arrival there, Wilkinson wished to turn the vessel over to the agent for Fraser, Trenholm & Company, but the agent refused to have anything to do with the matter, well aware, no doubt, that blockade running was dead and buried. Finally the vessel was placed in the hands of Captain Bullock, an agent of the Confederate States government. Wilkinson also deposited with him all government funds in his possession and received a receipt for them.

So ended the blockade-running career of Captain John Wilkinson, a bold, efficient and resourceful naval officer who had little or nothing in the way of profit to show for his valuable and arduous services to the Southern cause. In his memoirs, he makes this observation: "I might have accumulated a fortune . . . there were many opportunities . . . during the war, without detriment to the cause, and consistent with every obligation to the Confederate government. There are times when I cannot decide whether I acted the part of a fool, or a patriot."

History may well award him the latter title, for he risked his life time after time for "the cause for which so much blood has been shed, so many miseries bravely endured and so many sacrifices so cheerfully made."

THE ELUSIVE CAPTAIN "ROBERTS"

The excitement, narrow escapes and quick profits of blockade running were front-rank topics of conversation in the wardrooms of the men-of-war of Her Britannic Majesty's Navy. Compared to the dull routine of naval life in peacetime, the game of eluding Federal cruisers and dodging shot and shell beckoned temptingly. Officers of all ranks applied for leaves of absence, but few were fortunate enough to receive official consent. What counted most was an outstanding record and strong connections at the Admiralty.

The handful of gentlemen-adventurers who became blockade runners pro tempore were a charming and carefree lot, according to the memoirs of Tom Taylor, who knew them all. They soon became friendly with Colonel and Mrs. Lamb at Fort Fisher and were often entertained at their home near by. "This cottage," Taylor recalled, "was famed for the frugal but tempting meals which its charming hostess would prepare for the distinguished guests." But the frugality was quickly altered to sumptuousness after the Britishers made their next trip through the blockade, for they brought in all sorts of delicacies for the Lambs, including the best of champagnes. In addition to English guests, Colonel and Mrs. Lamb entertained many Confederate Army and Navy officers "who delighted to find a bit of soothing civilization on the wild and sandy beach, ensconced among the sand dunes and straggling pines."

No one was supposed to know that these Britishers, faultlessly attired in the height of civilian fashion, were actually naval officers on leave. Officially they were "merchant captains" with surnames quite different from those on their service records back in London. It scarcely needed to be pointed out to anyone curious enough to inquire that it would be quite embarrassing to Her Majesty's government if a well-known British naval officer was caught by a Union cruiser in the act of blockade running.

Several of them became famous along the Carolina coast. There was debonair Captain Burgoyne, who, after the war, lost his life when his ironclad, H.M.S. *Captain*, foundered with all hands in the Bay of Biscay. Another was Captain "Murray" (Murray-Aynsley mentioned by Tom Taylor). On returning to the Navy after a successful career outwitting Union blockaders, he was rapidly promoted for gallantry and meritorious service and was an admiral at the time of his death.

The most noteworthy of all was Augustus Charles Hobart-Hampden, a younger son of the sixth Earl of Buckinghamshire. He was a favorite of Queen Victoria and at one time was the commander of her yacht, *Victoria and Albert*. He was tall, commandingly handsome, the living image of a salty hero; and indeed he was, for he had won the Victoria Cross during the Crimean War while serving under Admiral Sir Charles Napier. It was this tough seadog who issued the famous order, "Lads, sharpen your cutlasses." And it was Hobart-Hampden who led a boarding party of British tars against the Russian warships defending Kronshtadt. The British swarmed aboard and captured the Russians, enabling Napier to storm the seven forts which guarded the entrance to the harbor and sail up the Neva clear to St. Petersburg.

As a blockade runner, Hobart-Hampden operated under many aliases: Hewett, Ridge, Gulick and A. Roberts. His first command was the sleek and speedy twin-screw steamer *Don*.

"Roberts" considered her one of the finest of blockade runners. Especially built for the trade, she was of 400 tons burden, 180 feet in length, with a 22-foot beam. Her powerful engines developed 250 horsepower. Besides the captain, the *Don* carried three deck officers, three engineers and a twenty-eight man crew. They were all Englishmen, carefully selected for experience and courage. If the truth were known, a good many of these seamen had at one time or another served aboard vessels of her Majesty's West Indian squadron and it was nobody's business how they happened to be aboard a blockade runner. According to Captain Roberts' description, the *Don's* graceful hull showed only about eight feet above the waterline and was painted blue-gray to merge with the horizon and become virtually invisible at night. Only anthracite coal was burned. When steam had to be blown off, it was done under water to stifle the noise. Although chickens were commonly carried aboard to grace the captain's table, he issued strict orders that no cocks were to be included, lest a cockcrow at dawn alert a prowling cruiser.

Captain Roberts' maiden run past the Union squadron off the mouth of the Cape Fear was uneventful. While refueling in Wilmington he was entertained by a number of the town's elite families and heard stories of the immense profits that could be made by bringing in scarce merchandise for civilian use. When he asked one of his hostesses what was most needed by Southern ladies, she replied curtly, "Corsages, sir, I reckon." So Captain Roberts determined to load up with corsets to embellish the figures of Southern womanhood. On arriving in Glasgow he

astonished the manager of a large emporium by ordering 1,000.
For good measure he also bought 500 boxes of Cockles pills and
a large supply of toothbrushes.

Once again in Wilmington, safe and sound, Captain Roberts
began to have qualms about his ability as a merchant, for it had
never occurred to him until that moment how to get rid of the
merchandise. It was piled in his cabin in ominous volume. To
make matters worse, the Cockles pills had burst their boxes and
were rolling about the cabin in all directions. But soon to his
relief a somewhat furtive individual appeared aboard and asked
whether he wished to "trade." The captain greeted him with
open arms, plied him with brandy and ended the session by selling his entire shipment of corsets at 1,100% profit.

Heartened by the deal, Captain Roberts next tried to sell his
customer the Cockles pills. But the fellow merely sniffed and
opined that he had never heard of such things. Then the stealthy
one plucked at his host's sleeve and said hoarsely, "Say, Captain,
have you got any coffin screws on trade?"

"His question rather staggered me," Hobart-Hampden wrote
later in his book, *Never Caught*. But the fellow explained that
"they had no possible way of making this necessary article in the
Southern states and that they positively could not keep the
bodies quiet in their coffins without them, especially being sent
any distance for interment."

A few days later, the last of Roberts' personal cargo, the
toothbrushes, were on the way to Richmond, where they were
sold for seven times their cost. "So ended my first speculation,"
wrote Hobart-Hampden. "The vessel's cargo consisted of blankets, shoes, Manchester goods of all sorts, and some mysterious
cases marked 'hardware' about which no one asked any questions,
but which the military authorities took possession of."

Not long afterward the *Don* loaded cotton and prepared for
the dangerous eastbound voyage. His description of the trip is
worth quoting:

We left the quay at Wilmington cheered by the hurrah of
our brother blockade-runners, who were taking in and discharg-

ing their cargoes, and steamed a short distance down the river, when we were boarded to be searched and smoked. This latter extraordinary proceeding, called for perhaps by the existing state of affairs, took me altogether aback. That a smoking apparatus should be applied to a cargo of cotton seemed almost astounding. But so it was ordered, the object being to search for runaways, and strange to say, its efficacy was apparent, when, after an hour or more application of the process (which was by no means a gentle one) an unfortunate wretch, crushed almost to death by the closeness of his hiding place, poked with a long stick till his ribs must have been like touchwood, and smoked the color of a backwood Indian, was dragged by the heels into the daylight, ignominiously put into irons and hurled down into the guard boat. This discovery nearly caused detention of the vessel on suspicion of our being the accomplices of the runaway; but after some deliberation we were allowed to go on.

After steaming down the river for about twenty miles, the *Don* anchored off Fort Fisher at two o'clock in the afternoon. There would be a wait of some nine hours until the blackness of the night made it possible to creep out from the shelter of the fort and start the run through the cordon of Union war vessels. Meanwhile Captain Roberts went ashore and toured the fortifications with Colonel Lamb. Looking seaward from the Mound battery, Roberts counted twenty-five Federal vessels on patrol. Occasionally one of them ventured within range of Fisher's guns, but was soon chased off by a shot from one of the big Columbiads.

Continuing his narrative, Hobart-Hampden explained that the time chosen for starting the run was eleven o'clock, because at this time the tide was at its highest on the bar at the entrance of Cape Fear River:

Fortunately the moon set about ten, and as it was very cloudy, we had every reason to expect a pitch-dark night. There were two or three causes that made one rather more nervous on this occasion than when leaving Bermuda.

In the first place, five minutes after we had crossed the bar we should be in the thick of the blockaders, who always closed

nearer on the very dark nights. Secondly, our cargo of cotton
was of more importance than the goods we had carried in; and
thirdly, it was the thing to do to make the double trip in and
out safely. There was also all manner of reports of the new
plans that had been arranged by a zealous Commodore lately
sent from New York to catch us all. However, it was of no use
canvassing these questions, so at a quarter to eleven we weighed
anchor and steamed down to the entrance of the river.

Very faint lights, which could not be seen far at sea, were set
on the beach, having been thus placed for a vessel coming in;
and bringing these astern in an exact line, that is, the two into
one, we knew that we were in the passage for going over the
bar. The order was then given: "Full speed ahead," and we shot
at a great speed out to sea.

Our trouble began almost immediately, for the cruisers had
placed a rowing barge, which could not be seen by the forts,
close to the entrance, to signalize the directions which any vessel
that came out might take. This was done by rockets being
thrown up by a designed plan from the barge. We had hardly
cleared the bar when we saw this boat very near our bow, nicely
placed to be run clean over, and as we were going about fourteen
knots, her chance of escape would have been small had we been
inclined to finish her. Changing the helm, which I did myself,
a couple of spokes just took us clear. We passed so close that
I could have dropped a biscuit into the boat with ease. I heard
the crash of their broken oars against our sides; not a word was
spoken.

I strongly suspect every man in that boat held his breath until
the great white avalanche of cotton, rushing by so unpleasantly
near, had passed clear of her.

However, they seemed very soon to have recovered themselves, for a minute had scarcely passed before up went a rocket,
which I thought a very ungrateful proceeding on their part.
But they only did their duty, and perhaps they did not know
how nearly they had escaped being made food for fishes. On the
rocket being thrown up, a gun was fired uncommonly close to
us, but as we did not hear any shot, it may have been only a
signal to the cruisers to keep a sharp lookout.

We steered a mile or two near the coast, always edging a

little to the eastward, and then shaped our course straight out
to sea. Several guns were fired in the pitch-darkness very near
us. (I am not quite sure whether some of the blockaders did
not occasionally pepper each other.) After an hour's fast steaming we felt moderately safe, and by the morning had a good
offing.

Daylight broke with thick, hazy weather, nothing being in
sight. We went all right till half-past eight o'clock when the
weather cleared up, and there was a large paddle-wheel cruiser
(that we must have passed very near to in the thick weather)
about six miles astern of us. The moment she saw us she gave
chase. After running for a quarter of an hour it was evident that,
with our heavy cargo aboard, the cruiser had the legs of us, and
as there was a long day before us for the chase, things looked
badly. We moved some cotton aft to immerse our screws well;
but still the cruiser was steadily decreasing her distance from us,
when an incident of a very curious nature favored us for a time.

It is mentioned in the book of sailing directions that the course
of the Gulf Stream (in the vicinity of which we knew we were)
is in calm weather and smooth water plainly marked out by a
ripple on its inner and outer edges. We clearly saw, about a mile
ahead of us, a remarkable ripple, which we rightly, as it turned
out, conjectured was that referred to in the book. As soon as
we had crossed it we steered the usual course of the current of
the Gulf Stream, that here ran from two to three miles an hour.
Seeing us alter course, the cruiser did the same; but she had not
crossed the ripple on the edge of the stream, and the course she
was now steering tended to keep her for some time from doing
so. The result soon made it evident that the observations in the
book were correct; for until she, too, crossed the ripple into the
stream, we dropped her rapidly astern, thereby we increased
our distance to at least seven miles.

It was noon, from which time the enemy again began to close
with us, and at five o'clock was not more than three miles distant.
The sun set at a quarter of seven. By then she had got so near
that she managed to send two or three shots over us.

Luckily as night came on the weather began to get very
cloudy, and we must have been very difficult to make out though
certainly not more than a mile off. All this time she kept firing

away, thinking, I suppose, that she would frighten us into stopping. If we had gone straight on we should doubtless have been caught, so we altered our course two points to the eastward.

After steaming some distance, we stopped quite still, blowing off steam under water, not a spark or the slightest smoke showing from the funnel; and we had the indescribable satisfaction of seeing our enemy steam past us, still firing ahead at some imaginary vessel.

Hobart-Hampden's success as a blockade runner was not only due to his excellent navigation and seamanship, but also his quick thinking and resourcefulness. On another voyage from Bermuda to Wilmington he made a remarkable getaway when it seemed that destruction or capture was inevitable.

It was a moonless, cloudy night as the *Don* approached the coast. Captain Roberts set his course west by north, directly for Masonboro Inlet, intending to swing sharp around to the southwest as soon as he sighted land. Then he planned to steam along the beach until he came within the protection of Fort Fisher's guns. This was the same course favored by Wilkinson and other canny blockade runners.

Confidently the *Don* plunged through the night at thirteen knots, straight for Masonboro Inlet. There was nothing to guide Roberts except the compass, for his knowledge of the coast at this time was scant. But luck was with him. A half-hour later a welter of tide rips signaled the turning point and soon the gun emplacements of Fort Fisher loomed through the gloom. At that moment a rain squall blotted out all sight of land, but Captain Roberts did not slacken speed, for the water was deep and the swells less severe. As the squall passed he saw, dead ahead, a long black shape close aboard—a Federal cruiser guarding the entrance to New Inlet.

Hobart-Hampden graphically describes the encounter: ". . . suddenly a stentorian voice howled out, 'Heave to in that steamer, or I'll sink you!'

"It seemed as if all was over, but I answered, 'Aye, aye sir, we are stopped . . .'

"The cruiser was about eighty yards from us. We heard orders given to man the quarter boats; we saw the boats lowered into the water; we saw them coming; we heard the crews laughing and cheering at the prospect of their prize. The bowmen had just touched the sides of our vessel with their boathooks when I whispered down the tube into the engine room, 'Full speed ahead.'

"I don't know whether the captain of the man-of-war thought that his boats had taken possession, or whether he stopped to pick up his boats. All I can say is that not a shot was fired, and that in less than a minute the darkness hid the cruiser from our view."

After passing several other cruisers, some unpleasantly near, Captain Roberts saw through his night glasses another steamer, dead ahead, lying almost across his bows and so close that it would have been impossible to pass on either side of her without being seen. But the quick-witted Englishman was equal to the crisis. "A prompt order given to the engine room (where the chief engineer stood to the engines) to reverse *one* engine, was as promptly obeyed, and the little craft spun round like a tee-totum.

"Having turned, we stopped to reconnoiter and could still see the faint outline of the cruiser, crawling slowly into the darkness, leaving the way open to us, of which we at once took advantage."

One more audacious dash past another cruiser anchored closer in, and the *Don* reached New Inlet, "thanks to disguise and great speed. As we were now perfectly safe, lights were at once lighted, supper and grog served out *ad libitum*, everybody congratulated everybody else, and a feeling of comfort and jollity, such as can only be experienced after three days and nights of intense anxiety, possessed us all."

Not all of Hobart-Hampden's voyages through the blockade ended as happily as that one. Although he could rightfully claim that he had never been caught, he had a narrow escape from the U.S.S. *Niphon* when he had to beach the *Condor* to avoid striking another wrecked blockade runner. The true story of that stormy night and its tragic dawn is told in the next chapter.

After resuming his naval career, Hobart-Hampden apparently became bored with the dull routine of service ashore, for he accepted command of the entire Turkish Navy at the outbreak of the Russo-Turkish War. Known as Hobart Pasha, he became Admiral in Chief of the Sultan's Navy. He died in 1886 after receiving many honors and was buried in the English cemetery at Scutari.

CHAPTER 6

Ladies in Danger

DURING the first two years of the war, the hazards of blockade running were considered to be so slight that Southerners* thought nothing of traveling back and forth between Bermuda, Nassau and Southern ports. The fares were exorbitant, but that was of little account to the rich or those on government business or merchants making fortunes in cotton. The Confederate States government made no attempt to regulate or restrict passenger traffic through the blockade until comparatively late in the conflict. Seagoing travel was not confined to men by any means. Pretty young women and comely matrons often accompanied their menfolk. Small children frequently went along with their parents.

In the fall of 1864 a young matron of Wilmington and her baby endured a harrowing night aboard an outward-bound blockade runner that nearly cost them their lives. Good seamanship plus a large measure of luck enabled them to reach shore wet and cold, but otherwise unharmed. The lady was Mrs. L. H. deRosset, a passenger aboard the steamer *Lynx*.

The *Lynx* was enroute to Nassau on a dark night and had successfully crossed New Inlet Bar and was heading to sea when she was discovered by the Federal cruiser *Niphon*. Captain Reed of the *Lynx* put on all steam pressure and determined to run north along the coast in the hope of shaking off his heavy-draught pursuer. Unfortunately he was sighted by two more Union cruisers.

"Immediately the sky was illuminated by rockets and broad-

---

* Probably the most sinister passenger was John Wilkes Booth, who is said to have traveled through the blockade to Canada on several occasions, in connection with a plot to kidnap Lincoln.

side upon broadside poured upon us," wrote Mrs. deRosset afterward. Captain Reed sent her to the wheelhouse for safety. A moment after she got there a round shot passed through the bulkhead, scarcely three inches above her head, wounding the man at the wheel. A large piece of wood, torn off by the cannon ball, struck Mrs. deRosset on the head but did not inflict a serious wound. As she hurried below to her cabin to attend to her baby a shot struck the *Lynx* below the waterline and the steamer began to sink. Terrified, Mrs. deRosset remained in her cabin as the water stealthily crept up around her knees.

Although a frightful sea was running at the time, Captain Reed managed to head the *Lynx* for shore and with a shudder the ship struck bottom. Lifeboats were manned. Captain Reed brought Mrs. deRosset and her baby on deck. One small boat was heaving wildly alongside and the crew was having a hard time to prevent it from being torn away. As Mrs. deRosset was about to get in the boat, she handed her baby to a sailor expecting that he would hand it down to her. When she was seated, a great sea swept the lifeboat fifteen feet away from the ship's side. Mrs. deRosset screamed and threw out her arms in a gesture of despair. At the same moment the quick-witted seaman tossed the baby across the intervening waves into the arms of its frantic mother. Thanks to the skill of the boat's crew Mrs. deRosset and her infant were brought safely through the surf and sent to Fort Fisher where they were dried, fed and put to bed. The next day, none the worse for their experience, mother and baby returned to Wilmington.

Through the old records, now dimmed by the years, shines a bright gleam of feminine excitement and the thrill of adventure, fortified by a gay disregard of shot and shell. Captain Wilkinson, who always kept a weather eye cocked in the direction of pretty passengers, remarks in his memoirs, "We rarely made a trip either way without as many passengers as could be accommodated and many ladies among them. My observation of the conduct of the fair sex, under trying and novel circumstances, has convinced me that they face inevitable dangers more bravely and with more composure than men. I have frequently seen a frail, delicate woman standing erect and unflinching upon the deck as the shells were whistling and bursting over us, while her lawful protector would be cowering under the lee of a cotton bale. I pay this humble tribute of admiration to the sex, but a cynical old bachelor, to whom I once made this observation, replied that in his opinion their insatiable curiosity prevailed even over their natural fears!"

Captain Maffitt's daughter Florie, returning from Bermuda in charge of one of her father's blockade-running friends, insisted on remaining on deck during the vessel's bombardment by a Federal cruiser. She also offered to conceal about her person part of the captain's hoard of gold so that it would not fall into enemy hands.

The two most notorious women to penetrate the blockade were both Southern spies: dark-eyed Mrs. Rose O'Neal Greenhow and gay, devil-may-care Belle Boyd. For Rose Greenhow, her return to Dixie spelled terror and death. For Belle, traveling in the opposite direction, her voyage brought romance, adventure, love and marriage.

Rose Greenhow was a tall, statuesque brunette who could turn on such charm that United States government officials, army and navy officers and even lowly clerks kept her supplied with a constant stream of information invaluable to the South. Rose enjoyed an unassailable social position in Washington and from the very beginning of hostilities used it to further the Confederate cause. The author of a recent book on spies of the North and South characterizes Mrs. Greenhow as the Perle Mesta of her day. She entertained lavishly and numbered among her guests such VIP's as the chairman of the Senate Military Affairs Committee, many high-ranking army and navy officers, department heads and others of similar caliber.

It has been said that she charmed certain army officers to such an extent that they turned over to her top-secret maps, blue prints and army orders. At one time she claimed to have received copies of the minutes of Lincoln's cabinet meetings and General McClelland's military conferences.

An able organizer, Mrs. Greenhow built an efficient spy ring composed of trustworthy men and women secretly dedicated to the Southern cause. She is credited with warning President Davis of the first major offensive move by the Union Army. After the Confederate victory at the First Manassas, President Davis told her, "But for you, there would have been no Bull Run." Later on, the slow-moving Northern authorities got around to putting her in jail. Yet even behind the bars she contrived to operate her spy ring, at the same time making plenty of trouble for her jailers. Finally, in desperation, they hustled her back across the Mason and Dixon Line and told her to stay. She traveled widely throughout the Confederacy, building morale and trying by every means at her command to stiffen the spines of her people.

By the summer of 1863 the general situation was becoming worse. Lee had suffered his greatest defeat at Gettysburg. Southern optimism had faded into weary fatalism. Soldiers were slinking off home. Gold was selling at fantastic prices and Confederate currency was looked upon with increasing suspicion, its purchasing power shrinking each month.

Rose Greenhow, short of funds herself, sold her jewelry and silks to keep going. She had written a book about her experiences and felt that if it could be published in England it would rekindle the British public's now cooling sympathy for the South. There was also a chance that she could help promote new plans for buying ships, guns and other war goods through the use of Cotton Certificates issued by the Confederate States Treasury. So she sought and received permission to go to England, with the added prestige of an official emissary. Jefferson Davis himself wished Mrs. Greenhow godspeed when she left Richmond in August 1863.

Arriving in Wilmington, North Carolina, Mrs. Greenhow interviewed Major General W. H. C. Whiting, who was in command of the local Army district, and persuaded him to raise a cavalry brigade and send it North to aid Lee. Supplies of men and animals were getting tragically short. Rose wrote President Davis of Whiting's promise, adding that she was amazed at the number of blockade runners who thronged the city and "who should be in the Army." Her letter intimates anxiety over her excursion into the unknown, for she had never before traveled outside the United States. "The Yankees are reported as being unusually vigilant, a double line of blockaders block the way. Still, I am in nothing daunted and hope by the blessing of Providence to get out safely . . ." She did. With her young daughter Rose, she sailed aboard the *Phantom*, whose skipper skillfully stole past the grim lines of Federal cruisers.

To Rose Greenhow and her excited little girl, the blue-and-green waters of Saint George's and the verdant tropical foliage and white houses were enchanting. Their spirits perked up immediately. Since Rose enjoyed official status as a representative of the Confederate States government, she was allowed to take passage for England aboard a British man-of-war. This was somewhat out-of-the-ordinary procedure. The Royal Navy rarely took aboard female passengers except wives or relatives of high-ranking officers. The fact that President Davis requested this courtesy no doubt turned the trick.

Rose Greenhow's European trip was more of a personal triumph than an official one. In Paris she was received in the Tuileries by the Emperor of France, but failed to secure his support for the South. His government had definitely turned a cold shoulder to the Confederacy. At a formal presentation at court Mrs. Greenhow caught the fancy of the Empress and shortly afterward was a marked favorite at a magnificent state ball. Rose had replenished her wardrobe from the best Paris couturiers and friends had donated enough jewels to make her sparkle. Intrigued as she was by the gay social life of Paris and the fascinating shops, she did not for a moment forget the objectives of her mission. She interviewed bankers, statesmen, businessmen—anyone who might be willing to aid the Southern cause.

The English publisher of her book, *My Imprisonment and the First Year of Abolition Rule in Washington*, reported good sales. This first-person narrative undoubtedly aroused some pro-Southern sentiment in England, for it was blunt, factual and named names. Current literary giants of the time, including Thomas Carlyle and Robert Browning, paid her flattering attention and she found herself engulfed in a colorful wave of parties among the cultured set of London.

Mrs. Greenhow was not neglected by prominent figures at court, including Lords Palmerston, Russell, Napier and Lyons. Gossip had it that she was engaged to Lord Granville, a recent widower. However, some of the wives of those notables were alarmed at her grim and unrelenting attitude toward the "lords of abolition" . . . her "frantic sense of bitter wrong . . . when from her breast the rushing tide of vengeful anger came." Gradually under the benign influence of peaceful England, her manner softened.

Mrs. Greenhow worked closely with Commodore Matthew Fontaine Maury and Commissioner Mason in their frantic efforts to barter cotton for gunboats, rams, blockade-running steamers, food, medicines and other war supplies. Nor did she overlook the importance of maintaining the confidence of Alexander Collie, head of the shipping company of that name. He was the man whose fast ships had already run out a million Federal dollars' worth of cotton from Southern ports in the third quarter of 1863.

Events at home seemed always to neutralize and even set back all of Rose Greenhow's efforts. News from the fighting front was constantly bad. U. S. Grant had taken charge of Federal forces in the East. The battles of the Wilderness, Spotsylvania and Cold Harbor filled Rose with horror at the bloody fighting and tragic Confederate losses in men and material. Letters from home spoke pitifully of shortages of food and clothing. It was time to go back to Dixie, Rose decided, and bring with her clothing and other necessities for Southern womanhood. At the same time she was busy making notes for a report to President Davis on the shipping situation and the cotton bonds.

Rose had also reached another major decision: she had made up her mind to marry Lord Granville. But first she felt she must fulfill what to her was a sacred mission back in Richmond. When this was accomplished (and she hoped to do it as speedily as possible) she would return to England to become Lady Granville.

Rose bought and packed a large supply of female clothing and, after bidding good-by to her London friends, traveled north to Greenock and sailed from there on August 10, 1864. She had with her two thousand dollars in gold, the proceeds of her book. This consisted of nearly four hundred gold sovereigns at the current rate of exchange—a considerable weight of metal for a woman to carry about her person.

Rose Greenhow was not afraid. She had run the blockade going out and would do so going in. She loved the sea and never suffered from *mal de mer*. She reveled in the tang of the salt spray and the wild roar of the waves. Her sense of safety was enhanced by the fact that she was traveling on a stout ship and with an able commander.

The vessel on which Mrs. Greenhow embarked was the *Condor*, a new three-funneled steamer of Scottish build. She was a beautiful craft, with the long, low lines of a yacht. The extreme rake of her masts and funnels gave her a fast look—and fast she was for her time. Her draught was only seven feet to enable her easily to clear the bars at Charleston and the mouth of the Cape Fear. Her crew of forty-five were known to be veterans of the sea and the blockade. The route of the *Condor* on her maiden voyage was to Halifax and from there through the Federal blockaders to Wilmington.

The commander of the *Condor* was none other than tall, bearded Augustus Charles Hobart-Hampden, the Captain "Roberts," whose exploits were described in the preceding chapter. But on this voyage he used the alias "Samuel S. Ridge." He had been fully briefed on Mrs. Greenhow, her background and her mission to Richmond. In fact he had received several dispatch bags from his friend Commissioner Mason, who asked him to turn them over to Mrs. Greenhow at the proper time for conveyance straight to Richmond.

On the voyage across the Atlantic Rose kept to herself, although she walked the decks regularly and seemed to enjoy thoroughly the brisk breezes and the brilliant sunlight. Her fellow passengers noted an unusual thing about this tall, commanding woman with the firm mouth and piercing glance: invariably she wore a reticule of leather, apparently quite heavy, for it was suspended about her neck by a long chain. This she was never seen without, whether on deck or in the dining salon. Perhaps Captain "Ridge" knew that it contained her precious two thousand dollars in gold, worth many times that amount in depreciated Confederate currency. In any case, no one else suspected what the reticule contained.

On September 7 the *Condor* steamed proudly into Halifax harbor bringing with her a heavy cargo of war supplies destined for the hard-pressed Southern armies. At Halifax a man well known to Mrs. Greenhow came aboard to take passage to Wilmington. He was James B. Holcombe, who for several months had served as a Confederate commissioner in Great Britain. He had just quitted an ill-advised and unofficial attempt at peace negotiations at Niagara Falls. Undoubtedly Rose and Holcombe had many conversations about the current war situation. They had plenty of time, for the *Condor* delayed her departure until the moon had waned and the blockade runner could slip through the Federal cordon off the Cape Fear in total blackness.

Meanwhile the U.S. consul at Halifax had prudently informed Secretary Seward of the *Condor's* imminent departure; also the fact that she was loaded to the gunwales with war supplies. If he knew that Mrs. Greenhow was aboard, he failed to mention the fact to Washington. In any event Seward notified Gideon Welles, who lost no time in alerting Acting Rear Admiral S. P. Lee, in charge of the North Atlantic Blockading Squadron, with headquarters at Beaufort.

An hour before dawn on October first the *Condor* nosed cautiously toward New Inlet. For days the Federals had kept on extra special watch for the new steamer and her load of contraband. The U.S.S. *Niphon* was the first to sight her long, gray hull, a mere shadow in the darkness. Up shot the warning calcium flares and the chase was on. Captain Ridge felt no anxiety as he stood on the bridge next to the Cape Fear pilot who was conning the steamer. The *Condor* was thrashing toward the Inlet with every ounce of steam her boilers could produce. A cloud of black smoke belched from her triple stacks. The *Niphon's* bow chasers barked and shells tore through the *Con-*

dor's sparse rigging, then plunged into the sea in white geysers of brine.

Ridge knew that he could outrun the *Niphon*, for the bar was close. To starboard loomed the Mound Battery at Fort Fisher. It would be only a matter of minutes now before the *Condor* would plunge within the protective range of those big Confederate guns. Just then, out of the blackness ahead, loomed a vessel's hull and spars. To the *Condor's* pilot that meant only one thing—"a damned Yankee" gunboat barring the way. In instant response to his cry of "Hard a-starboard," the *Condor* heeled and swung away. Seconds later her keel struck the treacherous shoals to the right of the channel. She lurched, scraped, then came to a jarring halt, her safety valves spurting steam. In the misty dawn those aboard the stranded *Condor* saw that it was not a Federal man-of-war that had loomed in their path, but the wreck of the British blockade runner *Night Hawk*, one of the steamers operated by Tom Taylor, British supercargo extraordinary.

The impact of the *Condor's* grounding catapulted Mrs. Greenhow from her berth. As she dressed rapidly, she could hear the frightening shouts of seamen, dash of waves and howl of wind. Reaching the deck, she stood uncertainly, buffeted by the wind, clutching her precious reticule.

To a British Naval officer of long experience like Captain Ridge, the pilot's sudden panic was infuriating and embarrassing. The *Condor* carried a precious cargo consigned to the Confederate States government. In addition, she carried distinguished passengers whose lives must be safeguarded. Ridge hoped that with daylight and subsiding wind and waves he could get her hauled off.

Meanwhile the *Niphon* moved in for the kill. More calcium flares soared skyward as the Union cruiser again fired at the helpless *Condor*. Instantly Fort Fisher replied and drove off the eager *Niphon* with a barrage of shells. Commander Kemble of the *Niphon* reported later that when daylight came he deemed it wise to stand offshore and not risk running aground himself or being hit by the shells from Fort Fisher. His anxiety to destroy the blockade runner was frustrated, for nature herself succeeded in putting a finis to her brief career. The heavy pounding of her light frame on the reef broke her back and eventually she became a total loss.

Meanwhile Rose Greenhow was terrified by the cold, wind and confusion aboard the stricken vessel. As her eyes bridged the few hundred yards of storming surf that lay between her and the land, she made up her mind that she must go ashore as soon as possible. She told this to Holcombe and a young lieutenant named Wilson. They agreed to speak to the captain and request him to put them ashore. Captain Ridge told them there was nothing to fear. The northeaster was subsiding. The *Condor* was hard aground and would not soon break up. Later in the day, he said, everyone would be taken off.

The commander's words calmed the fears of Holcombe and Wilson but failed to assuage those of Rose Greenhow. She made up her mind that she was going ashore—and by heaven she meant to do so! With grim determination she faced Ridge and demanded to be put on dry land. With all the patience he could summon, he told her that she would be running a far greater risk by trying to make land through the raging surf than by staying aboard until the weather moderated.

Rose was adamant. She had important business in Richmond and a vital dispatch to deliver to President Davis. She turned on all of her charm, trying to persuade the tall, bearded seadog to do as she wished. When he again refused she gave full vent to anger—and the anger of Rose Greenhow was like a hurricane. Face pale, soaking wet from the flying spray, she clutched her reticule tightly and her voice soared wildly above the gale. Ridge shouted back at her, repeating all his former arguments for staying aboard. But Rose, tight-lipped now, refused to listen. All she wanted was to be put ashore. At last Ridge reluctantly consented. It would be foolhardy and dangerous, he told her. Never mind, she answered, she had risked all sorts of dangers before; this was but a new one to add to her list.

At the captain's orders one of the lifeboats was made ready. The pilot, two seamen, Holcombe and Rose Greenhow were to go. Somehow they managed to push off from the stricken ship and the next instant were riding the giant combers that surged toward the shore. But the steersman allowed the little boat to swing broadside to the waves just long enough to be rolled over and swamped. Wilson and the two seamen fought their way to the surface, clung to the keel. Holcombe, swept away, was washed ashore and revived. Wilson and the seamen peered anxiously through the murk for Mrs. Greenhow. She was nowhere to be seen, for she had strangled deep in the icy brine, her precious gold weighing her down. Wilson and his two companions managed to hold on long enough to drift ashore where they lay battered and bruised until taken in charge by a squad of soldiers from the fort.

Hours later, a young recruit walking along the beach north of Mound Battery, saw what looked like a dark bundle of clothes awash in the shallows. Coming closer he saw to his amazement that it was the body of a woman, lying in the distorted posture of death, her face livid and bruised, her voluminous clothing in pitiful disarray. He stood staring down at her and then noticed what looked like a heavy handbag half concealed under her coat. He stooped down and removed the chain that held it around her neck. It was heavy. Seating himself on the sand he loosened the catch of the bag and out poured a golden stream of British sovereigns. Cautiously the soldier looked around and saw that no one was near by. He stuffed his pockets with the coins and scuttled off to find a safe hiding place.

By now it was full daylight. Captain Ridge came ashore and with part of his crew organized a search for Mrs. Greenhow. No one had seen her. It was almost certain that she was dead. As it turned out, it was not Ridge who found her. Tom Taylor, of the *Night Hawk*, the wreck of which had inadvertently brought disaster to the *Condor*, noted in his memoirs, "It was I who found her body on the beach at daylight and afterwards took it to Wilmington. A remarkably handsome woman she was, with features which showed much character."

When the young recruit heard he had robbed the famous Mrs. Greenhow, he was filled with such shame and remorse that he sought out Colonel Lamb and returned all of the gold.

Mrs. Greenhow's body was tenderly conveyed to the cottage

of Mrs. Lamb where it was prepared for burial before being
taken to Wilmington. Here she lay in state at the Seamen's
Bethel, guarded by picked troops and her corpse was mourned
by thousands of Southerners. After an impressive service at St.
Thomas' Church, Mrs. Greenhow was laid to rest in Oakdale
Cemetery with full military honors. Here she sleeps to this
day beneath a simple marble cross:

> Mrs. Rose O'N. Greenhow,
> a bearer of dispatches
> to the Confederate Government.
> Erected by the Ladies Memorial Association.

Rose Greenhow had often expressed her willingness to die
for the sacred cause of the South. Her wish had been fulfilled,
and as Lady Fullerton wrote after Rose's death, "She had been
faithful to the last to a fond, hopeless dream. . . ."

Belle Boyd, born at Martinsburg, Virginia (now West Virginia), May 9, 1843, was the other woman spy to brave the
blockade. She was an intelligent and well-read young woman
with a charming personality and witty tongue. While she might
not have been termed beautiful, her lovely blond hair and striking blue eyes were most attractive. Something of a hoyden,
Belle had a hair-trigger temper and a large amount of courage
bordering on recklessness. She was an excellent horsewoman and
that ability was put to much use in running the land blockades.

As an ardent Southerner, she longed to do something more
than roll bandages or make jelly for sick soldiers. She was intrigued by Mrs. Greenhow's spy ring and wanted to carry messages through the Union lines. Her chance came shortly after
the first battle of Manassas when friends got her placed as a
courier and official member of the Confederate intelligence service. Her first mission was carrying messages for Generals Beauregard and Jackson.

Although blockade running is generally associated with the
ships and the sea coast, another sort was in full swing throughout
most of the war—*inland* blockade running. This involved smug-

gling much-needed supplies from Northern areas into the South. Belle Boyd performed valuable service on this inland route, passing back and forth across the border with messages sewn into her riding habit or concealed in her coiled hair.

Belle was caught twice by Federal authorities and imprisoned both times. On the first occasion she was captured on orders of Secretary E. M. Stanton and lodged in the Old Capitol Prison in Washington. When she became ill there, because of the close confinement, she was released along with a number of exchanged Confederate soldiers.

When she recovered her health, Belle returned to her spying, but once more fell into Northern clutches in July 1863. How Belle managed to be released less than six months later has never been made clear, although it has been said that Lincoln interceded in her behalf, and that perhaps she was exchanged for a Federal prisoner. The exchange point was Fortress Monroe, in charge of General ("The Beast") Butler. His appearance even without his reputation was enough to frighten a young girl. Butler was a short, chunky man with heavy jowls, a red-veined face, small, crafty eyes and a sullen, irritable expression. His repulsiveness was further enhanced by a droopy eyelid, crooked smile and irregular, tobacco-stained teeth.

A record of the brief interview between Belle and "The Beast" has been preserved and even today reads like a real-life drama:

As Belle entered General Butler's headquarters he looked up from his desk and said, we suspect with heavy sarcasm, "Ah! So this is Miss Boyd, the famous Rebel spy! Pray be seated."

Belle answered in a low voice, "Thank you, General Butler, but I prefer to stand."

Glancing at her face he could see that she was upset, whether from anger or fear, he could not decide. So he said again, "Pray be seated. Why do you tremble so? Are you frightened?"

Quickly Belle saw the opening and made the most of it. "No . . . ," she began, then ". . . ah! That is, yes, General Butler. I must acknowledge that I do feel frightened in the presence of a man of such world-wide reputation as yourself."

We can almost see the pompous general smiling his crooked smile and preening himself at her reply. Rubbing his pudgy hands together he said for the third time, "Pray be seated, Miss Boyd." Then after a pause during which he raked her with his little eyes, he asked, "What do you mean when you say I'm widely known?"

Belle took a deep breath and fixed him with a devastating look of contempt. "I mean, General Butler, that you are a man whose atrocious conduct and brutality, especially to Southern ladies, is so infamous that even the English Parliament commented on it. I naturally feel alarmed at being in your presence."

The records merely say that Butler rose angrily and ordered Belle out of his office. Yet we can imagine that furious red face, the quivering chops and bared teeth. "The Beast"—bested by a woman!

Belle hastened home after leaving prison and toured the South to help rally flagging morale. Again her health had suffered from fetid air and bad jail food. She felt ill, depressed and restless, especially since her father's recent death. On her return to Richmond in March 1864 she decided she wanted to travel to Europe. She interviewed President Davis, who quickly gave his consent and arranged to have her carry important dispatches.

On March 25 the dispatches were ready, but Belle was not, for again she had been laid low by illness. Recovering, she arrived at Wilmington a scant two hours after the blockade runner upon which she booked passage had left port. To add to her dismay was the news that no other steamer was scheduled to make the run through the Federal squadron for two weeks, since the moon was waxing.

Belle waited impatiently until several steamers arrived, including the *Greyhound*, commanded by a captain to whom Belle refers merely as "Captain Henry." But it is known that before the war he had been a U.S. Naval officer and afterward held equal rank in the Confederate States Navy. The *Greyhound* was a fast British vessel of 400 tons, especially purchased for the blockade-running trade.

It was not until May 8 that the *Greyhound* was ready for the eastern run and Belle was invited to take passage aboard her. She gave her name as "Mrs. Lewis," although all hands knew who she was. In her reminiscences, written a few years later, Belle recalled that she knew "the venture was a desperate one," but she reassured herself that by posing as a civilian passenger traveling for her health she would, in case of the steamer's capture, be merely detained as a witness at the prize court proceedings. Conversely she knew what to expect if she was recognized as an official Confederate courier running the blockade on a vessel commanded by an officer of the Confederate States Navy. Apparently Belle did not fully realize how notorious she was in the North and how well known her face, which had appeared in numerous magazines and newspapers.

The other two passengers were Mr. E. A. Pollard, editor of the Richmond *Examiner* and a Mr. Newell. At 10:00 P.M. the waning moon had disappeared. The *Greyhound's* captain curtly ordered anchors aweigh and she pointed her graceful prow seaward. Six miles away waited a shadowy flotilla of blockaders, the larger ones at anchor, the smaller gunboats cruising about restlessly in search of prey.

Every available inch of the *Greyhound* was loaded with cotton bales, closely packed on deck and about the wheelhouse. On top perched the lookouts, alertly scanning the horizon. From the mainmast flew Confederate colors. "It was a night never to be forgotten," Belle wrote later, "a night of almost breathless anxiety."

If Belle had known of the eagerness of the Federal Navy to track down and capture the *Greyhound*, she would have been even more perturbed. Union officers had barely missed seizing her on the inward voyage and were determined to end her brief career outward bound.

It is not clear why the blockade runner's captain delayed his departure so long, but it was dawn before the *Greyhound* was clear of the land and breasting the Atlantic swells. Belle, standing in the shelter of the deckhouse, suddenly remembered that it was her birthday. We can imagine her somewhat forced smile, for already she was suffering from seasickness.

A light haze hung over the water. Hoping to elude pursuit, Captain Henry passed close to the wreck of the Confederate ram *Raleigh*. This maneuver did more harm than good, for a Federal cruiser spied the gray-hulled runner and gave chase. Captain Henry hauled down the Confederate colors and raised the British ensign, at the same time calling for more steam pressure. Staysails were set to steady the tossing vessel. Nevertheless the distance between pursuer and pursued gradually lessened.

Belle was quick to assess her dangerous situation. If the Yankees discovered that she was carrying important Confederate dispatches, she would face a third term in prison with all its attendant privations, discomfort and indignities. To her, death would be preferable. Now she saw that the Union cruiser had come within range and as she watched she saw "a thin white curl of smoke rise high in the air as the enemy luffed up and presented her formidable broadside. Almost simultaneously with the hissing sound of the shell, as it buried itself in the sea within a few yards of us, came the smothered report of its explosion under water."

The Federal cruiser began firing her guns rapidly. Some of the shells fell close, others wide. Enough of them burst over the *Greyhound* to frighten even the most hardy men aboard. Meanwhile the crew was busy jettisoning the deckboard of cotton. There was a vague hope that the pursuer would stop and try to salvage the precious bales, giving the *Greyhound* an opportunity to escape.

Captain Henry paced the bridge, his face as gray as the steamer's paint. He kept demanding, "More steam—more steam!" But every ounce of pressure was in the boilers already. At this juncture, Belle Boyd's memoirs contain a graphic (and somewhat florid) description of her conversation with the captain:

Captain Henry: "Miss Belle, I declare to you that, but for your presence on board, I would burn her to the water's edge, rather than those infernal scoundrels should reap the benefit of a single bale of our cargo."

Belle (with spirit): "Captain Henry, act without reference to me. Do what you think your duty. For my part, sir, I concur with you; burn her by all means. I am not afraid. I have made up my mind and am indifferent to my fate; if only the Federals do not get the vessel."

Captain Henry did not reply. He swung away and talked with his officers. In a few moments he returned to Belle. Captain Henry (bitterly): "Too late to burn her now. The Yankee is almost on board of us. We must surrender!"

Belle did not make any further attempt to influence the captain, for she could see that there was no chance for escape or destruction of the *Greyhound*.

A hush fell over the steamer as she came into the wind and stopped her engines, waiting for the enemy to draw close. Yet the cruiser continued to fire. One of the missiles drove just above the heads of Belle and the captain with what she described as a deep humming sound.

"By Jove," cried Henry, "don't they intend to give us quarter or show us some mercy at any rate? I have surrendered!"

What caused the continuance of the cannonade was that Captain Henry had neglected to strike his colors, a traditional signal of surrender. Now a loud coarse voice thundered across the lane of water between the two vessels: "Steamer ahoy! Haul down that flag or we will pour a broadside into you." Quickly Henry obliged, at the same time gesturing to two of his seamen to roll a keg containing nearly $30,000 in hard money over the side. Down below, Belle was feeding her precious dispatches into the firebox in the engine room.

By the time she had hurried back on deck a boat from the U.S.S. *Connecticut* was approaching. In a few moments Lieutenant Louis Kempff, U.S.N., climbed aboard. Politely he asked for the ship's papers. Captain Henry retorted shortly that he possessed no papers.

Mr. Pollard, one of the two male passengers, observed this scene on the quarterdeck and noted that the naval lieutenant was accompanied by a very young midshipman whose hair was slickly panied in the middle, meticulously uniformed and sporting a pair of lavender kid gloves. Lieutenant Kempff was unconcerned by Henry's answer, saying merely that the captain would have to go back with him to the *Connecticut* and be examined by her captain, Commander John J. Almy.

Almost immediately after Captain Henry of the *Greyhound* stepped into the wardroom of the U.S.S. *Connecticut*, his identity became known, for he was recognized by several of the cruiser's officers as George Henry Bier, erstwhile lieutenant in the United States Navy and currently a lieutenant in the Confederate States Navy.

Meanwhile, the kid-gloved midshipman had been appointed the boarding officer aboard the *Greyhound*. His name and title soon became known to all hands: Acting Ensign William H. Swasey. He strutted about the quarter-deck bellowing orders and made himself as disagreeable as can be imagined. Of him Belle wrote: "An officer as unfit for authority as anyone who has trodden the decks of a man-of-war."

Apparently Belle's identity had become known just about as soon as the captain's, for she describes in her book how grossly impolite were the remarks of the bumptuous little acting ensign. Seeing her in her cabin he bellowed, "Sergeant of the guard! Post a man in front of this door and give him orders to stab this woman if she dares come out."

Remarks Belle with heavy sarcasm: "This order, so highly becoming an officer and a gentleman, so courteous in its language, and withal so necessary to the safety and preservation of the prize, was given in a menacing voice and in the very words I have used."

Not only did the kid-gloved ensign act badly but his prize crew took their cue from him, drank up the captain's wine, went in and out of Belle's cabin, poking about inquisitively and, as she recalls, "swearing and sulking." A buxom Negro maid servant was overheard remarking in the midst of the hubbub that she "hadn't seen a Christian" since she left Petersburg.

As Belle stood by stiffly, watching the uncontrolled actions of the Federal prize crew, another acting ensign walked up to her and said with a malicious smile, "Do you know that it was I who fired the shot that passed close to your head?"

"Was it?" Belle retorted coldly, then she told him that he was an arrant coward to fire on a defenseless ship after her surrender. This remark caused the young man acute embarrassment and he hastily left her.

Belle was sitting in her cabin and when she glanced toward the doorway she saw another Federal officer. He had just come aboard and was looking about curiously. She describes him as having "dark brown hair that hung down to his shoulders. His eyes were large and bright. Those who judge of beauty by regularity of features could not have pronounced him handsome," she wrote some years afterward, "but the fascination of his manner . . . was so much that of a refined gentleman that my 'Southern proclivities,' strong as they were, yielded for a moment to the impulses of my heart, and I said to myself, 'Oh, what a good fellow that must be!' " This Federal naval officer was Sam Hardinge, who was to play opposite her in a real-life wartime romance; a giddy mixture of rapture and heartache for them both.

Seeing Belle, Lieutenant Hardinge bowed and asked permission to enter her cabin.

"Certainly," she answered with assumed passivity, "I know that I am a prisoner."

"I am now in command of this vessel," Hardinge told her, "and I beg you will consider yourself a passenger, not a prisoner."

From then on, neither of them could scarcely take their eyes off each other. It was love at first sight. While the captured *Greyhound* steamed northward there were plenty of happy hours during which they could talk and make love. The weather was mild, the sea calm, the starry nights spangled with moonbeams. Well sheltered from the wind they stood close together at the rail while Hardinge softly quoted from Shakespeare and Byron. Recalling those precious minutes, Belle wrote that Hardinge then "endeavored to paint 'the home to which, if love could but fulfill its prayers, this heart would lead thee!' And from poetry he passed on to plead an oft-told tale. . . ."

Belle had a good deal more to think about than love right then. She had no idea what the Federal authorities would do with her, although she felt sure the grim shadow of prison loomed. So she told the impetuous Hardinge she could give him no definite answer until the *Greyhound* reached Boston.

The steamer stopped briefly at Hampton Roads and for several terrifying hours it looked as if Belle would be brought ashore to face "Beast" Butler once more. To her immense relief no such thing happened and she remained aboard and the steamer resumed its journey.

Another stop was made at New York. Here, surprisingly, Belle was allowed to go ashore and stay at the home of a friend. Apparently her promise to return to the *Greyhound* was considered sufficient security. Yet she carried with her a heavy money belt containing a substantial amount of gold belonging to herself and Captain Henry. Presumably she had concealed this wealth just before the *Greyhound* was captured.

In a day or two the ex-blockade-running steamer headed out of New York Harbor en route for Boston. The passionate Hardinge continued his pleas of marriage. Belle accepted him, although she gives no details of the proposal in her memoirs. She did note, however, that she was well aware of the wide differences in their political principles. But she felt that her lover's generous nature and nobility of mind, together with a new tolerant attitude on her part would overcome these divergencies. Secretly she hoped that in time, and for her sake, he would learn to love the South.

In Boston Belle lived up to her reputation as a spy. Captain George Henry was in serious trouble. As a former U.S. naval officer he had forsworn his allegiance to his country and had cast his fortunes with the South. It was certain that he faced a long term in prison. Belle realized this; also she felt he had done his utmost to conceal her identity, and she owed him something in return. If he could escape he might find a temporary hiding place in Boston until he could make his way to Canada and from there back to the Confederacy. After a number of secret conferences the two decided that the captain would make a break for freedom as soon as possible after the *Greyhound* entered Boston harbor.

With cool courage Captain Henry commandeered the first boat that came alongside and before Hardinge or anyone else aboard the prize realized it (thanks to distractions provided by Belle) the blockade-running skipper disappeared shoreward through the harbor mists. Word came back later that he reached Canada safely.

The arrival in Boston of a comely female spy and the escape of Captain Henry splashed across the front pages of all the local papers. When Belle stepped ashore she was met by large crowds and alternately cheered and booed. She was repeatedly interviewed. A few days later the papers announced that Miss Boyd had been sent to Fitchburg jail. This report turned out to be premature. Neither she nor Hardinge had lost any time in trying to square themselves with the powers in Washington. Hardinge rushed to the Capitol to answer for the escape of Captain Henry and to see what he could do in Belle's behalf. To this end he applied for a leave of absence, hoping to convey Belle to Canada and there make her his wife. She wrote a long letter to Secretary of the Navy Welles admitting frankly who she was and stating that her presence aboard a "British" ship was because she was en route to Canada to settle there "until this cruel war is over." Welles's reply was in the form of an order, instructing Belle Boyd to be escorted over the Canadian border within twenty-four hours. She was to be informed also that if she was ever again caught within the United States she would be summarily shot.

If Lieutenant Sam Hardinge expected his superiors to listen sympathetically to his pleas, he was promptly disappointed. Instead, Admiral Stringham had him put behind bars and charged with having assisted in the escape of Captain Henry. Hardinge tearfully begged permission to return to Boston and bid good-by to Belle before she entrained for Quebec. He was paroled just long enough to do it, which is indeed surprising, considering Northern bitterness against Belle and all her doings. Soon afterward, Hardinge was dismissed from the service, charged with "neglect of duty in permitting the captain of the prize steamer *Greyhound* to escape."

From Quebec, Belle took an ocean steamer to England. In London she was the guest of the Confederate commercial agent, Mr. Hotze. It was to him that the dispatches had been addressed which she had burned just before the *Greyhound* was boarded. Her official connection with the Confederate States government was now terminated, at least for the time being.

The trials and tribulations of Belle and Hardinge had not in any degree cooled their ardor for each other. Letters flowed back and forth across the Atlantic. At last, in August 1864, the cashiered Hardinge arrived in London. There was a joyous reunion and they were married on the twenty-fifth. The ceremony and reception were attended by a large number of persons of high rank in the Confederate government, as well as British personages who sympathized with the Southern cause. Their presence at Belle's wedding is an indication of their esteem for her and her exploits.

Not long afterward Hardinge returned to the United States. Although he had been dismissed from the United States Navy, he felt he had no further cause to run afoul of the law. In this he was sadly mistaken, for he was almost immediately arrested, charged with being a spy and a deserter and lodged in the Old Capitol Prison where both Belle and Mrs. Rose Greenhow had once languished. During his confinement, Hardinge's health suffered a decline. Later he was moved to Fort Delaware prison outside of Wilmington, Delaware, where he remained until his release in February 1865.

His exit was abrupt. He was told he was free and on his own. The weather was severe; his clothing was threadbare; he had no shoes; his feet were wrapped in rags. Weak and ill, he had to trudge more than sixteen miles through the snow before reaching Wilmington. Somehow he managed to get home to Brooklyn and after a period of recuperation sailed for England to join Belle. Meanwhile Belle had finished writing her book which soon became a best-seller of the day, *Belle Boyd in Camp and Prison*. It first appeared in May 1865.

Sam Hardinge did not live very long to enjoy the extra notoriety that came to his wife in England as the result of her book. He died late in 1865 or early in 1866; the date is uncertain.

After the birth of an infant daughter, Belle Boyd accepted an offer to go on the stage. She was only a moderate success. During her latter years she married twice and died at Kilbourne,

Wisconsin, on June 11, 1900. During her whole life her love and loyalty for the South never wavered. Not even "Beast" Butler could stop her. In an age of feminine timidity and indecision, she was a courageous and forthright woman of action and a credit to her beloved Confederacy.

The final chapter in the history of the steamer *Greyhound* is ironic. After she was condemned and sold to the United States Government, in the late fall of 1864, she became the floating head-quarters of General Butler, the very man who had been worsted by Belle Boyd in her verbal battle with him at Fortress Monroe. At this time Butler's troops were occupying an important position on the James River and he had to make frequent trips back and forth. Also at this time Admiral David Porter was helping to plan the joint operations of the army and navy against Fort Fisher. Butler came up to Dutch Gap aboard the *Greyhound* to see Admiral Porter. In his book *Incidents and Anecdotes of the Civil War*, Admiral Porter describes the visit. The *Greyhound*, he wrote "deserved her name, for she was a long, lean-looking craft and the fastest steamer on the river." Porter had an urgent summons to confer with Assistant Secretary of the Navy Fox at Hampton Roads, and since Porter's flagship, the *Malvern*, was notoriously slow, Butler offered to take him down the river.

The crew of the *Greyhound* did not wear regulation uniforms, but a special "Butler uniform" which he had designed himself. But, as Porter recalled, "There was not so much as a pop-gun among them."

Dutch Gap was a kind of neutral ground between the Northern and Southern armies where prisoners were exchanged. Porter noticed a good many "hang-dog-looking rascals" skulking around. He had no doubt that there were a number of Confederate spies among them. As the steamer left Dutch Gap and sped down the river, the Admiral took a turn through the upper saloon which had been luxuriously furnished and decorated on Butler's orders. Here to his surprise he found a half dozen of those cutthroat-looking fellows such as he had seen at Dutch Gap.

"What are you doing here?" Porter demanded of them. "Does the *Greyhound* carry first-class passengers?"

They glared at him and one fellow said impudently, "We are just lookin' round to see how you fellers live. We ain't doin' no harm!" Porter did not reply but walked about the saloon appearing to admire its fittings, but not failing to notice that one by one the suspicious-looking men had slunk below.

Porter went immediately to Butler and warned him, suggesting that he take action against them before they did harm. Butler moved promptly. He ordered the *Greyhound* to put in at Bermuda Hundred (a hamlet on the river), rounded up the evil-looking characters and turned them over to an army guard ashore. Then the steamer proceeded on her way. No one attached much importance to the affair, merely supposing that the men had tried to get a free trip down to Hampton Roads.

What happened next is best told in Admiral Porter's own words: "We had left Bermuda Hundred five or six miles behind us when suddenly an explosion forward startled us and in a moment large volumes of smoke poured out of the engine room. The engineer at once closed the throttle-valve; the steam rushed out and the *Greyhound* howled louder than her living namesake would have done." Most of the frightened crew jumped overboard while Butler demanded to know what had happened.

"Torpedo!" Porter answered. "I know the sound!"

Before being put ashore the suspicious-looking scoundrels had planted a torpedo in the bunkers so that when it was thrown into the ship's furnace with the coal it exploded and set fire to the vessel. By now the flames had moved amidships and the Admiral knew it was time to abandon ship. He was a powerful man and with the aid of the steward launched General Butler's gig and assisted with another smaller boat. Thanks to Porter's quick action, Butler and all hands got away safely from the fiercely burning steamer, including several of the crew struggling in the water.

"The *Greyhound* was now wrapped in flames from one end to another." It was a "grand spectacle"—the dramatic end of one of the fastest and handsomest blockade runners of the Confederacy.

CHAPTER 7

Beleaguered Cities

THE STORY of the beleaguered cities of the South is a story of slow strangulation. It is also a story of patriotism versus the selfishness and greed of a minority of merchants, speculators and not a few officials of the Confederate government. But in those early spring days of 1861 the wholesalers and retailers located below the Mason and Dixon Line did not worry much about where their future supplies were to come from. Their shelves were well stocked and business was brisk. For months all sorts of merchandise and food supplies kept flowing into the South from Northern states until at last the Federal government put a stop to all trade.

From among all the blockaded cities of the South, Wilmington, Charleston and Richmond have been chosen as examples, for what happened there was duplicated for the most part elsewhere.

As might be expected, the first effect of the blockade was a disruption of shipping facilities. Foreign vessels left hurriedly. The few merchant vessels owned by Southern concerns remained in port waiting to see if it would be safe to venture out. Many business firms handling raw materials were dismayed to see them piling up on the wharves in alarming quantities.

Although Charleston and Wilmington managed to keep contact with the outside world until almost the very end of the war, other Southern ports were less fortunate. Mobile was securely bottled up during the greater part of the conflict. New Orleans ceased to be a factor in blockade running a year after hostilities began. Admiral Farragut and his powerful fleet saw to that. Galveston, lost early in the war, was recaptured by General

Magruder on New Year's Day 1863. From then on, this Texas seaport played an active role in blockade running.

Along the coasts of Georgia and eastern Florida there was slight activity. Only thirty-five steamers took part in blockade running in this area, although small schooners, sloops and brigs engaged in coastwise trade through many of the unguarded inland waterways. But they too were choked off by the end of 1861, due to the vigilance of Federal men-of-war which worked tirelessly to stop all the leaks along the coast.

Prior to 1862, Savannah was a busy port favored by blockade runners. They experienced little difficulty steaming in and out, as witnessed by the following excerpt from a letter written in September 1861 by an officer aboard the U.S.S. *Iroquois*: "We are stationed some twelve miles from the shore; we can just see the outlines of the land and that is all. The U.S.S. *St. Lawrence* is here also. The blockade is a perfect farce, I think, for we can see steamers run up and down the coast every day and we are so far off that we are useless; before we could get under way they would be out of sight."

All this was changed the following spring, for on April 10, 1862, Federal forces captured Fort Pulaski, commanding the entrance to the Savannah River. With U.S. men-of-war patrolling outside and captured Fort Pulaski's guns looking out upon the long, narrow channel of the river, there was little chance for a blockade runner to sneak in or out. By piecing together the written accounts left by the people who lived and worked and bucked the blockade at home, it is possible to reconstruct a relatively clear picture of what went on there.

CHARLESTON

Always a gay romantic city, Charleston made a brave show of keeping up a carefree atmosphere and an active social life almost until the bitter end. When the first cannon boomed out the signal for the Confederate attack on Fort Sumter, several ladies and gentlemen had scarcely gone to sleep after returning home from a round of parties. They jumped out of bed, flung on their dressing gowns and rushed to the rooftops to see the show. Some of the more pious ladies fell on their knees and began to pray. Eye witnesses said that the bombardment looked like a thousand Fourth of Julys rolled into one. There were speeches from the piazza of the Charleston Hotel; shouts, songs, brass bands and round after round of cheers. One woman was heard to say, "We will surely win. God is on our side."

"Why?" asked her companion.

"Because," answered the other, "God hates all Yankees."

When the news of Lincoln's blockade proclamation reached the city, the newspapers ridiculed it as being merely boasting and almost everyone agreed the blockade could never be enforced. In the first two years of the war, British and Confederate-owned steamers went in and out of the harbor with comparative ease, in spite of the sunken hulks of the Stone Fleet. There was a deal of cannonading offshore. A few runners were damaged and several captured or beached. But no one in Charleston thought the harbor would ever be bottled up completely or that the city would be cut off from trade with Europe. Cotton cargoes went out and munitions, food, champagne and luxury goods came in. Prices were high, naturally, but Charleston's upper crust always managed to pay what was asked. They seemed determined to maintain their old way of life, no matter what happened in the outside world.

Mrs. James Chesnut, Jr., that indefatigable Southern diarist, recorded in April 1862 that, "Today the ladies in their landeaus were bitterly attacked by the morning paper for lolling back in their silks and satins, with tall footmen in livery, driving up and down the streets, while the poor soldiers' wives were on the sidewalks. It is the old story of the rich and poor."

The following month Mrs. Chesnut, visiting Columbia, South Carolina, observed: "Family dinners are the speciality . . . they have everything of the best—silver, glass, china, table linen and damask, etc. . . . From the plantations came mutton, beef, poultry, cream, butter, eggs, fruits and vegetables. It is easy to live here, with a cook who has been sent for training to the best eating-house in Charleston."

Fifteen-year-old midshipman James Morris Morgan was stationed in Charleston in August 1862 and while roaming the streets noted that the "war as yet has had no effect on the style kept up by the old blue bloods, for I was amazed to see handsome equipages, with coachmen in livery on the box, driving through the town. Little did their owners dream that before very long those same fine horses would be hauling artillery and commissary wagons, and those proud liveried servants would be at work with pick and spade throwing up breastworks!"

A few weeks later, young Morgan was a guest at the home of George A. Trenholm, head of the rich import-export firm of Fraser, Trenholm & Co., of Charleston and Liverpool, which already had become the biggest blockade-running organization in the Confederacy. Mr. Trenholm later became Secretary of the Treasury of the Confederate States.

Midshipman Morgan was awed by Mr. Trenholm's stately, pillared mansion, guarded by massive gates. "The parlors," young Morgan wrote later, "were all very grand and the sofas luxurious." Mr. and Mrs. Trenholm soon put the young man at his ease. There were two pretty daughters who also helped. One of them became Morgan's wife a few years later.

"Oh, but it was a good dinner I sat down to that day," Morgan recalled long afterward. "After all these years the taste of the good things lingers in my memory and I can almost smell . . . the aroma of the wonderful old Madeira."

After dinner there was music and conversation in the drawing room. That night young Morgan slept soundly between snow-white sheets in a huge walnut bed. It was a welcome luxury after months of service afloat and ashore. Following breakfast next day, he went on a long horseback ride with one of the Trenholm sisters. Their horses were of the finest breed, one of them a famous racer. Riding became an every morning affair during his stay. In the afternoon he would accompany the Misses Trenholm in a landau drawn by a superb pair of bays with two men on the box. In the evenings the Trenholm family and their friends would sit on the wide piazza while tea, cakes and ice cream would be served, "and the gentlemen could smoke if they felt so inclined."

"Just at this time," Morgan recalls in his memoirs, "the life of a midshipman did not seem to be one of great hardship for me." But his luxurious way of life was fast drawing to an end. One day the distinguished hydrographer and naval astronomer Commodore Matthew Fontaine Maury was a dinner guest of the Trenholms. There was a gay party on the piazza afterward and young Morgan was enjoying himself, laughing and talking with the group of young people. Apparently Mr. Trenholm had taken a great liking to Jim Morgan, for he suddenly came up to him and asked him if he would like to go abroad with Commodore Maury and serve on a Confederate cruiser that was about to be fitted out to destroy U.S. shipping. Morgan was delighted and accepted on the spot. Next morning when he returned from his usual ride he was handed a telegram which read, "Report to Commodore M. F. Maury for duty abroad." It was signed by S. R. Mallory, Secretary of the Navy, C.S.A. Mr. Trenholm had arranged everything, including Morgan's passage aboard one of Trenholm's own blockade runners.

The vessel on which Commodore Maury, his twelve-year-old son and midshipman Morgan took passage was the little, light-draught steamer *Herald*. She was lying in the harbor loaded almost to the gunwales with cotton. At ten o'clock on the night of October 6, 1862, the *Herald* got under way and steamed toward the harbor's mouth. At her gaff flew the Stars and Bars. In command was Lewis M. Coxetter, one of the most fearless of the Southern blockade-running skippers. He was a thick-set, gentlemanly mariner of middle age with florid complexion, and round face set off by a mustache and goatee. Captain Coxetter had been commander and part-owner of the private armed brig *Jefferson Davis*, which had sailed from Charleston on June 28, 1861, on a successful privateering voyage during which she captured or burned a number of Northern sailing vessels. After a seven-weeks' cruise the *Davis* grounded off St. Augustine, Florida, and was lost. The crew and Coxetter came ashore and were

hospitably treated by the Floridians. On arrival in Charleston
two weeks later, Coxetter was welcomed as a hero and presented
with a gold watch and fob.

On the night that the *Herald* left port there was a half moon.
But fortunately it was obscured by a heavy bank of clouds to
eastward. The little steamer passed between the frowning ram-
parts of forts Moultrie and Sumter and was feeling her way
cautiously across the bar when the clouds suddenly parted and
revealed a large sloop-of-war, dead ahead. Instantly Coxetter
spun the wheel hard to starboard and the *Herald* turned tail and
headed back into the protection of Charleston Harbor, followed
by several shells from the Union warship. "Two or three more
days were passed delightfully in Charleston," young Morgan
recalled, "then there came a drizzling rain and on the night of
the ninth . . . we made another attempt . . ." It is not difficult
to imagine Midshipman Morgan's excitement as the *Herald* made
her second dash for Bermuda, all lights doused, not a word
spoken except by the pilot who gave his whispered orders to the
wheelsman.

According to Morgan, Captain Coxetter had been posted as a
"pirate" by the Federal government because of his former privateering activities, and had no wish to be captured. "He was
convinced that the great danger in running the blockade was in
his own engine room," Morgan remarks in his reminiscences, "so
he seated himself on the ladder leading down to it and politely
informed the engineer that if the engine stopped before he was
clear of the [blockading] fleet . . . the engineer would be a dead
man. As Coxetter held in his hand a Colt's revolver, this sounded
like no idle threat."

Presently the *Herald* reached the bar. The waves were high
and it could not have been flood tide, for the iron steamer scraped
the bottom several times, causing her to "ring like an old tin
pan." But she safely bumped her way across the shallows, plunging and tossing, with scarcely five feet of freeboard. On she
went through the blackness about as much under the water as
on top of it. She managed to elude the Federal cruisers and got
safely into the open sea.

Illustrated London News

Blockade runner *Lizzie*.

From RUNNING THE BLOCKADE *by Thomas E. Taylor*

The burning of the *Night Hawk.*

It is interesting to record that the *Herald* could make only six or seven knots in good weather, eight if pushed. She was one of the slowest of all the blockade runners, yet one of the most successful, making about fifty round trips. Her ability to flit in and out through the U.S. Naval cordon so often was due principally to good timing, reliable information as to the position of enemy ships, knowledge of the coast and cool determination.

On the trip described by Midshipman Morgan it took the *Herald* seven days to negotiate the 600-mile distance to Bermuda, usually accomplished in two and a half to three days by a fast steamer. The reasons for this long voyage were two-fold: One of the engines broke down and Captain Coxetter couldn't find Bermuda. On the fifth day the gale died and two schooners were sighted. Coxetter headed for one of them and when he came close asked for his position. The skipper of the schooner gave him the latitude and longitude and Coxetter resumed his eastward course. It is not recorded whether this was Coxetter's first experience as the skipper of a blockade runner. However, Morgan relates that Coxetter knew nothing about navigation except by taking bearings on landmarks along the coast. In fact, during his commerce-raiding voyage in the privateer *Jefferson Davis* he had scarcely ever been out of sight of land. Before that, his experience had consisted entirely of trading trips along the coasts of the Carolinas and Florida.

Less than twenty-four hours after speaking with the schooner, Coxetter became lost again. At this point let us find out what happened in the words of Midshipman Morgan himself: "Such was the jealousy, however, of merchant sailors toward officers of the Navy that, with one of the most celebrated navigators in the world aboard his ship [Maury], he [Coxetter] had not as yet confided to anybody the fact that he was lost. On the sixth day . . . he told Commodore Maury that something terrible must have happened, as he had sailed his ship directly over the spot where the Bermuda Islands ought to be!"

The taciturn Maury must have smiled at this, even though he was always seasick whenever any kind of sea was running. Maury told Coxetter that he could not work out a position until that night and only if it was clear. "At ten o'clock the great scientist and geographer went on deck and took observations, at times lying flat on his back, sextant in hand, as he made measurements of the stars."

At the end of his calculations, Maury gave Coxetter a course that he said would bring the *Herald* within sight of Port Hamilton light by 2:00 A.M. provided the *Herald* maintained a certain speed. Then the commodore went back to his bunk. The rest of the passengers and crew were too anxious to turn in and remained on deck, waiting. When four bells struck, no light was in sight. Five minutes went by. Still no light. Whether or not Captain Coxetter whispered "I told you so!" to the mate is open to conjecture. After ten minutes, a passenger was heard to grumble that there was "too much damned science aboard and we shall all be on our way to Fort Lafayette in New York Harbor as soon as day breaks."

He had scarcely spoken when the lookout at the masthead sang out, "Light ho!" The learned commodore's reputation had been saved and all hands were happy, especially when the *Herald* ran around the islands and entered Saint George's harbor without being chased by any Union cruisers.

Midshipman James Morris Morgan went on to England and served under Commodore Maury aboard the Confederate cruiser *Georgia*, which raided U.S. merchant shipping in the South Atlantic and off the coast of Africa.

Local supplies of civilian clothing had been exhausted, for they had been sent to the army or had been worn out on the backs of their owners. So the country people of the Carolinas and other Southern states were forced to return to the primitive methods of their forefathers—hand carding, spinning and weaving. Spinning wheels of a past generation were still stored in many houses. No time was lost in dusting off these machines and putting them back to work. Yet almost all of the hand cards, which were indispensable for carding the wool and cotton, had disappeared or been lost. In response to the cry for cards, the blockade runners brought them in as part of their cargoes and they were widely distributed. Also a number of machines for making cards were brought safely through the blockade.

In Charleston the ladies spent many hours each day sewing shirts and trousers for the soldiers. Negro tailors from inland plantations were brought in to help make the coats. Knapsacks were made from any kind of fabric. Women knitted constantly.

In June 1862 Union forces nearly succeeded in fighting their way into Charleston by the back door. Fortunately for that city, General Hagood, with three South Carolina regiments, reinforced the badly outnumbered Confederates and drove back the attacking force. This repulse saved Charleston.

A young Confederate officer who had been in the thick of the first fight and received a bullet in his leg was asked by a Charleston lady, "When so outnumbered did you not think of retreat?"

"Where could we have run to?" he answered. "The bottom of the Ashley River would have been the only refuge. Had we crossed to Charleston, you would have driven us out with your broomsticks!"

Even though the blockade had drawn tighter by the autumn of 1862, gaiety still prevailed, especially since an expected attack from the sea had not taken place. Parties of pretty girls dressed in their best crinolines went by boat to Fort Sumter and danced on the parade ground with brightly uniformed officers of the First South Carolina Regulars. At the great Beauregard Ball, "every man was in uniform with his leave in his pocket and his heart on his sleeve."

Practically everything which civilians wore, ate and used was in short supply and terribly high in price. Civilian merchandise brought in by blockade runners was auctioned off to Charleston merchants who bid fabulous amounts and then resold again for big profits.

Inland, the people suffered much more than those of the coastal cities. Very little civilian merchandise ever reached the plantations, for it was all bought up before it had a chance to get there. So it was necessary to substitute and improvise on almost everything. A letter written by the mistress of an upriver plantation at about this time reveals how much they were in need of necessities. They had no whale oil for their lamps so they made their own oil from peanuts. Bolted corn meal was used in place of wheat flour. Lacking real sugar, they contrived sugar syrup from watermelons. Since they could not buy leather, they made their own from the hides of horses, mules and hogs and tanned it with red oak bark. Shoe blacking was a mixture of soot and cottonseed oil. The women were constantly at work spinning and weaving their own cloth and wherever one went on the plantation "the hum of the spinning wheel and clang of the loom is borne on the ear." Dyes were obtained from bark, leaves, roots and berries. Buttons were carved from wood and covered with cloth. Drugs and medicines were absolutely unobtainable. The products of the woods and fields were sought to replace them. Herbs of various kinds were pressed into service by those who knew how to use them. After experimenting with various concoctions of parched meal and acorns, a passable coffee substitute was developed from dried okra seeds. Instead of tea they served dried raspberry leaves. So it went, everyone feeling the pinch but somehow managing to keep cheerful and reasonably healthy.

All through the bombardment of forts Sumter and Wagner by Union ironclads in April 1863 the people of Charleston never lost heart for a moment. Nor did the shelling of the city by the Swamp Angel, that long-range gun planted on Morris Island, in August of the same year, cause the citizens to lose faith or hope. They simply moved uptown or into the country. Yet there was much indignation when ten shells penetrated St. Phillips Church, wrecking the chancel and demolishing the organ.

In the midst of Charleston's hunger, bombardments and shortages of all sorts, the blockade runners, both British and Confederate, continued to carry the cotton past prowling lines of Federal cruisers and on to Bermuda and Nassau. Between July 1, 1861, and March 30, 1863, 130 steamers cleared Charleston carrying a total of 32,050 bales valued at $3,054,476. Some of the incoming cargoes of war materials ran in value as much as $1,500,000 each in Confederate currency.

Profits were in proportion, especially during the last year of the war. The Anglo-Confederate Trading Company, a Charleston firm organized specifically for blockade running, paid two dividends in 1864 of $1,000 per share in Confederate notes. The shares themselves had originally sold for $100 each, Confederate. Another Charleston firm, the Palmetto Importing and Exporting Company, paid a dividend of $2,000 in Confederate currency in 1864.

Through Charleston passed some very strange cargoes brought through the Union cordon, the origins of which were open to question. According to records stolen in 1863 by a Union spy from the Confederate Secretary of War, barreled beef and pork were shipped from New York and Boston aboard a British steamer, the destination of which was supposed to be Liverpool. Actually, however, the vessel showed up in Nassau. From there the meat was run into Charleston. One paragraph in the report is amusing. Some of the barrels of beef "bore marks of previous condemnation by the inspecting officers of the U.S. Navy." The report solemnly recommended that Confederate inspectors should be placed in Northern ports to make sure that no more spoiled meats were shipped into the South, especially since the Confederate inspectors in Nassau were known to be inefficient!

By 1864 the whole life and business of Charleston had been crammed into a few squares above Calhoun Street and along the Ashley River, where the hospitals and prisons were located. This area was safe, for it was out of range of enemy guns. The lower part of town was deserted—Federal shells were falling there. Grass and bushes had grown up in the streets. Houses with fallen chimneys, broken windows and shell-torn walls stared blankly at the harbor. As a city Charleston was only a shadow of its former self. As a blockade-running port it had virtually ceased to exist. The few shops that remained open sold the poorest wares at the highest prices. Again it was the old story of supply and demand: the supply coming from the dwindling number of blockade runners making port and the demand coming from everywhere in the South. For example, a red tin cup holding about a gill sold for $10, Confederate money. Enough brown sugar to fill the cup fetched an additional $10.

Endless experiments were being carried on in new methods of defense. Torpedoes were contrived of copper taken from roof gutters; old river boats were converted into rams; great trees were cut and chained together to make booms to impede enemy war vessels; and the bells of St. Phillips had long ago been melted down and recast into cannon.

By February 1865 Sherman was storming up from Savannah with 70,000 troops, burning as he came. As he neared Charleston his men destroyed all but one of the great mansions along the Ashley River. Sherman sent a corps to occupy the city, and received formal surrender from the municipal authorities. Meanwhile General Hardee, who had been in command at Charleston, withdrew his small force of 14,000 to North Carolina where he hoped a last stand might be made.

At last the old city's gaiety turned into the bitterness of defeat. All who were able went out ahead of the army, in trains, carriages, carts and on foot. It was in the middle of winter and there was much hardship. After a siege of 567 days, Federal iron-clads entered Charleston Harbor with tooting whistles and flying flags. During the entire war, Charleston had held fast against the enemy's incessant battering. But now that gallant defense was over and soon there would be peace on land and sea.

WILMINGTON

The port of Wilmington had certain natural advantages that made it strategically important as a blockade-running center. It was situated twenty-eight miles up the Cape Fear River and was thus safe from direct attack from the sea. Unlike Charleston and other Southern ports, there were at that time two separate and distinct approaches to the Cape Fear. One was from eastward, called New Inlet. The other was to the south, by Old Inlet. Although the distance between the two by land was only six or seven miles, the presence of dangerous Frying Pan Shoals and Smith's Island made the distance by sea nearly forty miles.

The Confederate Army quickly realized the natural advantages of these two inlets and lost no time in fortifying them early in the war. What had once been called Federal Point, commanding New Inlet, was rechristened Confederate Point and fortified by a shore battery. This later grew into the great earthwork called Fort Fisher. Confederate Point was flat and sandy, thrusting itself out into the water like the head of a giant snake. On the seaward side of the point a long line of sand dunes stretched northward, their flanks covered by brown sea grass. It was among these dunes that Fort Fisher was built.

Through New Inlet streamed part of the great flow of the Cape Fear River to meet the Atlantic in an endless battle of waters. Below the surface of the channel and unseen except for tide rips, was New Inlet bar. Here silt from the river and sand from the sea churned and eddied and piled up to form a barrier scarcely fourteen feet under water at flood tide. On either side of the channel there was even less depth. To make navigation more difficult, New Inlet bar had an annoying habit of shifting its position according to the season of the year or the vagaries of tides and currents. Captains and pilots who failed to familiarize themselves with the shifting character of New Inlet often ran their vessels aground.

When the blockade of the Cape Fear River became a serious objective of the Union Navy, both entrances to the river were closely watched by Union cruisers. From Smithville, both groups of blockading vessels could be distinctly seen. This gave outward-bound blockade runners an advantage, for they could take their choice as to which inlet to use, depending on the positions of the Federal men-of-war. But on the inward-bound run, pilots had to be guided by wind and weather as well as the location of Federal vessels. The soundings both north and south of the river entrances were deep and remarkably regular. With a light-draught steamer the pilot could run her close to shore, almost to the first line of breakers without danger of going aground.

In the 1860s, there were a number of flourishing rice plantations along the Cape Fear River, notably Lilliput, Green Field, Spring Garden, Pleasant Oaks, Belgrange, and Orton. Of these, Orton was the most famous, for it had been established by "King" Roger Moore in 1725.

When a steamer came within about two miles of Wilmington,

she passed a famous landmark near the east bank called the
Dram Tree. It was a great and ancient cypress that stood in the
water a few yards from shore. The story goes that early in
colonial times the captain of an English sailing vessel on his
first voyage up the Cape Fear had been told to look for this landmark because when he came abreast of it he would be close to
his destination and his worries and dangers would be over. Sure
enough, he found it, standing there like a sentinel, festooned with
Spanish moss. He shouted to the steward to bring him a bottle
of spirits. When it was brought he poured himself a dram and
had the crew and passengers do likewise. Then they all drank to
their safe arrival. On that day a tradition was born that continued throughout the era of blockade running and persisted until
World War II when the Dram Tree was removed to make way
for a shipyard.

The first glimpse of Wilmington's steeples above the treetops
must have given weary North Carolina captains and pilots a
warm and pleasurable feeling, for they were all well-known
friends: the white cupola of the Front Street Methodist Church,
and further inland the tall spire of the First Presbyterian and
the sturdy square tower of old Saint James Episcopal. Above the
rooftops on rising ground was the classic façade of the town
hall with its rows of Corinthian columns. Down by the water
front two other buildings stood out prominently: the dingy
bulk of the customhouse and, beyond, the columned tower of
the town market house between Front and Water streets. The
town hall was unique among buildings of its kind anywhere in
the United States for it possessed within itself a full-sized theater.
It belonged to the Thalian Association, an amateur theatrical
organization which already was years old before the outbreak of
the Civil War. All the best people in Wilmington belonged to
the Association and acted in the plays. Shakespearian dramas
were among the favorites. The whole population flocked to see
these productions, said to be of nearly professional caliber. During the war the fame of Thalian Hall seems to have spread to the
Federal blockading squadron, for on one occasion a couple of

bold young Yankee officers came ashore at night in a small boat, stole a pair of saddle horses and rode into Wilmington just in time to catch the opening curtain of a current production. Since they were in civilian clothes and were careful not to reveal themselves by their speech, they passed unnoticed. They returned safely to their man-of-war and were much envied by their brother officers.

News of North Carolina's secession was received in Wilmington by bonfires of tar barrels and patriotic speeches. Lincoln's declaration of the blockade was greeted with resentment and derision. Nevertheless the shipping of this small port came to a standstill and there was great uncertainty as to what destiny had in store for the town. Although Wilmington's population was only 4,000 at the outbreak of the war, the town furnished a full quota of volunteers for the Army.

Aside from rice, the chief exports of Wilmington in the decade prior to the Civil War were cotton, lumber and naval stores. The pine lumber was cut along the upper reaches of Cape Fear River and floated down to Wilmington on rafts. Naval stores was a common term given to products extracted from Carolina pine trees: crude turpentine, spirits of turpentine, resin, tar and pitch. During this period the turpentine territory contributing to the commerce of Wilmington had been greatly expanded with consequent increases in the exports of naval stores. These increases continued throughout the blockade-running era as the British Navy filled a large portion of its needs from this source.

Immediately following President Lincoln's call for volunteers, Fort Caswell and Fort Johnson were occupied by the 30th Regiment of North Carolina Militia.

At this time what was then known as Federal Point had no fortifications whatever. But late in the spring of 1861 the state of North Carolina placed a battery there and sent the Wilmington Light Infantry to man the guns. This fortification, known then as Battery Bolles, was the beginning of Fort Fisher.

At the time of the Civil War there was no bridge across the Cape Fear River at Wilmington. The Market Street ferry consisted of a flatboat operated by sweeps. Consequently there was very little road traffic between Wilmington and Brunswick County on the south side of the river. Most of the commerce and transport was by water. The plantation owners had their own sloops and used them to go back and forth to town and to carry their cargoes for shipment abroad. There was also a small steamer that ran down the river as far as Smithville, now called Southport. The steamer made regular calls at all the important plantations.

The social life of Wilmington was active and pleasant. Many of the leading families had intermarried and there was much visiting back and forth between those who lived in town and friends and relatives on the plantations along the river.

There were many good stores stocked with attractive merchandise from New York and other Northern cities as well as London and Paris. At 23 Market Street, M. N. Katz offered staple and fancy dry goods, silks, merinos, alpacas and French millinery; also Balmoral and hoop skirts, double elliptical skirts, and mourning and fancy veils. After decking themselves out in silks and satins from Mr. Katz's emporium, the ladies could then order their coachmen to take them to C. N. Van Ardsdell's extensive Stock Depot and Photographic Rooms were they could choose "photographic portraiture of every known style, beautifully colored in oil, pastel, watercolor or india ink."

The leading druggist in town was William L. Lippsett at 55 Market Street. His advertisement in the Wilmington *Journal* proclaimed him to have available "chemicals, dye stuffs, perfumery and soaps. Prescriptions accurately and neatly filled. Store open 6 A.M. to 9 P.M. Persons wishing prescriptions filled at night call at my residence at 2nd Street between Dock and Orange."

There was no lack of good things to eat and drink. William Patton, baker, offered many delectable oven-fresh delicacies including crisp breakfast rolls, arrowroot crackers and pilot bread. "All orders for cake and so forth for weddings and parties will be executed in the most approved manner and on the shortest notice." As for beverages, there was a wide selection, both hard and soft: lager beer, ale, French brandy, old rye and bourbon whisky, rum, gin and all kinds of wines and, possibly for use in cocktails, Drake's Plantation Bitters. Sarsaparilla, ginger pop and soda water were popular with the ladies and children.

Wilmington was one of the cultural centers of North Carolina and its upper classes were well read and kept abreast of political, social and economic developments at home and abroad. There was a public reading room as early as the last decade of the eighteenth century. The wealthy planters had large private libraries and subscribed to the best English and American periodicals.

For more than a year after the beginning of hostilities life was still comparatively placid, comfortable and pleasant. Blockade running had not yet developed into big business, for the Federal Navy was unable to spare enough ships and trained crews to patrol effectively the twin mouths of the Cape Fear. As late as July 20, 1861, only one Union cruiser, the *Daylight*, operated off Confederate Point. She was so far offshore that she was never considered a menace.

Each state member of the Confederacy was expected to furnish food, clothing and ammunition for its own troops. North Carolina took her obligations most seriously. By October 1861 the price of materials for clothing had risen 100 per cent and the state adjutant general was desperately scouring markets from Richmond to New Orleans for yard goods, shoes and other supplies for the 36,000 North Carolinians then in service. In this emergency Governor Ellis appealed to the people for such articles of clothing and camp necessities as they could spare from their homes. The response was prompt and heartwarming: blankets, quilts, overcoats, home-knit socks and gloves, throat scarves, tin plates and pans poured into the destitute camps. When the supply of blankets gave out, the women fashioned comforts. When cloth was exhausted, carpets were stripped from the floors, cut into blanket size and made into "carpet blankets." These emergency measures kept North Carolina troops fairly comfortable during the bitter winter of 1861-1862.

By July 1862, North Carolina troops had increased to 67,000. New cotton mills were going up all over the state; existing mills were enlarged. Woolen mills took on new life. Shoe factories were established and state agents were sent traveling into every county, buying wool and hides.

Zebulon Vance, newly elected governor of North Carolina, not only saw the need for importing war materials from Europe but also realized the necessity for owning one or more ships in which to transport these vital items. On his own responsibility he decided to put the plan in operation and selected John White of Warrenton as a commissioner of purchases, together with Captain Thomas M. Crosson, a former U.S. naval officer and Theodore J. Hughes, of New Bern, a businessman. It was Captain Crosson's responsibility to buy a vessel suitable for blockade running, load her with war supplies and sail her through the blockade to Wilmington.

After much searching, Captain Crosson found what he was looking for—a swift-heeled vessel that could outrun any Federal ship on blockade duty. She was the *Lord Clyde*, an iron side-wheeler that had formerly plied between Glasgow and Dublin. The price of the vessel plus extra fittings and nautical equipment cost the state of North Carolina $170,972.30. With a pressure of twenty pounds of steam per square inch, the steamer developed seventeen knots without difficulty. This was a phenomenal speed for that day.

The *Lord Clyde* was rechristened the *Advance*, not the *Ad-Vance* or *A.D. Vance* as she is sometimes referred to in official and unofficial documents. Her name had nothing to do with Governor Vance. The true fact is that when Captain Crosson bought the steamer and pointed her bows westward he said, punning, that she was going *ad* Vance, to Vance. He later spelled the name *Advance* and thus it appears on her cargo manifests.

In the meantime White had engaged the English firm of Alexander Collie & Company as agents for the state. This able and well-established company handled the blockade-running affairs of North Carolina right up to the capture of Wilmington. To avoid technical delays and complications, Collie & Company received and paid for all purchases made by White, arranged for the sale of cotton bonds, was consignee for all of North Carolina's cotton shipped to England and finally became a joint owner with the state of three other blockade-running steamers: *Don, Hansa and Annie.*

On her maiden voyage as a contraband carrier, the *Advance* safely negotiated the blockade and landed her assorted war goods in Wilmington amid an enthusiastic welcome by the citizens. Her cargo was immediately shipped under guard to Raleigh on a special train. A large part of the cargo consisted of cloth which, on arrival at the capital, was seized by a corps of eager women and quickly converted into uniforms.

White continued to make heavy purchases in England and Collie & Company forwarded them in chartered vessels to Bermuda. Throughout the war it cost the state approximately two dollars to get one dollar's worth of goods delivered at Bermuda or Nassau—which illustrates the great outlay necessary to do business where heavy risks were involved. The same John T. Bourne of Bermuda who was agent for the Confederate States government was also the agent for the State of North Carolina.

It seems strange that the Richmond government did not co-ordinate all purchases of supplies abroad under one central control early in the war. Perhaps one of the reasons was the attitude of some states like North Carolina which preferred to shoulder the task of feeding, arming and clothing its own troops, thus making certain its soldiers were being well taken care of. North Carolina was fortunate in having not only cotton to exchange for food and war supplies but also another product that had a ready sale in Europe, a product extracted from her own forests of jack pine—*resin*. Resin warrants as well as cotton warrants were issued by the state and were readily sold abroad.

As the war went on and the Federal Navy tightened its strangle hold on the Cape Fear, Governor Vance seriously considered giving up the state's share in blockade running as being too risky. However, he reconsidered and North Carolina continued in the trade until the very last moment. Nevertheless, Vance's political opponents termed the business a financial failure. Smarting from these accusations, the governor appointed a committee early in May 1864 to "investigate all matters relating to the blockade running business." No definite conclusions were reached by the committee except to praise the results of the state's activity: ". . . the soldiers of North Carolina are clothed and furnished in a manner that is the admiration of the Confederacy—giving them a degree of comfort and efficiency that cannot be measured in dollars and cents."

As the outward flow of North Carolina cotton and the inward flow of war goods increased, state cargoes became more than the *Advance, Don, Hansa* and *Annie* could handle. They were augmented by three Collie steamers, *Constance, Edith** and *Pet*, which busily plied between Wilmington and Nassau and Bermuda.

It was rare that a blockade runner dared to run through the entire Federal fleet in broad daylight. But such was the case on the third inbound voyage of the *Advance*. The Rev. Moses D. Hoge, a passenger, describes the affair thus:

Captain Crosson prepared to run up near enough to see what blockaders were within view and I supposed that he would then stand out to sea, lie off until night and then run in at his leisure. But to my astonishment, although it was about eight o'clock in the morning, the sun shining brilliantly and the sea as level as a floor and three blockaders guarding the entrance [New Inlet], he steamed straight on for Fort Fisher. The blockaders seemed confused for a few moments by the audacity of the movement, but presently they came about and all but three struck for the shore, intending to cut us off. They came on very speedily, but finding that we were running so swiftly they opened upon us with shrapnel, shell and solid shot. It was a scene of intense excitement. We could see the people on the shore watching the

* The *Edith* was later armed and converted into the Confederate cruiser *Chicamauga*.

result . . . the shells were plowing up the water and tearing up the sand on the shore, bursting over and around us and yet not one struck us.

Soon the courageous little *Advance* came within range of Fort Fisher's guns,* and they promptly boomed in a hoarse chorus, driving off the eager Union vessels. The gunners cheered wildly as the *Advance* rounded the point and came safely to anchor.

All of the steamers working for the state were captured, one after another during 1864. The *Pet* was overhauled and seized in February. The *Don* was made a prize by the U.S. steamer *Pequot* in March. Her cargo was valued at close to $200,000. On the last trip of the *Advance* luck seemed to have deserted her. Between August 8 and September 10 she made eight attempts to leave the mouth of the Cape Fear. Each time she had to turn tail and return because, as General Whiting put it, "both bars are swarming with boats." On the ninth try, the *Advance* got through the regular line of cruisers. But just as officers and crew began to breathe easily, the *Advance* was spied by the U.S. war vessel *Santiago de Cuba*, en route to Norfolk for coal. This steamer was exceptionally fast and she hung on the heels of the *Advance* from half-past ten in the morning until nearly eight at night, and finally overhauled and boarded her. No better epitaph for the plucky *Advance* could be written than the words of Daniel H. Hill in his two-volume work, *Bethel to Sharpsburg*, when he said it was tragic that the *Advance*, which "had contributed so much to the welfare of the war-harassed state and was regarded in an affectionate personal way by a half million people, was compelled to strike her colors." In reporting her loss Governor Vance wrote that she was the "pride of the State and the benefactor of our soldiers and people."

During the closing year of the war, the Federal squadron off the mouth of Cape Fear was augmented continuously until at

* In a letter to Secretary Seddon, General Whiting in charge of the district complained, "My men, who ought to be at their work and at their drill, have to be transformed into boatmen and wreckers and at night have to stay on those wrecks to keep off the enemy's boats . . . I mention this only to show what sort of work this little garrison is daily and nightly at."

the height of the blockade it numbered thirty or more vessels. These formed a cordon every night in the shape of a crescent, the horns of which were so close inshore it was difficult if not impossible for a small boat to pass without discovery. Federal picket barges also patrolled the bars and sometimes even crept in close to the forts. In November 1864 a second cordon was formed and cruised up and down the edge of the Gulf Stream to sight and chase blockade runners approaching from Bermuda or Nassau and drive them into the arms of the inshore squadron.

Early in 1863 when the British firms began sending numbers of speedily built steamers against the blockade, Wilmington underwent a marked change. Speculators from all parts of the South flocked there to attend weekly auctions of cargoes of luxury items brought through the blockade. According to Captain Wilkinson, "The town was infested with rogues and desperadoes, who made a livelihood by robbery and murder. It was unsafe to venture into the suburbs at night, and even in daylight there were frequent conflicts in the public streets between the crews of the steamers in port and the soldiers stationed in town in which knives and pistols would be freely used; and not unfrequently a dead body would rise to the surface of the river near one of the docks with marks of violence upon it. The Civil Authorities were powerless to prevent crime."

Representatives of British blockade-running firms and their captains and officers lived in magnificent style, paying a king's ransom in Confederate money for their household expenses and nearly monopolizing the supplies in the market. Wilkinson describes how his family servant, newly arrived from the country in Virginia, would sometimes return from market with an empty basket, having flatly refused to pay what he called "such nonsense prices" for a bit of fresh beef or a handful of vegetables. At the time about which Wilkinson writes, toward the close of the war, a quarter of lamb sold for $100, a pound of tea for $500. He notes that Confederate money which in September 1861 was nearly equal to specie in value, had declined in September 1862 to 225; the same month in 1863 to 400 and before September 1864 to 2,000. During the height of the blockade-running era, houses rented for enormous prices. It was also noted the elite did not mix with the blockade-running fraternity but kept to themselves and confined their social activities to friends and army and navy officers.

It was not always good things that were brought through the blockade. On August 6, 1862, the little steamer *Kate* arrived in town with a valuable cargo. But aboard lurked the dangerous virus of yellow fever. Several of her crew came down with the fever and it quickly spread throughout the city. It raged for ten consecutive weeks and killed a total of 446 people. It was thought that a noxious miasma was the cause, and tar barrels were burned in the streets to clear the atmosphere. Many of the Wilmington families who could afford to, fled to the country to escape contagion.

Wilmington was a stopover point for convalescent soldiers being shipped from Virginia hospitals to their homes further South. Mrs. Armand J. deRossett was the founder of the Soldiers Aid Society, organized to alleviate the suffering of these wounded. The ladies set up long tables at the depot and fed delicacies to the sick. Many dressed the wounds of the men in the railroad cars. At other times the ladies worked diligently, making underwear, clothing and haversacks for the men at the front. They also covered canteens, made cartridges for rifles and powder bags for the great Columbiads at forts Fisher and Caswell. The gathering place for the ladies was the City Hall, where the hum of sewing machines and female conversation blended with the voices of the city fathers, intent on matters of administration.

In commenting on Wilmington at this time, Wilkinson wrote, "It is true that a class of heartless speculators infested the country, who profited by the scarcity of all sorts of supplies, but it makes the self-sacrifice of the mass of the Southern people more conspicuous, and no state made more liberal, voluntary contributions to the armies or furnished better soldiers than North Carolina."

Across the Cape Fear River from Wilmington was a low, marshy flat. Here was erected one of the first steam cotton presses in the Southern states. Up to this time cotton bales had been so loosely packed that they took up a large amount of cargo space for their weight. The steam cotton press, by exerting tremendous pressure, contracted the cotton until the finished bale was half the size it was before. Thus a great many more bales were stowed in the holds of blockade runners than was possible before the invention of the cotton press.

Sentries were posted on the wharves day and night to prevent deserters from the army from stowing aboard blockade runners. An additional precaution was established by the government to flush out these stowaways by fumigating all outward-bound steamers at Smithville. But in spite of this vigilance many persons succeeded in getting free passage abroad. One captain, annoyed at the frequent stowaways discovered in spite of all precautions, turned four of them adrift in the Gulf Stream in an open boat with a pair of oars and only a few days' allowance of bread and water. They managed to make their way ashore and apparently spread the news of their treatment, for the number of stowaways decreased remarkably thereafter.

A contemporary writer describes conditions in Wilmington with special reference to the English blockade-running fraternity. "At every turn you met up with young Englishmen dressed like grooms and jockeys, or with a peculiar coachmanlike look, seeming out of place in a foreign land away, when they should have been at home with their mothers. They indulged their fancy in extravagant dress to the utmost. These youngsters had money, made money, lived like fighting cocks, and astonished the natives by their pranks and the way they flung the Confederate stuff about. Of course, they were deeply interested in the Confederate cause and at the same time wanted cotton.

"They occupied a large house at the upper end of Market Street. There these youngsters kept open house and spent their pa's and the company's money while it lasted. There they fought cocks on Sundays, until the neighbors remonstrated and threatened prosecution. A stranger passing the house at night and seeing it illuminated with every gas jet lit (the expense no doubt charged to the ship) and hearing the sound of music, would ask if a ball was going on. Oh no! It was only these young English Sybarites enjoying the luxury of a band of Negro minstrels after dinner. They entertained every and anybody."

When President Lincoln issued his Emancipation Proclamation in January 1863, the colored people of Wilmington took little notice of it. One colored woman attracted some attention by striding along the downtown streets crying out, "Thank de Lord, freedom done come!" She was looked upon as being very queer and different from the devoted household servants.

A red-letter day in Wilmington's history during the war was the visit of President Jefferson Davis. He arrived in Wilmington on November 5, 1863, and lodged at the headquarters of General W. H. C. Whiting. His purpose was to inspect the defensive works of the port. After surveying them, he gave his approval and appealed to the people to stand up for the Confederate cause and do their fullest duty. He gave them many assurances of ultimate and glorious success. The day ended with a parade of soldiers.

There were two large shipyards in Wilmington at this time. Beery's, the larger of the two, was located on the west bank of the river. Here the ironclad *North Carolina* was constructed in 1862. She was stationed off the lower part of Cape Fear, near Smithville. She was so clumsy in construction that she was considered unsafe in rough water, so she remained anchored most of the time and only occasionally used her guns. Finally, rotten with shipworms, she weakened and sank. An attempt was made to build a submarine at Beery's, but it never saw service.

The ironclad *Raleigh*, constructed at Cassady's shipyard, near the foot of Church Street, had a more impressive career. She was finished in 1864 and was commanded by the famous Confederate Navy Captain J. Pembroke Jones. The *Raleigh* created quite a stir among the Federal blockading fleet off the mouth of the Cape Fear. One night she and two consorts steamed out among the blockaders and frightened them out to sea. But on her return to New Inlet the next morning she ran aground on the bar. Attempts to salvage her were unsuccessful, for she broke in two amidships and sank.

During the latter years of the war, salt became a very scarce commodity throughout the Confederacy. The only possible way to manufacture salt was by evaporating sea water. Salt works were constructed in many places along the South Atlantic Coast and sufficient salt was made by this means to provide for the minimum requirement of the army and the civilian population. Yet, as in so many instances, speculators reaped excessive profits from this essential commodity. A large salt works was located at Greenville Manor, Shandy Hall and other estates along the lagoons near Greenville Sound in the Wilmington area. Large iron kettles were used to boil the salt water and the fires were kept burning day and night. It was a slow process and required large supplies of wood for fuel. At night the fires from the salt works could easily be seen by Federal naval forces cruising offshore a few miles away. Every once in a while a Federal man-of-war would lob a spherical shot across to disrupt operations. It was more of an annoyance than a danger. Salt making along the coast continued with little interruption throughout the war.

According to a gentleman who once lived on one of these estates near Greenville Sound, one of the shots from a Federal cruiser almost had fatal results. One fine summer day in 1863 a group of ladies was playing croquet on the lawn of Shandy Hall. Suddenly there came the scream of a shot followed by the distant boom of a cannon. A great 11-inch cannon ball fell in the middle of the greensward and kicked up a shower of dirt and sod. Several of the good ladies swooned and had to be revived with smelling salts and generous portions of blackberry cordial.

The citizens of Wilmington suffered as much from lack of adequate food as any of the people of any other seaport in the South. One of the present citizens of the city was told by her grandmother that a typical "blockaded meal" consisted of milk, one wheaten biscuit and a bit of honey. As an alternative there would be a corn muffin with plenty of hominy. Coffee was made from parched corn or acorns and for tea there was always the ever-plentiful youpon.

Wilmington was spared many of the horrors of war experienced by other Southern cities in the path of the enemy. Except for a small amount of shelling, just before its occupation by Union troops, the city came through the conflict unscathed.

RICHMOND

When the news of Lincoln's call for 75,000 volunteers reached Richmond, the *Examiner* declared angrily: "Lincoln declares war on the South, and his secretary demands from Virginia a quota of cut-throats to desolate Southern firesides." Rugged old ex-Governor Wise, after exclaiming over the news, said fiercely that Southerners were skilled in the use of the bowie knife and would not hesitate to draw it in defense of their land. He also questioned whether the Federal government would blockade Southern seaports in spite of the threat to do so, for this would contravene treaties between the United States and European powers.

Richmond's celebration of the passage of her ordinance of secession was in no way less noisy and enthusiastic than the celebrations of her sister cities of Charleston and Wilmington. Parades, music, orations, bonfires, fireworks, singing and dancing all merged together in one great spectacle. Enthusiasm overwhelmed common sense. "I am neither a prophet nor the son of a prophet," shouted a youthful speechmaker, "yet I predict that in less than sixty days the flag of the Confederacy will be waving over the White House."

All during the spring of 1861 and well into the summer, the supply of civilian goods was plentiful in Richmond. Somehow or other, all sorts of products continued to reach the city from the North and Europe with a minimum of delay and interference. By this time, Richmond was a boom town. Its population had doubled in a matter of months, for it had become the mecca of politicians, government workers, army and navy personnel, gamblers, speculators, refugees and visitors from all parts of the South.

Business life was changing rapidly. New stores were opening and the older ones were being bought out by newcomers. The city's industries were in peak production and the chimneys of the city belched smoke continuously. Such items as portable steam engines, plows, stoves and furnaces were advertised for sale. All types of military merchandise were actively bought and sold along with books on military science. Luxuries such as perfume, tea, and coffee, scented soap and olive oil were still in good supply.

The first indication of a shortage came when the government began printing its passports on brown paper. The wealthier people of Richmond continued to enjoy Clermont hams and other choice meats, a wide variety of vegetables and of course the beverages that went with them, such as brandy, claret, Madeira and sherry. People were saying the Yankee blockade would never become really effective. There were always means of getting shipments of necessary food and merchandise through "underground channels" in Baltimore and other Northern seaports. Foreign vessels continued to arrive in Southern ports and no time was lost in shipping their cargoes of civilian merchandise by fast train to the capital of the Confederacy. From many parts of the South came such delicacies as canvasback ducks, oysters and terrapin. Prices were high but many could still afford them. The punch served by Governor Letcher at his traditional New Year's Day party was just as potent as ever. Dress goods were available in quantity. However the ladies of Richmond felt they should select quiet tones in keeping with the seriousness of the war situation. It would seem the men thought otherwise, for their uniforms were quite gay and brilliant in contrast. Perhaps this was a show of bravado on their part.

Gradually scarcity began to show itself. Newspaper advertisements gave clues. For example, greatcloth suitable for military purposes was advertised as "very cheap for the times." A beverage called dandelion coffee was proclaimed to be "equal to the best java." One Richmond druggist felt it necessary to explain his reduced stock by an advertisement which said, "the usual avenues through which our supplies are obtained have now been closed."

Although the general scale of prices had increased during the winter of 1861-1862, there was actually no suffering except among the very poor and the refugees who crowded the city. These had been driven from their homes on the Eastern shore of Maryland, Alexandria and the lower valley. For them the holiday season was grim and freighted with uncertainties. Because of high prices and lowered earnings these people were already experimenting with rye, corn and wheat parched as substitutes for coffee. For tea they were using the leaves of currant and blackberry bushes.

Rents were exorbitant and every boardinghouse crowded. Profiteering was a common practice and those who had to depend on low government salaries found it difficult to make ends meet. By early January 1862 butter had climbed to 50 cents a pound, with bacon at 25 cents and beef had soared from 13 cents a pound to 30 cents. The only item which remained plentiful and fairly cheap was flour.

Well-born young ladies, whose families had suffered financial reverses on account of the war, used patriotism as a cloak for necessity and found employment at the Treasury Department and other government offices. Many of them began making over their old dresses and using anything they could find to trim their hats.

Youth and gaiety could not be suppressed. The girls gave cooperative parties at which each contributed some refreshment. Officers and "high privates" were invited with no discrimination being made between commissioned officers and those in the lower ranks. Costume parties were also popular and the young ladies searched attic trunks for old dresses and materials which they could make into fancy costumes. Many people in Richmond still had relatives living in Washington and other points in the North and kept in touch with them through letters smuggled in and out of the blockade. News of events among the Yankees reached Southern cities through newspapers and also came through on blockade runners.

Like most all the women in other Southern cities, the ladies of Richmond devoted many hours a week to tending the wounded and ill soldiers who crowded the hospitals. They read them the

Bible, said prayers, cheered them, fed them delicacies, wrote letters to their loved ones and did everything in their power to ease their pain and contribute to their comfort. Those whose menfolk were wounded and lying in hospitals in other Southern cities spent great amounts of time and money to travel to their bedsides.

In August of 1862 the government clamped down on the activities of enemy aliens and ordered them to leave the country. A number of rich Northerners were arrested and their money confiscated. Passports were forbidden to be issued to enemy aliens and any who applied for them were arrested. Nevertheless certain Jewish merchants apparently found ways of entering and leaving the Confederacy any time they chose, or so the popular rumor ran. It was also said that they were cornering the market in foodstuffs. It was further declared that "foreigners from Maryland" (merchants from Baltimore) had opened retail establishments in Richmond and were bringing in goods through the blockade and making profits as high as $50,000 a month. The reason for this, it was stated, was that these merchants had bribed officials on both sides of the dividing line. If a person wished to send a letter to, or from, Washington or into Maryland he could easily do so by paying a "letter carrier" a delivery charge of $1.50 a letter.

During this period there was practically no provision made for the thousands of soldiers who went through Richmond on leave or on their way back to the front from the hospitals. Hotel rates were high and practically no one in the enlisted ranks could afford to pay them. There was no free shelter of any kind and the Richmond keepers of saloons did a land-office business selling fighting men poor whisky and then kicking them in the gutter when they had too much. Prostitution flourished, crimes and murders were common. Richmond was not accustomed to this lawlessness and marshal law became inevitable. The same law required all saloons and distilleries within Richmond and for ten miles around the city to close their doors. Whisky could be purchased only on a physician's prescription. This of course led to bootlegging and if one knew the right people and had the right price it was not hard to get a drink of liquor.

In spite of these annoyances and the slackness of the government in enforcing law and order, the war effort continued in full force. A foreign visitor who stayed in Richmond at this time said that, "It reverberated with the roar of forges, echoed with the clatter of army wagons, rang with the band music of marching regiments. Of evenings officers and ladies came and went on the tree-shadowed sidewalks or sat chatting in rose-embowered porticoes in a quiet broken only by the falls."

As the war dragged on and the number of Confederate wounded increased in Richmond, the capacity of the city to take care of them lagged. These wounded soldiers were a pitiful sight:

They came walking, limping with a musket for a crutch, red-eyed, under bloody bandages, with powder-blackened faces and lips sore from the powder of bitten cartridges. They came in ambulances, in hired hacks and private carriages that had been driven to the dressing stations, in wagons and trucks so thickly that the vehicles stood massed in the streets, waiting to be unloaded.

Wounded men lay on the bare board floors of the Saint Charles Hotel, their faces stiff with blood and thick with flies. The Kent Payne Company threw open its building to them. Churches sent their pew cushions, rich folk their treasured wines. Women and girls who chanced to be passing were stopped and implored to come in and help. It was worse than it had ever been. There was not enough of anything. Bandages, lint, stretchers, beds and bedding all were exhausted. Many soldiers died of the mortification of their wounds because essential care could not be given to all in time to save them.

There was hardly a Richmond family that had not at least one member in the field. Every house, it seemed, was either a hospital or the abode of mourning. To one family enjoying the cool of the evening on their porch rolled a caisson escorted by walking wounded and bearing the body of their son. Nursing the wounded and burial of the dead became the city's two leading occupations. Such was the congestion in the fifty hospitals that presently the streets were full of men who had lost an arm three days before. Erysipelas added loathsomeness to the horror of gangrene. Between them they tainted the air.

New made graves spread over the hillsides. The grave diggers, work as they would, could not keep up with the demands upon them; and bodies left out all night swelled until they burst the flimsy coffins. Funerals were so many—even the funerals of friends—that none could be more than sparsely attended. Again as in the days after Manassas a crowd of strangers poured into the city: women mostly, searching the hospitals for wounded relatives or among the raw, red mounds and common trenches for a trace of their beloved dead. Again there could be no formal celebration of victory, no fanfare of trumpets, illuminations, and hundred gun salutes—only the farewell volleys over flag draped coffins and the lonely notes of taps.*

By the beginning of 1863 keeping clothed became one of the chief occupations of the people of Richmond. The blockade had shut off all but a trickle of cloth from abroad. The women of Richmond spent hours sewing, mending or knitting. Civilian men wore the coarse Confederate gray, a sign of patriotic sacrifice. Ordinary dress muslin cost $6 to $8 a yard, calico $1.75. On the other hand, good North Carolina homespun sold for reasonable prices. Occasionally when relatives came through the lines from the North under a flag of truce they would bring patterns of the latest Washington styles and distribute them among their friends. There was also a deal of smuggling across the border involving stockings, gloves and gray woolen dresses that could be made over into Confederate Army uniforms. Sometimes even a hoop skirt got through the Potomac blockade. To stretch out sinking family incomes, ladies of society who had never even thought of hard times before, made up things to sell, such as pickles, sparkling gooseberry wine and soap.

When diarist Mrs. Chesnut's husband, James, was made aide-de-camp to President Davis, she took up residence in Richmond.

---

* Alfred Hoyt Bill, *The Beleaguered City* (New York: Alfred A. Knopf, 1946), pp. 135, 137, 138.

There, on September 7, 1863, she recorded in her diary that "Mrs. Auld and Mrs. Davis came home with me. Lawrence [Negro servant] had a basket of delicious cherries. 'If there were only some ice' said I. Respectfully Lawrence answered, 'Give me money and you shall have ice.' He had heard of an ice house over the river, though its fame was suppressed by certain Sybarites, as they wanted it all.* In a wonderfully short time we had mint juleps and cherry cobblers."

On Christmas Day 1863, Mrs. Chesnut dined with the Prestons (wealthy and prominent South Carolinians). They regaled themselves with oyster soup, roast mutton, ham, boned turkey, wild duck, partridge and plum pudding. Beverages included sauterne, burgundy, sherry and Madeira, all of which had not long before nestled in the hold of a fast steamer dodging Yankee shells off New Inlet bar. Noted Mrs. C. gloatingly, "There is life in the old land yet."

In contrast to Mrs. Chesnut's luxurious fare, here is what a Confederate officer had to subsist on during the winter of 1863-1864. McHenry Howard of Baltimore, attached to General George H. Steuart's headquarters, recalled that dinner usually consisted of corn bread and soup made of water thickened with corn meal and mashed potatoes cooked with a small piece of meat. When the soup was done, the meat was carefully removed and kept to be cooked over again in mashed potatoes for the next morning's breakfast. Howard wrote bitterly, "A dog could not have lived with the mess that was left; there was, in fact, nothing left."

As for the men who owned and operated the blockade runners, as well as the officers who manned them, they got along very well, not in the slightest disturbed by the hunger and hardships of the poor. Tom Taylor, jolly and prosperous supercargo, recalled that, "Money still purchased most things and we blockade runners who were well supplied with coin, managed to live in comparative comfort and at times even fared sumptuously. I remember a great dinner I gave to a few heads of [government]

---

* Where did the ice come from? Most probably imported via blockade runner from Halifax.

departments; it was a banquet no one need have been ashamed of. But oh, the bill! A little over $5,000 for a dinner for fourteen. When one has to pay $150 for a bottle of champagne, $120 for sherry or Madeira, and as much in proportion for the viands, the account runs up." However, he adds smugly, "it was a great success and well worth the cost." Worth it, no doubt, in government influence favorable to his thriving blockade-running business.

To the hard-working and patriotic people of Richmond the sight of shopwindows filled with luxuries from Europe and Baltimore, smuggled in via the blockade-running route, was enough to infuriate them. These rich items of merchandise were on sale for the benefit of the profiteers and speculators who were growing fat and wealthy from the blockade-running trade. All sorts of tempting fruits, champagnes and *paté de fois gras* were there to tempt the palate. Even mutton, brought all the way from England on ice, could be had by those who could pay the price.

Outside the city, country women were "digging with their own hands in the earth of their smoke houses and tobacco barns to extract from it nitre for the manufacture of gunpowder. In the towns, in every spare moment, they sewed or knitted stockings for the soldiers, undeterred by the jibes of the male idiots who, in this as in every war, apparently found something humorous in such activity. To beat the blanket shortage which had now become deplorable among the troops in winter quarters in Fredericksburg, they pulled up many a costly Brussel's carpet, cut it into suitable sizes, and bound the edges."*

Some of the commonest items of everyday necessity were practically unobtainable and none of the ladies in Richmond hesitated to accept sewing kits taken from Union prisoners or from enemy dead. These contained sorely needed needles, pins and thread.

Even as the war entered its most serious stages, there was still the desire on the part of the government and the people to "eat one's cake and have it too." For example, when flour to feed the troops became short, Secretary Seddon confiscated all the

---

* Alfred Hoyt Bill, *The Beleaguered City*, p. 157.

flour in the mills and warehouses. As a consequence the price in the open market soared from $30 a barrel to $40 and of course the people of the city had to pay. There was great public indignation and as a result Secretary Seddon was prevented from continuing his policy by a court injunction.

Properly to evaluate economic conditions in Richmond and throughout the South at this time, it is illuminating to investigate briefly the unrealistic financial policy pursued by the Confederate government throughout the war. In the beginning there was a total lack of understanding of the potential scope and duration of the struggle. Yet everyone realized the necessity for substantial revenues. At the start donations of money, jewelry, food and clothing served to supply the army with sorely needed items; but they were a mere drop in the outsized bucket.

In February 1861 the first Confederate loan of fifteen million dollars was launched, quickly followed by additional loans and taxes. At the same time the South was flooded with millions of dollars of Confederate paper currency.

Financial analysts and historians are fairly well agreed that, immediately upon its organization, the Confederate government should have seized control of every bale of cotton within its borders; then, using it judiciously and with political foresight, it should have been doled out to Europe. If properly used, cotton could have been used as a powerful lever for forcing recognition of the Southern Confederacy by England and France and other foreign powers. Instead, President Davis withheld practically all Southern cotton from world markets, hoping to force recognition. When this plan failed, and the Confederacy was critically in need of war supplies and knew it had to pay cash or the equivalent in cotton on the barrelhead, Davis released a flood of cotton. While this helped pay for his war wants, it did not bring the long-sought-for recognition of his government by world powers.

Another important use for cotton which was neglected by Confederate fiscal officials was its use as a means of maintaining Confederate paper at par; also as a means of profiting handsomely from an inevitable rise in the price of the staple itself.

That is exactly what happened. Between 1862 and 1864 cotton prices soared. If Christopher G. Memminger, Confederate Secretary of the Treasury, had possessed a minimum of foresight, he could have bought all the cotton he could lay his hands on before a shot was fired at 5 cents and 6 cents a pound and given notes and bonds to the growers in exchange. Although in those early days there were not nearly enough cargo vessels to transport this enormous crop to England (to get it out of the country for safekeeping and release it abroad according to the needs of the European market), it is quite likely that British mill owners would have arranged with British shipowners to send over a monster mercantile armada to fetch it. Certainly those same Britishers were quickly able to marshal a sizable flotilla later on, in order to run the blockade and bring home much-needed cotton, at the same time making enormous profits.

The "Cotton Loan" for fifteen million dollars floated in March 1863 could with the proper perspective, have been put out one or two years earlier. Jefferson Davis, in his writings, does not mention any effort as having been made in this direction prior to 1863.

General William C. Oates, C.S.A., in his book, *The War Between the Union and the Confederacy*, describes the "Cotton Loan" as follows: "The security of the bonds was an obligation of the Confederate Government to deliver cotton to certain Southern ports. Each bond, at the option of the holder, was convertible at its nominal amount into cotton . . . at the price of six pence per pound or about twelve cents. Almost immediately the loan stood in the London market at 5% premium. And the loan was oversubscribed."

Then General Oates asks significantly, "Why on earth did he [President Davis] not sell them [the British public] all the bonds they wanted at the high price offered and use the gold obtained to stop the depreciation of the Confederate notes [and] the inflation of prices, and have gold to aid in carrying on the war and maintaining the credit of the Confederacy? When the day came for the bonds' payment there need not have been any shortage of cotton with which to pay off the bonds, and if there had been, the stringency would not have been so great as were the needs of the armies and government for good money at that date."

From across the span of nearly a hundred years no voice has been raised to answer General Oates's pertinent questions. After the Civil War was over, Salmon P. Chase, wartime U.S. Secretary of the Treasury, told General Oates that he, Chase, kept a close watch on Memminger, his opposite number, hoping against hope that Memminger would not use Southern cotton as the basis for European credit for war material. How well Chase's hopes were at least partially fulfilled is spread broadly across historical records.

In the face of the muddled and ineffective financial policy of the Richmond government, it is hardly surprising that at this time the Confederate armies were existing on half rations or less. Most of the civilian population was undernourished while the speculators, blockade runners and birds of similar feather (not excluding certain Confederate politicians and commissary officials) waxed sleek and fat.

As money shrank in value, government clerks and many others who had to depend on fixed incomes became shabby and ill-fed. Because of the paper shortage, newspapers were printed on half sheets and sometimes even on brown wrapping paper. Envelopes were in short supply and people turned the ones they had received in the mail inside out and used them again. An ingenious stationer made some envelopes from old wallpaper with the pattern inside.

When President Davis proclaimed a day of fasting and prayer there was grim laughter by many. "Fasting in the midst of famine!" Nevertheless the people of Richmond overflowed the churches and observed the day. It is indeed remarkable that it was not until April 1863 that President Davis called upon the people of the Confederacy to plant food instead of cotton and tobacco.

Riots were not unknown. A crowd of women and free Negroes armed with pistols, knives, axes and other weapons marched past the War Department and through the main streets of town smashing windows and pillaging stores, not only of food but of shoes, clothing and jewelry. The government read them the Riot Act and threatened military force. The mob finally scattered and dispersed.

One of the greatest causes of worry and misapprehension throughout the long war was the lack of proper communication between the capital of the Confederacy and the armies. Rumors, half-truths and enemy-circulated lies washed back and forth through the city like a poisonous tide. Women whose loved ones were at the front suffered hours and days, and sometimes weeks of agony, fearing that their men had been killed. Others, swept to heights of ecstasy by false news of victories, were then plunged into the depths of despair when truth and defeat were known. Newspapers were misled and had to resort to conjecture and word-of-mouth information. Even at this comparatively late period in the war the people of Richmond refused to accept the idea that their men could be defeated by a superior fighting force. They still were sure that one Southern soldier could kill a dozen Yankees. Bred in a tradition of integrity, they kept the ideals of duty and devotion steadily before them, day after day. Old and middle-aged men cheerfully exchanged pens and ledgers for muskets or picks and shovels when their home-guard leaders called them into the trenches protecting Richmond.

After the fall of Vicksburg, sugar became scarce in Richmond. Households omitted desserts containing sugar and the shabby gentility felt the pinch on all items of food and clothing. Even so, the upper crust continued to demand and pay for ice, oysters and every sort of alcoholic beverage. Red auction flags hung in front of many establishments where luxury items brought in by blockade runners were sold to the highest bidder. Buying was brisk and prices kept pushing higher and higher.

About this time there was a meeting of the presidents of the various Southern railroads to decide what could be done to speed up shipments of war supplies from the coast to the interior and also to relieve the distribution bottleneck on food for civilians. If this meeting produced any tangible results, they were not apparent to the general public. Wrote a Richmond dweller: "It is mysterious how the overtaxed railroads manage to bring

From PICTORIAL *and* HISTORICAL NEW HANOVER COUNTY,
by William Lord deRosset

Colonel Lamb in command of Fort Fisher.

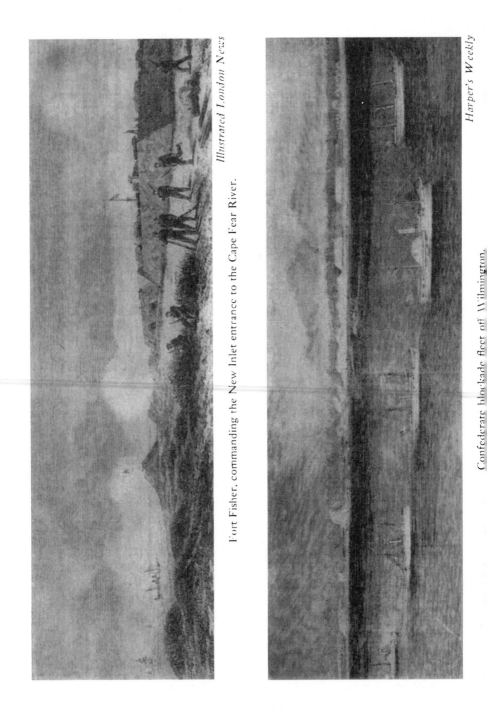

Fort Fisher, commanding the New Inlet entrance to the Cape Fear River.

Illustrated London News

Confederate blockade fleet off Wilmington.

Harper's Weekly

expensive non-essentials up from Wilmington and Charleston so promptly while masses of grain and bacon and other supplies for the army rot in freight cars on the sidings or in depots along the line."

Another citizen remarked on the astonishing number of jewelry stores that had mushroomed along the principal streets. In other stores, calico at $2.50 a yard was considered a bargain. In October 1863 cotton stockings cost $6 a pair, a 50-cent handkerchief $5, and a merino dress $150. People on small fixed incomes found everything scarce except paper money and that was of little value.

By the autumn of 1864 the city had resigned itself to grim hardship and self-sacrifice. Mrs. Jefferson Davis, who had sold her horses and carriage, had them returned to her anonymously by friends. Although they were accepted, she was afraid it would be impossible to find enough oats to feed them.

Rather than organize blockade running on an efficient and effective basis, whereby only the most essential war goods and civilian items would be imported, the government vacilated and wasted time by interfering with the blockade runners owned and operated by the state of North Carolina. These vessels brought in strictly essential goods. This interference by Richmond so annoyed Governor Zebulon Vance (who had also efficiently organized state clothing factories) that he threatened to join Georgia and South Carolina in withdrawing from the Confederacy and combining with them for the defense of Charleston. But he cooled off and did not make good his threat.

Fancy viands eaten by Richmond bigwigs served to allay their fears that the city would soon be captured. The true story is told of Secretary Benjamin accepting an invitation from Secretary of the Navy Mallory to eat "pea soup," which turned out to be oysters and champagne. Meanwhile, plain folk were eating cowpeas.

Mrs. Chesnut noted late in 1864 that "We are in a sad and anxious state here just now. The dead come in, but the living do not go out so fast." Nevertheless commissaries and quartermasters continued to be well-fed and rode down Richmond's streets on sleek and well-groomed horses. A group of wealthy socialites, tired of the austerities of Richmond, moved to Columbia, where the women occupied their time in nursing at the hospital, gossiping and sewing for the army. Former Confederate Secretary of War Randolph took his family to Europe. Some took temporary abode in Bermuda and Nassau. Still others "refugeed" into the country, feeling that if Richmond were invaded they would be safer among scattered farms.

In spite of these exits, the city remained full of people. One group of newcomers would be replaced by another. Furnished rooms, when available, rented for as much as $100 to $110 a month, a small fortune in those days. Fantastic prices prevailed for other things such as: twenty-five bushels of coal, $90; a cord of wood, $100. A salary of $13,000 a year could not support a household of seven even with the most stringent economy. Among the very poor, rats, mice and pigeons mysteriously disappeared. Cats and dogs prowled hungrily through the streets at night.

As Christmas approached, the gold dollar rose in value until it was the equivalent of $2,000 in Confederate paper money. When the year of 1864 came to a close, the volume of Confederate notes in circulation swelled to the fantastic total of one billion dollars. Those who had sizable amounts of Confederate money did not care how lavishly they spent it. An army officer who was charged $200 for a pair of boots tossed a $500 bill to the bootmaker and did not wait for the change. Some transactions were made on the basis of barter. A private school advertised that it would accept tuition for payments in flour, wheat, bacon and lard.

Because of the now almost watertight blockade of Southern ports, communication with the North and vice versa was extremely difficult and often impossible. "There were columns of paid personal notices [in the newspapers] charged with distress and sorrow—'New York newspapers please copy': queries as to missing soldiers mostly, and news of deaths and other family matters, which might by this means reach men in Northern prison pens. And the New York papers did copy. Since early in the war this method of communication across the lines had been the resort of many when regular channels failed them and spies and other secret agents found it highly convenient."*

Christmas of 1864 offered little in the way of jollity and happiness or even a well-fed feeling. A turkey fetched $100 or more. One of the most acceptable gifts a person could give was a box of sugar, captured from the enemy. Those who had to travel during the holidays found the railroads in deplorable condition. The cars rattled and swayed, not a lamp or stove remained in the cars and hardly a window was unbroken. The track and roadbed were in a dangerous state of disrepair; the same was even more true of the battered locomotives and rolling stock.

Everywhere in the South this was a Christmas of solemn self-sacrifice, especially in Richmond. People stripped their pantries in order to give delicacies to sick and wounded friends and relatives, for Confederate currency would buy very little and there was pitifully little to buy. However, churches and homes were decorated with evergreens that cost nothing and the New Year was greeted by the young boys with salutes fired from the cartridges of soldiers home on leave. Those who had fought to keep a cheerful exterior found it difficult to maintain their outward composure when the news of Savannah's fall came through on Christmas Eve.

Few of the Christmas boxes, lovingly prepared for front-line soldiers, reached the half-starved men. It was not known exactly what happened to the boxes, but it was suspected that the commissaries fared especially well over the holidays. The greatest holiday treat enjoyed by the lady clerks of the Confederate States War Department was on the second day of January 1865, when a kindly major in charge of the office treated them to real coffee. No one knew where he got it, nor cared.

Finally, severe legal penalties were imposed for buying merchandise or food for resale. Nevertheless the threat of the Union Army and Navy against Wilmington in December 1864 caused

---

* Bill, *The Beleaguered City*, p. 245.

speculators to ignore the law, corner all available sugar and coffee and sell it on the black market. Typical prices: sugar, $15 per pound, up $5 from $10. Coffee jumped from $15 to $45 per pound.

One of the most painful shortages of all was that of medical supplies. Since the South depended entirely on blockade runners to bring in medicines, hospital stores and surgical instruments, profiteering in these precious commodities was scandalously common. Morphine, quinine and chloroform brought exorbitant prices and were favored by blockade runners because such items occupied a small amount of space in relation to their value. At this time morphine was sold for $100 per ounce, quinine the same; calomel was $20 per ounce, blue mass the same.

Because of the lack of these and other medicinal necessities, especially anesthetics, together with a certain amount of incompetency among Confederate army surgeons, amputations were the order of the day, even for comparatively mild flesh wounds. Arms and legs were hacked off in shocking quantities, sometimes piling up in a grisly heap outside field hospitals.

An article in the New York *Semi-Weekly Tribune* complained: "Our severely wounded are living monuments to the incompetency of rebel surgeons . . . legs were cut off after the fashion of the 1600s . . . who use no chloroform because they have none. That their own wounded suffer from similar causes is undoubtedly true." As a matter of record, Union army surgeons amputated with a celerity equal to their brother professionals on the opposite side. It was a time of medical ignorance, compared to modern times, lack of sanitation and callousness to suffering and death.

There was little cause for celebration on Washington's birthday 1865, for this day marked the capture of Wilmington, North Carolina, thirty-eight days after the fall of Fort Fisher and the consequent termination of blockade running in the Cape Fear area. Morale in Richmond reached a new low. A lady diarist wrote that "People did not believe the croakers. But they were restless by evil surmising." At this point she gave up her diary in despair, "because," she said, "there was nothing but evil to write about."

Even the hardworking lady social service workers of Richmond slacked off their efforts. In one case only five showed up when they were asked to gather at a church and knit for the soldiers. Hoarding of flour and other foodstuffs was common. There was a rumor that the government was going to seize all food supplies. A barrel of flour now commanded $1,250 in Confederate money. Rationing was instituted by the Richmond Common Council, which doled out cornmeal, sorghum, flour and bacon in small quantities to the famished poor. For the first time, beggars appeared on the streets, and many generous people kept others less fortunate than themselves from starving by donations of food which they could ill spare. The Negro slaves fared better than anyone else, for their masters refused to reduce their diet. Hopes flared briefly when it was reported that four blockade runners had succeeded in penetrating Charleston Harbor with cargoes of commissary stores.

Railroad service was in a deplorable condition. Passenger travel had been completely suspended by government order, and the Central Railroad, angered at this, refused to furnish enough cars to move troops. The Piedmont Railroad callously left great piles of salt and grain along its right-of-way to be ruined by rain and mud. In Charlotte, North Carolina, a fire carelessly allowed to get out of hand destroyed great quantities of clothing, blankets and provisions in several army storehouses. What was saved from the flames was loaded into freight cars by half-naked and starving soldiers.

To add to the general misery, the weather during January 1865 was one of the coldest in history. There was little fuel. The poor burned their furniture and everything else inflammable that they could get their hands on.

As the end of the month approached, Richmond "seemed to be crazed on the subject of gaiety," very much like Paris at the height of the French Revolution. Amateur shows and dances were common. A Miss Carey invented a "Starvation Party," with only James River water as refreshment. Some people said that the whole town was "dancing on the edge of the grave." Owners and operators of blockade runners still reveled in luxuries—the last black market operations—even after the fall of Wilmington. There were many weddings and somehow or other the parents of the happy couples managed to scrape together enough food for wedding breakfasts. Everyone knew that blockade running was dead and nothing more could be expected from Europe. The fast little steamers which had served so faithfully were now huddled disconsolately at anchor in the Cape Fear River, their captains and crews waiting to find out what would become of them. And most important of all, the trickle of supplies from abroad that had been reaching Lee's armies had stopped entirely.

Richmond was less crowded now, for during the winter many people left town to refugee in Charlotte, Salisbury, Columbia and other cities further south. Government factories were being dismantled and ordnance machinery, guns and ammunition sent to safe locations outside the capital of the Confederacy. War and Navy department officials were busy packing their archives for shipment.

During these death throes, the spirit of resistance burned once again briefly. The few generous and self-sacrificing people who had already lost almost everything they possessed still gave what little was left to help keep the bankrupt government alive. Women gave their last jewelry and silverware. Men donated family heirloom watches. Some of the more impulsive ladies declared that they would cut off their hair and send it to Paris to be sold for the benefit of the Confederacy. Even if they had made good their intentions, there would have been no way to get their lovely tresses to the hair market of France!

Merchants and speculators who had profited hugely from blockade running now uncovered hoarded stocks of merchandise and put them up for sale, sure in their belief that if they did not do so now, the Yankees would get all when Richmond fell. Prices remained sky high. Flour soared to $1,500 a barrel. Auction sales of personal furniture and belongings were numerous.

With the army, food was at its most critical point. It was said that six Confederate soldiers received as much to eat as one Federal soldier. The average day's ration was one pint of cornmeal and one-third of a pound of "Nassau bacon." Men in the lines said that the Yankees allowed the bacon to come through the blockade in order to poison them.

About this time, Captain John Wilkinson, the famous blockade runner and officer of the Confederate Navy, was called to Richmond on official business. He describes his entry into the city as follows: "There now remained to the Confederacy only the single line of rail communication from Wilmington, via Greensborough and Danville to Richmond. The progress of demoralization was too evident at every step of my journey, and nowhere were the poverty and the straits to which the country was reduced, more palpably visible than in the rickety, windowless, filthy [railroad] cars, traveling six or eight miles an hour over the wornout rails and decaying roadbed. We were eighteen hours making the distance [about 140 miles] from Danville to Richmond. As we passed the rear of General Lee's lines, and I saw the scarecrow cattle there being slaughtered for the troops, the game seemed to be at last growing desperate. We were detained for perhaps an hour at the station where the cattle were being slaughtered. Several soldiers who were on the train, left us there; and as soon as they alighted from the cars, they seized portions of the offal, kindled a fire, speared the scraps on the points of their ramrods and devoured the unclean food with the avidity of famished tigers."

Soldiers were filthy because they had no soap. Their uniforms were ragged and their blankets in tatters from long use. Only about fifty men in a regiment had shoes. As for munitions, bullets were so short that Confederate soldiers had to dig them out of the earth and fire them back at the enemy.

During the last few hectic days of Richmond's wartime life as a city, banks remained open for business and their depositors formed long lines to draw out what little hard cash they could get. Bonfires in the streets were made of Confederate paper money. Cannon which had been intended for the defense of the city were rolled into the canal. The government was putting the last frantic touches to its packing before departure. Passengers crowded the trains leaving the city and others went out by any vehicle that could be hired or bought. Women made especially large pockets in their crinolines to accommodate food and valuables for the journey. Everybody—civilians, soldiers, wounded, all who could walk or crawl—was leaving Richmond as fast as possible.

The commissary, quartermaster stores and the government bakery threw open their doors to anyone who wished to take what they wanted of the food supplies. Crowds fought for hams, crackers, sacks of sugar and coffee. Other more greedy individuals loaded wheelbarrows or rolled away barrels of flour.

Mrs. Jefferson Davis had left the city weeks before and the President himself was ready to depart together with Secretaries Benjamin, Trenholm, Mallory and Postmaster General John H. Reagan. Mrs. Trenholm went along with her husband, who had thoughtfully brought with him a quantity of old peach brandy, which helped smooth the hard and jolting journey of escape.

By this time the city was in the hands of the mob. For hours, government commissioners had been pouring government whisky into the streets from staved barrels, kegs and hogsheads. Gutters ran ankle-deep in liquor. Men and women, black and white, deserters and the off-scourings of the slums fought for it, rolled in it and drank it in huge, greedy gulps.

At the Richmond depot stood a train loaded with government gold and specie: double-eagles, gold ingots and nuggets, silver bars and bricks from Mexico—$500,000 in all. Had it not been for an alert, armed guard of sixty young naval midshipmen, this treasure would have been pillaged by the mob. But thanks to the cadets, it reached its destination safely.

Soon, in the midst of the noise, confusion and looting came fire, and with it the end of Richmond, capital of the Confederacy.

CHAPTER 8

White Sails in the Gulf

As the war moved grimly into its third year, the blockade of Southern ports became tighter and more efficient. Union squadrons patrolling off the coast were augmented with faster cruisers. Better means of communication were also established. With the experience gained from a careful study of the methods used by blockade runners in slipping through the cordons, Federal war vessels were now able to track down, capture or destroy more and more British and Confederate vessels. Consequently, a good share of Southern traffic in cotton and war supplies was shifted to the Gulf of Mexico and the states bordering its shores. It was carried out in this area with great activity until the very end of the war in the face of a powerful blockading fleet.

It is not generally known that a large number of the cargoes which were successfully carried in and out of the blockade in the Gulf were transported in small sailing vessels. These fast, centerboard schooners, because of their shallow draught, could easily pass over the bars and shoals that lay at the entrances of many inlets and rivers of the Gulf States. Union cruisers, being deep-water vessels, could not get close enough to prevent the entrance or exit of light sailing craft. The best the Federals could do was to keep a strict lookout for the schooners once they fetched deep water and, when sighted, pursue them.

There were many hazards connected with blockade running under sail. For such small craft, the voyages between Mexico and Cuba and Gulf ports were often long and stormy, with the ever-present danger of being sighted and overhauled by a Union man-of-war. Moreover, most of these schooners sailed heavily overloaded because of the high freight rates on their cargoes.

201

They were manned by adventurous skippers and crews who drove their little craft with cheerful recklessness.

Aside from their shallow draught, centerboard schooners had other advantages that made them suitable for blockade running in Gulf waters. They were generally very weatherly, and were good sailers to windward, for they could come about quickly and in a small circle, having so little keel. The short centerboard acted as a pivot on which they turned. When they were sailing free or off the wind, the centerboard was partly drawn up which lessened the friction. But the principal utility of the small craft was in crossing shallow areas where a deep draught vessel could not go. When the centerboard was drawn up, the draught of the schooner was reduced to suit the depth of the water and then let down again when the water deepened.

The most famous of the little schooners was the *Rob Roy*, whose owner, Captain William Watson, became one of the most audacious blockade runners under sail. She was a graceful, yacht-like craft, of clipper build, with low bulwarks, tall masts and large sails of heavy cotton canvas. She measured 78 feet in length, with a beam of 22 feet 6 inches. Her depth of hold was only 6 feet. An idea of her light draught may be gained by the fact that her depth was only 4 feet 9 inches when loaded, with the centerboard up, and 13 feet with it down. In addition to owner Watson (who also acted as supercargo), the *Rob Roy* carried in addition to the captain, a mate, a cabin boy and four seamen.

Watson was an Englishman, an engineer by profession, who had lived in the South for about ten years prior to the outbreak of the war. He had been told of the very high inducements being offered for light-draught schooners such as the *Rob Roy*, which could cross the bar, sail up the river to Matamoros, land their cargo, take on a load of cotton, and go direct to Havana. He bought the *Rob Roy* in New Orleans in June 1863, ran past the forts at night and brought a small cargo to Belize, Honduras, where he changed the vessel's registry to British. This made it a neutral, trading between two neutral ports and free from risk of capture from either Confederate or Union men-of-war. After changing the registry he headed for Matamoros.

This small and dismal Mexican town was a key point in a long and winding route that led from the heartland of the Confederacy to the mouth of the Rio Grande and from there across the windswept Gulf to Cuba and the outside world. Matamoros was the Confederacy's extreme Southern escape hatch for cotton. Also at this time it was a far safer port of entry for the war material than any other on the Gulf. Mexico, being a neutral nation, had no objection to the use of Matamoros as a transshipping point for any sort of merchandise, provided the import and export duties were paid on the spot.

Matamoros was situated on the Rio Grande, about thirty miles inland from the mouth of the river. Directly across the Rio Grande from Matamoros was the Texas town of Brownsville. A ferry plied between the two towns. It was this ferry that provided communication between the Confederate states and the rest of the world which was not blockaded. The Rio Grande itself, being a neutral river, could not be sealed off by Union war vessels. It might well be asked at this point whether it would have been possible for small craft to have navigated the Rio Grande from its mouth to Brownsville and bring out the cotton direct without bothering to go through Mexico at all. As far as navigating the river was concerned, this was possible, although the Rio Grande was exceedingly twisting, being only eighty yards in width and varying in depth from seven to nine feet. But what made it impossible to use Brownsville was that the Federal government had declared it to be a blockaded port by sea, though not against Mexico. So it was necessary for the Confederacy to have all goods go through the neutral port of Matamoros. An immense amount of cotton left the Confederacy by this route and an immense tonnage of war supplies entered the Confederacy the same way.

Correspondence between the Confederacy and the outside world had, of necessity, to take a long, roundabout route to assure letters and dispatches getting through safely. Only a part of the distance was covered by rail or water transportation. Of the 1,500 miles from Richmond to Brownsville, several hundred miles were merely a rough track or trail. From Brownsville the mail had to travel another 270 miles to Tampico. British and Spanish mail steamers called at Tampico once a month—their sailings so scheduled to provide fortnightly service.

But it was in the transportation of the goods that the greatest amount of time, expense and labor was incurred. With only one exception, no port or harbor on the entire east coast of Mexico could be reached by a vessel drawing more than six feet of water. All ships with more draught had to ride at anchor in the open sea and discharge their cargoes into lighters, which carried the stuff across the dangerous shoals when the weather permitted. Much precious merchandise was lost in attempting to bring it ashore in the face of high winds and crashing combers. It is small wonder that any kind of merchandise brought in by this tortuous route commanded fantastic prices. In addition to sky-high freight rates, port charges had to be paid to the Mexican Government. There was also a flat 12½ per cent *export* tax! The ferry charges were also on a highway robbery basis.

After the shipments arrived on Confederate soil they still had a long way to go. The frontier town of Brownsville was more than three hundred miles from any other center of population—the nearest places were Austin and Houston. The only connecting link between Brownsville and the two towns was a winding trail, rough and parched. Across the seemingly endless plains crawled heavy wagons drawn by teams of oxen. The trip took from six weeks to two months. The greatest hardships occurred during the season of drought, when the sun beat down pitilessly, dried up the water holes and seared the grass. Oxen, mules and horses died by the hundreds and the dreary route could easily be followed by their bleached bones.

When the *Rob Roy* arrived off the mouth of the Rio Grande, those aboard could see nothing to indicate the existence of any port, for the coast appeared parched and barren. A fleet of nearly one hundred steamers and sailing vessels lay at anchor about four miles off this uninviting stretch of land. They were of all sizes and descriptions in various stages of discharging and loading. It was a windy day and most of the vessels had storm trysails set, to keep their heads to the choppy sea. Those that had discharged their cargoes were so light they were veered by the current into the trough of the sea, where they rolled and tumbled so their keels could almost be seen. Their bottoms had heavy coatings of sea grass and barnacles, showing that they had been at anchor for a long time.

The sight of these vessels was disturbing to Watson, for he had hoped to make a fast run with a load of cotton across the Gulf to Cuba. His hopes were further dampened by his own mate, who had been at this place the previous winter and who now recognized many of the vessels which he had seen at that time, waiting for freight, with apparently little difference in their stage of loading.

When he went ashore, Watson discovered that his forebodings were well founded. He had left the *Rob Roy* anchored inside the fleet of larger vessels, for the pilot who had come on board told him that he could not take the vessel in over the bar until about ten o'clock the next morning when it would be high water. So Watson decided to go upriver to Matamoros on board a small steamer which was leaving that afternoon. He had two ends in view: one was to enter his vessel officially at the port of Matamoros; the other was to find out what was going on and why so many vessels were lying idle at the mouth of the Rio Grande. At a place called Bagdad he saw several small schooners about the same size and class as his own and he thought it strange that they chose to discharge and load their cargoes there instead of going up the river direct to Matamoros. But it was not long before he found the answer. In his book called *The Adventures of a Blockade Runner*, Watson describes the course of the Rio Grande: "The river flowing through a level country was exceedingly tortuous, and many of the turns were so sharp that the steamer, though of no great length, could not be steered around them, but often had to butt up against the banks, which caused her head to bound off and push her round, and by backing and repeating this several times, she succeeded in getting round the corners. This showed that it would have been almost impossible to have sailed up, and none seem to have attempted it except some very small vessels, which worked up with the help of oars."

After having deposited the *Rob Roy's* register and the crew list and a copy of the manifest of the cargo with the British consul, Watson went to the Mexican customhouse and officially entered his vessel with the aid of a local broker. Afterward, while waiting for the steamer to leave down-river, Watson had an opportunity to look over the town of Matamoros and call on some of the merchants to see what his prospects were for selling his cargo and loading cotton.

He took a dislike to the place for a very uncomfortable reason: "The whole town was enveloped in a cloud of dust. By the long drought the soil on the roads and streets had by the enormous traffic been ground into a fine powder, which covered them to the depth of several inches; this was whirled about by the wind in every direction, and as windows and doors had to be kept open on account of the heat, no place was free from dust. Men looked like millers with clothes, hair and beards saturated, so that it was difficult to recognize one from another. Horses and mules shook their heads to throw the dust out of their ears, while the dust adhering to their perspiring hides made them appear all of one color."

Inside the houses and stores all the furniture and counters were covered with dustcloths. Watson recorded wryly, "I thought there must certainly be some strong inducement for people to live in such a place."

The houses themselves were nondescript, mostly one story in height with flat roofs. Watson noticed that many of the walls were pitted and scarred with bullet holes. Upon asking how this happened, he was told that it was quite usual for some revolutionary party to shoot up the town. When he inquired of an old resident if many of the citizens had died in these raids, the man replied, "Oh, no! they are great people here for shooting the houses; they don't shoot the people so much."

Every merchant that Watson talked to agreed that he could not have chosen a worse time to sell his cargo and load cotton.

He had come just too late. A great deal of business had been transacted recently, but it was now all over because the drought had completely halted all transport across the plains. Everyone hoped that a heavy rain would come, fill up the water holes, cause the grass to grow and so revive blockade running.

Several of the businessmen interviewed by Watson told him that they were expecting cotton from Texas and would prefer to ship it direct to Havana on a small vessel such as the *Rob Roy*. They added that if he could afford to wait until the rains came, he might do quite well. When that might be, no one had any idea.

On the following day, Watson returned to Bagdad and was relieved to find that his schooner had been safely brought in over the bar and was moored along the riverbank in a snug place. The big problem was to sell the cargo. The prospects were cheerless in the extreme, especially when he gazed at the immense piles of goods that had been landed from the other ships and lay wasting. The enormous charges for lighterage, when added to the freight, port dues and import duties, often exceeded the value of the goods themselves. In many cases the owners had disowned and abandoned the merchandise altogether and told those who had made the charges to take the stuff and go to the devil. "In fact," says Watson, "everything seemed to be in a state of chaos . . . everyone trying to grab what he could, and many schemes there were to make money out of the crisis."

Although Watson clearly recognized the bad situation he was in, he knew of no other port where he might go to sell his cargo. The only course open, he decided, was to "lie still and keep my cargo on board and wait to see if trade would revive again."

While waiting, he began to learn something of the way in which the Confederate government obtained large quantities of cotton for shipment abroad. He relates that some months previously the Confederate treasury in the Texas district was getting low and needed replenishing. To do this it was decided to "buy" a large number of bales of cotton and have it shipped from Mexico by way of Brownsville and Matamoros. "It was purchased," he says, "by what was called pressing, that is by forcibly taking possession of it on the plantations and paying the owners in Confederate money, or by a warrant on the Confederate treasury at a price fixed by the government."

The price paid for this cotton was usually high. But since payment was always made in Confederate currency or treasury warrants, some planters who had lost faith in the Southern cause were reluctant to accept the deal or else tried to sell at a low price for specie or take it to Brownsville on their own account. But the Confederate officials would not go along on any such scheme. If a planter refused their terms, they seized his cotton anyway. In any case, all cotton going out of Texas across the ferry to Matamoros required an exit permit from the Confederate States government.

The business of forcing cotton from the plantations was in charge of young Army officers working for what was called the Cotton Bureau. Watson characterizes them as generally of the stay-at-home class who had received their appointments through favoritism, preferring that kind of duty to fighting in the field. He recalls that they were often "pompous and overbearing, and endowed more with a sense of their own importance than business tact or discretion." Many of the officials thought of themselves as armed with absolute powers. It made little difference to them *what* cotton they seized. They grabbed what was handy, along with a sufficient number of mules or oxen to convey it to Brownsville.

The highhanded methods used by one of these arrogant young officers did not turn out as successfully as he anticipated. At this time there was an English agent who had brought a large quantity of merchandise into Texas, sold it at a good price and invested the proceeds in cotton. He loaded the cotton into wagons and started east across the plains. He had only gone a few miles when the teamsters refused to go further because word had reached them that there was no water ahead because of the drought. While the British owner of the cotton was having a heated argument with the teamsters, a couple of Confederate Cotton Bureau officers rode up. They promptly took possession of the entire lot of cotton in the name of the Confederate States government. It was of little use to protest, the officer blandly told the Britisher, for "the cotton was needed for the public service, which was paramount to all other rights." He tossed a receipt to the owner and told him to go to the office of the Cotton Bureau, where he would be paid—in Confederate money. Meanwhile the teamsters had deserted. This did not deter the determined Confederate official. He seized oxen and mules wherever he could find them and set out for Brownsville. After strewing the way with beasts that died from thirst, he finally reached his destination, mightily pleased with himself.

Since he was in charge of government cotton, he had no trouble getting a permit to take it out of the country and it was soon across the Rio Grande and piled up in Matamoros.

During all this time, the former owner of the cotton had followed the trail of the Cotton Bureau officer all the way to Brownsville and across the ferry to Matamoros. Here he confronted the Confederate and waved his original bill of sale under his nose, telling him in forceful language that it was mighty nice of him to have conveyed the cotton all the way across the plains and that now he need not give himself any more trouble but simply turn over the shipment.

"What the devil do you mean by that?" the Confederate officer demanded.

The Englishman pointed across the river to Brownsville and retorted, "You had it all your own way over there, but I have all the say here."

It now dawned on the official that he was on Mexican soil and that his commission had no authority whatever. The fellow apparently failed to realize what a difference the crossing of that ferry made.

An old Texan who lounged near by and had heard everything that took place and who had been disgusted by the tyranny exercised by the military, remarked to the young officer, "Ah, Mr. Ballroom Buttons, that old ferryboat has shaved your hair off," referring to Samson's lack of strength after he was deprived of his long locks.

Refusing to admit defeat, the Confederate officer protested to the Mexican customs officials. Logically enough, they would not recognize any other title to ownership than that of the Englishman, especially since his bill of sale corresponded to the marks and numbers on the bales.

After waiting for weeks for the rains to come, and with them cotton shipments from the interior, Watson made up his mind that there was no use staying around the Rio Grande any longer. So he shipped a new crew and headed for the Brazos River in Texas. In running the blockade it was not the custom on the Gulf to clear for the blockaded port, but rather for some port beyond, or in the direction of the blockaded port. This was to make the clearance easier. It did not contribute anything to the safety of the vessels, for the Federals watched and took note of each vessel that had run the blockade and would seize her, no matter what port she was cleared for. So Watson cleared for New Orleans, intending to use that port as a back door and last resource if he could not get into any Texas port. His plan was to head for New Orleans on a direct course, sailing past the blockaded Texas ports and run into one of them if an opportunity offered. Watson's choice of the Brazos River as a likely spot was because he had been told that no war vessels were anchored off the river mouth. This information proved to be false. He soon sighted two fast sailing vessels cruising back and forth, each armed with long-range guns. One of the craft was a barque, the other a three-masted schooner. The weather was foul, with heavy rain squalls. As the *Rob Roy* sighted the Confederate forts that guarded the entrance to the Brazos, a Federal gunboat hove in sight and opened fire. At first the shots fell short, but as the steamer came nearer, ricocheting round shot struck the vessel under the counter at the waterline. Fortunately for the *Rob Roy* and her crew, the water shallowed sharply and the gunboat could not pursue. After running up the river a mile or so, Watson careened his schooner on a sand bar, repaired the damage (which turned out to be slight) and anchored in the stream. Later they proceeded up as far as Columbia, where Watson left the vessel and went by train to Houston.

The service was irregular and the rolling stock and locomotives were so worn out from hard wear that the trains could not make more than fifteen miles an hour. In Houston, Watson found that he had to go to Galveston to report the arrival of the vessel and deposit the ship's papers with the British consul.

Galveston was in a dilapidated condition. Watson observed, "It had evidently been a prosperous place, but it was now virtually in ruins, and the grass was growing in the streets." Galveston had been taken by the Federal forces about a year previously, and had subsequently been retaken after a desperate battle by the Confederates, under General Magruder. The temporary earthworks across the streets and passes, the torn-up wharves, and the sunken war vessels in the harbor and bay remained the same as at the close of the struggle. Some of the Federal war vessels which had been captured lay at anchor, among which was the paddle sloop *Harriet Lane*.

One of the first things that Watson discovered in Texas was the absence of specie, for no gold or silver coin was in circulation. There was nothing but Confederate scrip. At this time a U.S. silver dollar bought twenty to thirty dollars' worth of Confederate currency. Watson looked at this money with a jaundiced eye, remarking, "Of course it was the circulating medium, and suited for marketing and domestic purposes, and, being declared by the existing Government to be legal tender, all articles were sold high in proportion, as no one dared refuse it or dared say or do anything to depreciate its value. Some, having implicit confidence in the ultimate success of the Confederate States, still valued it, and, as is too often the case in such times, the credulous masses were led astray by political jobbers who heralded reports of great Confederate victories and the assurance of the speedy triumph of the South, and were ready to execute summary vengeance on any one who should in any way attempt to depreciate the value of the national currency, whilst they themselves were using Confederate scrip to buy specie, and hoarding the latter away."

Although some of the *Rob Roy's* cargo suffered water damage, due to the shell hole, Watson sold the bulk of it for a good price and placed an order for a shipload of cotton. Now his troubles began in earnest. The Confederate Army seized his vessel and pressed it into service driving piles at the entrance to the Brazos River, for they had heard rumors that Federal war vessels planned an attack. After frantic efforts to recover his schooner, he finally succeeded, thanks to the intercession of General Magruder, who had been petitioned on Watson's behalf by a high-ranking officer.

This misadventure was nothing to what happened next. When the shipment of cotton arrived, no time was lost in loading it. The cotton bales, which had already been through the cotton press which squeezed them down to about half normal size (thus getting many more bales aboard), were jammed tight into the hold by means of screw jacks. In this way, every available square inch was filled with precious cotton. When the loading was finished, Watson and his mate went off to Galveston to clear the vessel. On returning to the river they were astounded to find that the vessel was sunk at her moorings, with only the tops of her rails above water. "I could scarcely realize my unfortunate position," Watson recalled. "Everything I possessed was sunk in the river. I had not even a change of clothing—all had gone down with the vessel."

It was discovered that in squeezing the cotton into the hold, the stevedores had put too much pressure on the screw jacks. This opened the seams in the casing, causing a leak high up in the hold and above the waterline. When the deckload of cotton was put aboard, the vessel was forced deeper into the water which seeped in rapidly during the night when the crew was asleep. After much difficulty and expense, the *Rob Roy* was refloated. Only the outer surfaces of the cotton bales were water-soaked, due to the tight compressing. The hearts of the bales were quite dry. But when Watson figured out the cost of repacking, he decided to take on fresh bales of cotton and try to recoup from the high rate of freight.

At this time, cotton was the one plentiful commodity in Texas. Everything else, including rainfall, was in short supply. The biggest problem (aside from the war itself) that occupied most Texans' minds was how to get the cotton out and bring back everything else that was needed by the Confederate armies and civilians. It was known, of course, that the North was suffering from a dearth of cotton and the Confederate government was bitterly determined that not a bale of the precious stuff should fall into Yankee hands. If the cotton famine in the North could be increased and the war thereby made unpopular, well and good. There was some satisfaction, also, in retaliating for the hardships and privations endured by Southern people and their soldiers because of the strangulation of the blockade. On land, whenever Confederate armies were forced to give ground, they invariably burned all supplies of cotton, regardless of who owned it. The same principle was followed at sea and on all navigable rivers: if a vessel carrying cotton was about to be run ashore and captured it was set afire before the enemy could salvage the ship or cargo. On inbound trips the orders were the same.

At the same time that Watson was having his troubles raising the *Rob Roy*, a powerful Union expedition including gunboats and troop transports appeared off the port of Galveston. They shelled the forts guarding the Brazos River, apparently to draw their fire and ascertain their strength. This was unfortunate for several bockade runners which found themselves boxed in. None escaped. Among them was a small schooner inbound from Cuba, commanded by Captain David McLusky, a Scottish resident of Galveston. He was a canny fellow with a genial disposition and was regarded by the local blockade-running fraternity as something of a daredevil. His resourcefulness in escaping with his vessel from the clutches of the Union Navy is illustrated by the following incident.

Since Captain McLusky's schooner was quite small, it was taken in tow by the Federal gunboat. McLusky and his men were left aboard and two seamen from the gunboat were also put aboard the prize to steer. Then the man-of-war headed for the mouth of the Brazos River and anchored for the night. Trailing astern and securely fastened to its captor by a stout rope was McLusky's little craft. Although the two Union sea-

men had been sent aboard as a watch, they did not like the
order at all and with good reason. It was Christmas time. A
grand party and celebration was going on aboard the Union
gunboat with plenty of grog for all hands.

Years later, in a letter to a friend, Captain McLusky described what happened next: "I sympathized with them in a
pleasant sort of way, saying it was certainly too bad; then as if
suddenly recollecting I said, 'Oh, by the by, I have got some
splendid brandy which I hoped to have drunk at a Christmas
jollification on shore tonight, but this confounded capture has
spoiled all that, and now I suppose that it will be taken from
me; so I think that we may as well drink it as let the officers of
the gunboat get it. We are a prize and we cannot help ourselves,
and we may as well be friendly, and I think Christmas is a time
that people should all be friends; so while they are having their
jollification on the steamer, we will have our little jollification
here: so come away down, boys, and we will drink to a Merry
Christmas, and peace and good will towards men.' "

It was a dark night with weather most foul. The wind was
whipping the open roadstead into whitecaps and the little
schooner was swinging wildly on her towline about fifty yards
from the gunboat. Nevertheless sounds of revelry came across
the water. After scarcely any hesitation, the two Union seamen
ducked below, sat down in McLusky's tiny cabin and accepted
a drink. McLusky thoughtfully instructed his mate to go on
deck and keep watch in place of their Yankee guests, just in case
a hail should come from the gunboat.

"The brandy was plied freely," McLusky related in his letter,
"and cigars and tobacco were brought in. I began to spin 'em
some interesting yarns and the drink soon made goodwill
amongst us."

Meanwhile the mate had passed the word to the crew what was
going on and told them to stand by.

By midnight both Union sailors were helplessly drunk and
lying asleep on the cabin floor. But McLusky did not act yet.
He waited until the middle of the midwatch when the sound of
revelry aboard the gunboat had died away and all was still except

the whine of the wind in the rigging. As McLusky peered through the gloom he saw that a rain squall was sweeping to windward of the steamer. Only four miles away lay the bar at the mouth of the Brazos River and safety. Quickly McLusky returned to the cabin and drew the cutlasses from the belts of the sleeping Yankees and hid them. By the time he returned on deck, the black squall had obscured the gunboat. McLusky cast off the towline and his schooner drove away through the squall. The crew smartly set sail and the small vessel was soon scudding toward the river mouth. There was no sound or movement from the Union gunboat. It was now but a shadowy outline in the murk. Not a gun was fired. All hands, including the deck watch, were evidently sunk in deep and alcoholic slumber.

Since McLusky knew the entrance to the river and the bar like the palm of his hand, he had no difficulty in reaching the Brazos, hailing the forts and identifying his vessel. With a spanking wind astern he sailed straight up the river until he reached a patch of woods where he came to the bank and made fast to the trees.

The rest of the story can best be told in McLusky's own words, for he wrote them with relish:

The two men having been so very drunk had never woke up and were still asleep on the cabin floor. I thought to have a joke over it, and determined not to disturb them until daylight, and the kindling of a fire on the bank—as was the usual custom, I made some coffee, and some men coming up from the forts to learn the news, I confided to them the night's adventure, and told them that the two men from the gunboat were still asleep on the cabin floor, and I wanted to have some fun over it . . .

As soon daylight began to appear, I slipped softly down to the cabin and threw myself on the sofa which was used as a bed, all the others keeping perfectly quiet.

At length one of the men waking up from his drunken sleep began to look around with a sort of stupefied gaze. A little light was coming down through the skylight but the high trees around made it still dark in the small cabin.

I now gave a yawn and looked around.

"Oh, I am mighty thirsty," I said. "Is there anything left in that bottle?" [The bottles had been replaced on the cabin table as they had been on the previous night.]

The man rose up and approached the bottle.

"Help yourself," I said, "and then hand some to me."

The man helped himself to a good pull, and then as his memory was cleared, he cried to his companion to get up quick and be on deck that they might be seen on the alert.

"It is surely not blowing hard," I said. "It must have calmed down."

"It must be dead calm," said the man as he ascended the little cabin stair.

Suddenly he uttered a loud exclamation and half tumbled back down the cabin stair.

"What is the matter?" I asked with the greatest simplicity.

"What is the matter!" cried the man. "We have got into hell or some other seaport!"

I jumped up, pretended great astonishment and ran on deck. The men . . . finding themselves in the midst of thick forests, their astonishment was great. . . . They at first imagined it to be some hallucination; but on coming more to their senses and finding their cutlasses gone, they did not know what to think of it; and seeing men standing by laughing, they thought that some devil's trick had been played. For the last thing they would have thought of was that the schooner could, or would, attempt to escape from under the guns of their man-of-war.

Their eyes were soon opened, however, when a corporal's guard from the forts came to take them along as prisoners.

During the last months of 1863 the blockade along the Texas coast became even tighter than before and by January 1864 the freight rate on cotton had risen to 14 cents a pound delivered to any neutral port. In addition, the owner of the vessel was given a bonus of $7 per bale for all cotton carried through the blockade. Considering the small size of the centerboard schooners that transported the precious cargo it was remarkable how much cotton they were able to carry. In the case of the *Rob Roy*, she carried eighty-one bales in her hold and ninety on deck, making a total of 171 bales. Since each bale weighed approximately five hundred pounds, the freight on the total cargo, if safely landed, amounted to $11,970; adding the $7 bonus per bale, the total income from one voyage of a week's duration amounted to $13,167. So it is quite understandable that skippers of fast schooners were willing to take long chances to elude the Union cruisers and gunboats.

In stowing the deckload, the bales were stood on their ends and dunnaged high up from the deck so that the water would run freely under them when the vessel was heeled over. This made the deckload about six feet high and it was necessary to work the vessel from on top of the cotton bales.

By the time that William Watson was ready for his first trip through the blockade, the whole of the Texas coast had been sealed off by Federal forces with the exception of the Brazos River where the *Rob Roy* lay. Brownsville and Corpus Christi had been occupied in November. The whole of the Mississippi was also in possession of the Union Army and Navy. Texas was not only close to being cut off from the Confederate States east of the Mississippi River, but her most important communication with the outer world through Mexico was in imminent danger. Galveston was so closely blockaded by a Federal squadron that entrance or exit was considered impossible and up to this time no vessel of any sort had tried to get through. This situation made the Brazos River the only possible export point for Confederate cotton. Even so, it was only the little centerboard schooners that could safely navigate those shallow waters.

One Federal steamer and sometimes two were stationed to the south of the river. But they had to operate three to four miles from the mouth, because of the shoals and sand bars. So it was possible for a light-draught sailing vessel to creep along the shore on a dark night and pass in or out, providing of course the captain knew the location of the bar or had a pilot aboard.

The Confederate government was desperately anxious to export as much cotton as possible. It also wanted to conserve the few vessels in Texas capable of running the blockade. The escape of Captain McLusky apparently had made quite an impression on General Magruder and the Chief of the Marine De-

partment in Texas, for they arranged to provide captains of
blockade runners with commissions or warrants showing them to
be officers in the Confederate Naval Service. "Such a commission," records Watson, "in event of their vessel being captured,
would serve them as a warrant in any attempt they might make
to recapture her should an opportunity present itself, and such
certificates . . . were granted to such men as the General might
approve of. I did not well see how any power under this certif-
icate could be acted upon, or carried out under a neutral flag.
[He was still under British registry.] However, it might be
acted upon after the vessel was captured, and the enemy had
placed their flag upon her."

Since no oath or other obligation was required, Watson
thought it a good idea to apply for one of the unorthodox "commissions" and was promptly handed one by General Magruder.
It was simple and brief, merely stating that William Watson was
an Acting Master in the Confederate States Navy and was to
be recognized, obeyed and respected as such.

Before setting out on his risky voyage, Watson had been
gathering all the information he could on the plans and movements of the blockading vessels. He discovered that one of the
big problems of the Union war vessels was coal. It was in such
short supply that all of the ships could not be on patrol at the
same time. Steamers not on patrol would lie at anchor near
shore with banked fires. The others would make short cruises
up and down. Further out in the Gulf the patrolling was done
by fast, well-armed sailing craft flying the Stars and Stripes.

Everything was now ready for the departure of the *Rob Roy*.
The nights were dark, for the new moon was nearly due. Two
other centerboard schooners, *Mary Elizabeth* and *Hind*, were
going to make the attempt in concert with Watson's craft. The
only thing that was wrong was the weather. It continued calm,
with scarcely a breath of wind—and this was not what Watson
wanted. He was waiting for a stiff norther so that he could
make the run under full sail.

At last the storm came, suddenly and with great fury, about
five o'clock in the afternoon. After the pilot came aboard the

Rob Roy, Watson and the two other captains waited until the menacing gunboats were hidden by the darkness. Then they hoisted sail and got under way. Eleven hours of darkness lay before them and they reckoned that if they could make ten knots an hour they would be 110 miles off the coast by daylight. The three small vessels moved cautiously under low canvas so that they could not easily be detected against the dark backdrop of the land.

All three cleared the bar safely, then were lost to each other in the blackness. The *Rob Roy* stood along the coast to westward, keeping in about two fathoms of water for the first three miles, then shook out the reefs from her sails and headed out to sea. As she got further off the land the wind increased and the little vessel surged through the water at a speed that some of the crew believed to be twelve knots. As Watson had no log line, he could not determine his vessel's pace. But everyone was exhilarated and happy that the first dangerous stage of the voyage was past.

Two nights later a dead calm overtook the *Rob Roy* and before daylight broke they took all sail off her and let her drift under bare poles. This was a precaution against discovery by an enemy vessel. It was well that they did so, for when the light got better a large square-rigged vessel was observed lying becalmed to the northward, about nine miles away. Watson thought she was some craft homeward bound from Matamoros, as they were near to such a course. The mate disagreed. He was sure she was a Union man-of-war.

As it turned out, he was right. As the two vessels drifted closer, those on board the *Rob Roy* identified the stranger as the *John Anderson*, a large armed barque, known to be a fast sailer. Soon the wind came to life again and the chase began. *Rob Roy* kept going about, forcing the enemy to do the same. The little schooner thus had an advantage since she could go about without losing an inch of ground while her opponent could not do so without making sternboard. Before the Federal vessel could gather headway, the *Rob Roy* would gain considerable distance.

But the Federal barque was not to be shaken off so easily. She

began making longer tacks and gradually began gaining. Then
the wind died away altogether. The two vessels lay helpless,
seven miles apart. Soon Watson and his crew grimly watched
the Union barque lower her boats and send them off toward the
Rob Roy with the plain purpose of taking her by the board.

"We got out the sweeps," Watson recalled, "and pulled with
great vigor . . . in hopes that a breeze would spring up again
before they reached us. There was, however, a slight sea against
us and we did not make great headway."

When the Federal boats had come within a mile, Watson's
crew decided that the game was up and there was no use straining at the sweeps any more. Watson thought so too and went
below to get a packet of dispatches entrusted to him by General
Magruder. These had been weighted with chain so that when
tossed overboard they would immediately sink to the bottom.
Soon the small boats had approached to within a quarter of a
mile and Watson watched the Union tars pulling with might and
main to reach their prize. Just then the breeze stirred and all
hands aboard the *Rob Roy* sprang to the sweeps with renewed
hope. Gradually the schooner began to move through the water,
picking up speed as the wind freshened. The boats were almost
within hail now, and the men in them were still pulling for dear
life. But it was no use. The *Rob Roy* was now heeling handsomely to the breeze. An angry but harmless fusillade from the
boats sped her on.

A few days later, Mount Tamana hove in sight over the western horizon and before nightfall the *Rob Roy* sailed safely up the
river to Tampico, Mexico. After the usual delays and red tape
with the authorities, Captain Watson received permission to discharge the schooner's cargo. While this was going on there was
a sudden burst of rejoicing in the city, for the news had just
reached Tampico that Maximillian had accepted the imperial
crown of Mexico. The mayor instantly declared a holiday and
the streets were decorated with flags and bunting. Cathedral
bells were rung and salutes fired from shore batteries. The populace never seemed tired of shouting *vivas* in the streets and
plazas.

While talking that day with one of the prominent Tampico merchants, Captain Watson asked him if he thought that the people were sincere in their demonstrations of joy.

"Sincere enough for the moment," the Mexican announced with a shrug, "but they would do the same tomorrow for President Juárez if he should come in and drive out the French and unseat Maximillian."

At the end of several more days in port, the *Rob Roy* sailed for Havana with a small cargo and ballast and arrived safely after an uneventful voyage.

At this time Havana was crowded to overflowing with businessmen, speculators, gamblers and shady characters of all sorts, from Southern and Northern states, Great Britain and Europe. All of them had the same end in view—to make money out of blockade running with a minimum risk to themselves and their capital. Their main hope was to feed on reckless blockade runners who had made successful voyages—had more money than their wildest dreams had conjured and were in the mood to spend it. Speculators and sharpers were so itchy to do business that as soon as the approach of a vessel which looked like a blockade runner was signaled from the Moro, a whole flotilla of small boats would put out into the harbor. Every occupant had something to sell. Most of these characters professed great "sympathy" for the Southern cause and proclaimed in loud voices that they were only too anxious to be of service to the captain and crew of a vessel that had so gallantly run the blockade.

Before the spring of 1864 most of the blockade runners plying between Havana and Gulf ports were unwilling to run a heavy risk on the western voyage by taking on a valuable cargo. It suited them better to run in a light cargo, knowing that they could always get a heavy load of cotton for the eastbound trip which would yield them astronomical profits.

But now the Confederate government stepped in and issued ironbound regulations, making it mandatory for blockade runners entering Southern ports to bring in full and valuable cargoes of war supplies. Consequently, Havana warehouses were brimming with all sorts of merchandise which their owners pro-

claimed were "expressly selected for the Confederate market . . .
all available at a low price because we wish the Confederate
States to get the benefit of them." This was sheer hypocrisy,
for these sharpers had only one aim: to sell their goods and get
their money without running any risk whatever. It was the
blockade runners who had to take the chances.

A favorite rendezvous of the blockade-running fraternity was
a large café called the Louvre, just outside the city walls. By
common consent the place was considered neutral ground where
men of the North and South could meet, exchange courtesies and
talk.

Captain James Martin, master of the *Calliope*, recorded his
friendly encounter with three Federal naval officers as follows:

"Here," I cried in a laughing way, "come and join us."

The three Federals looked surprised, hesitated a moment and
then came over to the table where I was seated.

"Who are you?" they asked, also laughing. "A blockade
runner?"

"Just that," I answered. "Will you all have a drink with me?"

"All right," said one of the officers, drawing up a chair, "I
never object to meeting a blockade runner."

"Especially at sea, eh?" I rejoined. "And with a good cargo of
cotton."

"You are right," replied the second Federal officer, "although
I sometimes think that if I had not been in the United States
Navy I would have been a blockade runner myself."

"And I too," said the third.

After the drinks arrived, the conversation became more general and Captain Martin asked them what had happened to Captain Corbin of the *Leander*, who had been captured several
months ago. They did not know of the case, but thought it most
likely since the capture was off Mobile that the prize had been
taken to Key West and the captain would be there.

"But cannot he get away from Key West?" Martin asked.
"Are not steamers often going from there to New Orleans?"

"Yes, but it is possible that he may be detained at Key West,"
the Federals answered.

"Detained! What for? You don't imprison blockade runners, I'm sure."

"No, but they are sometimes detained as witnesses to give evidence against the vessel, when the trial comes on in the prize court."

"How long would he be detained?" Martin demanded.

"Until the court sits, and that is uncertain; they are sometimes not in a hurry and generally like to keep a blockade runner a good long while. It keeps him out of mischief."

Captain Martin found out from these friendly enemies that the officers and crew of a captured blockade runner fared much better if they were taken to New Orleans instead of Key West. In New Orleans they were never held very long, as prize courts sat frequently. Also because New Orleans was a large city full of people from all parts of the world, the captured officers and men generally met with friends who would aid them, "whereas Key West was little better than a sand-bank and they were there little better than in a penal colony."

Although blockade-running captains and their vessels were in danger of pursuit, capture or destruction from almost the moment they left port, few of them had any personal animosity against the officers of the United States Navy. They knew these officers were only carrying out the orders of the Federal government in the face of wind, weather and the blackness of the night. Captain Martin and his fellow runners had a great respect for them. He found them, "like most of the officers who took a brave and active part on either side of the war, to be high-toned, honorable and sensible men, and quite free from the rancor and hatred indulged in by narrow-minded political partisans on both sides, who while keeping out of danger themselves, and often becoming rich by war jobbing, kept pouring forth the most scurrilous opprobrium against their respective opponents and inciting them to cruelties and outrage."

For years prior to the Civil War, a great deal of commerce between the United States and Cuba and the West Indies was conducted by merchant mariners, sea captains who not only owned all or part of their sailing vessels, but also owned all or part of the cargoes they carried. These adventurous skippers loaded their ships with whatever they believed would have a ready sale among West Indian merchants. When the cargoes were sold, the ships were then loaded with rum, molasses, sugar or anything that could be readily sold at the home port.

The same system was used to an even greater extent during the Civil War, except that Confederate agents in Havana and elsewhere saw to it that no cotton was sold to Northerners.

"Trading with the enemy" was an ugly phrase, not even whispered among the Northern seafaring fraternity. Yet it was openly indulged in, although somewhat indirectly. A merchant mariner from a Northern port would carry down a load of foodstuffs or merchandise to Havana and first of all try to make a quick sale to a local merchant who in turn would resell it at a large profit to a blockade runner or an agent of the Confederate government. If the Northerner was unable to sell to a local merchant, he would shop around among blockade runners and try to sell to them direct.

A case in point concerned the captain of a New England brig who brought down a large quantity of fine provisions "on spec." He had sold part of his cargo to Havana wholesalers and was anxious to get rid of what was left quickly and sail for home. He sought out the captain of a blockade runner that was about to try to run in to Galveston. The Yankee offered the runner thirty-six kits of mackerel at one dollar a kit and two dozen small cheeses at a half dollar each. The blockade runner promptly accepted the offer, for the prices asked seemed low. This turned out to be all too true, for when the skipper of the blockade runner returned to his schooner he found that the cargo of provisions he had ordered from a Cuban merchant included mackerel of the very same lot, charged to him at four and a half dollars a kit. Cheeses, identical to those bought from the New Englander, were listed on the Cuban's bill at two and a half dollars each. Such profits were the order of the day among Havana's wholesalers.

About this time several photographers came to Havana and set up studios. It became quite the fashion for blockade runners and other "gentlemen adventurers" and gamblers to have their pictures taken. They then exchanged the small photographs or *cartes de visite*, as they were called, among themselves and collected them in albums.

Captain Watson of the *Rob Roy* and devil-may-care Captain Dave McLusky, being good friends, exchanged *cartes*. Nothing more was thought of it until several weeks later. In the meantime Captain McLusky left Havana and ran his little schooner to the shelter of the Brazos River and then to Tampico, where he sold his cargo of cotton and the vessel as well. Then he took a steamer for Havana in order to buy a larger craft.

A week or so after his arrival at the Cuban capital, McLusky met his friend Watson and they began talking of their plans to make another western run to the Gulf coast. McLusky told Watson that he had no intention of risking $5,000 (the cost of a first-class small schooner) to run to Texas at that time of year. He added, "I have been looking at a thing today that will carry as much cotton as the *Roy Roy* in a foot and a half less water, and I can buy her for $500."

Watson, skeptical, remarked with a smile that even a silver-mounted coffin would cost that much. McLusky shrugged and told his friend to meet him next day at the shipyard and have a look for himself.

If McLusky expected to amaze Watson, he succeeded admirably. What they saw was a flat-bottomed barge, perfectly square at the ends, 75 feet long, with a 22-foot beam. Her bulwarks were six feet high and she was decked over. A long pole served as a bowsprit. There was also a rudder. Her bottom was strongly planked and a heavy log formed the keel and a bottom for the centerboard casing. There were two stubby masts. She was schooner rigged. McLusky claimed that at a distance she would look very much like an ordinary cargo vessel under sail. This strange craft had originally been built and used for carrying cordwood from the Trinity River to Galveston. Watson derisively christened her *Scow*.

In spite of the fact that McLusky had his vessel completely overhauled, adding a small cabin and forecastle, Watson was extremely dubious about his friend's chances of sneaking through the blockade. Yet McLusky was not at all worried. To Watson's bantering he retorted, "We'll see who is the wisest. If you had sold the *Rob Roy* and bought a thing like this for $500, you could have bought a cargo for yourself and had something left over to fall back on. If you got captured your loss would not be so great and if you made the run safely you would get yourself a big load of cotton and have the proceeds all to yourself."

Watson agreed that that was perfectly possible, but the slab-sided craft wouldn't stand much chance against the buffeting of wind and wave. McLusky brushed Watson's warnings aside, remarking that at this time of year the Gulf should be as calm as a frog pond and "the want of wind will be the trouble."

"I see, Dave," Watson said, in recording the conversation, "that, although you have become personally reckless, you still preserve your old Scotch characteristics in being cautious about the bawbees."*

"Ah," replied the skipper of the *Scow*, "you will find that this is the point they all steer by, Scotch and all others; and let me tell you this—keep your vessel always headed for the Almighty Dollar, and lay her course as close to it as you can." With this parting remark McLusky left his friend. They would meet again in Texas, weeks later. In between, Captain Dave McLusky was destined to become the hero of a true drama of the sea that is unique in the annals of blockade running.

Meanwhile the captain of the *Rob Roy* put his vessel in first-class shape for sea and began loading cargo consigned to the Confederate government in Texas. There were cases of Enfield and Belgian rifles with bayonets and accouterments: cavalry sabers, curry combs and brushes, saddlery, ammunition, blankets, clothing, boots and shoes, hardware and other goods. In addition, Watson considered it to be good policy to add special items that were in great demand by Southern civilians and which were absolutely unobtainable in Texas except through blockade runners:

* A small Scottish coin worth about a halfpenny in English money.

coffee, tea, cheese, spices, thread, needles, cloth. "Brandies and wine as well as spiritous liquors were forbidden* to be taken in," Watson declared in his memoirs, "but they were received with great thankfulness if given as donations for the use of the hospitals. All these might be entered as ship's stores."

Upon the advice of several experienced blockade runners, Captain Watson decided to shape for Galveston and take his chances of getting past the Union fleet by maneuvering in the shallow waters of Galveston Bay.

Captains McLusky and Watson sailed from Havana the same night, but they quickly lost sight of each other in the darkness.

The voyage of the *Rob Roy* was long and tedious, interspersed with variable winds and periods of flat calm. Before daylight each day he ordered all sail lowered, regardless of the wind. The vessel remained under bare poles until nightfall when she resumed her journey. It would have been very difficult for a prowling cruiser to have seen the little schooner under these conditions.

As Watson's craft crept toward Galveston a steamer was sighted. She looked like a United States naval vessel, but she passed within five miles without sighting the *Rob Roy*.

Not long afterward a small schooner hove in sight dead ahead. Watson identified her as the *Sylvia*, a blockade runner that had left Havana at the same time as the *Rob Roy*. Instead of making her way toward the land, as might be expected, the *Sylvia* changed course and pointed toward the other craft. This maneuver puzzled Watson and made him suspicious. The mate opined that perhaps the *Sylvia* had "changed captain and crew since leaving Havana and is now in the hands of the Yankees and they intend to make a prize of us."

Watson agreed and hauled up at once and kept to windward of the *Sylvia*. Then followed a sailing contest between the two swift schooners, whose size and design were similar. Watson

* This regulation was not in force during the early years of the war. Neither was it followed by blockade runners sailing to Wilmington at any time.

was not so much fearful of being overhauled as that the wind
might die. He knew that the *Sylvia* carried a large boat which
could be used with an armed crew to board the *Rob Roy* if
indeed she was now operated by the United States Navy. "As
neither vessel had hoisted their flag," Watson wrote of the incident, "I thought there would be no harm in making some display
of force." Apparently he believed that the "commission" he held
in the Confederate States Navy gave him such right. Yet his
crew were all civilians. Early in the war the Federal government
had declared that officers and crew of a blockade runner who
resisted capture by force of arms would be treated as pirates.
But this did not deter Watson. He called his men together and
told them he believed the *Sylvia* was on her way to New Orleans
in charge of a prize crew, and

they would like to make a prize of us if we would submit to go
quietly with them, but if they saw that we were not willing to
submit and had arms to protect ourselves, they would not make
any attempt, as there would not be more than six of them, and
there were eight of us, all as good men and well armed; and all I
would ask them to do would be to make a display of arms on
deck, which I had no doubt would be sufficient to warn them off,
as they knew that most of the captains of blockade runners now
held commissions in the Confederate service. The mate then told
them that a prize crew on a captured vessel had tried to board a
schooner from Mobile, and the crew of the schooner had beaten
them back with handspikes.

The men readily agreed; some expressed their determination
to fight rather than allow themselves to be captured. . . . We then
opened a case of Enfield rifles. In this we had some difficulty, as
the boxes were lined with tin, but we got out a sufficient number,
and brought them on deck and fixed the bayonets, every man
taking one except the man at the helm.

We were now to the northward of the *Sylvia*, and our course
clear before us, and the *Sylvia* to leeward. So I put the vessel
upon our course again, crossing the bows of the other vessel at
about a quarter of a mile distance.

We now made a display of our force in the best way we
could devise, taking care that at least seven men might be seen,

each with a rifle and fixed bayonet. This had the desired effect, and we soon saw the *Sylvia* luffing up and sailing away to eastward.

Several days later, after a tortuous passage through the shallow channels to windward of Galveston, and running aground several times, the *Rob Roy* was met by a Confederate guard boat and brought safely to anchor under the protecting guns of shore batteries. The voyage had taken eighteen days.

As if to make up for lost time, things began to move fast. The cargo was unloaded with utmost speed, for the Confederate armies were in dire need of the guns and ammunition brought in by the little schooner. Watson sent ashore urgent dispatches for General Magruder along with some delicacies and several bottles of liquor. Shortly afterward he was summoned to the general's quarters. His visit throws an interesting sidelight on the personality of this doughty Confederate warrior.

When Watson entered Magruder's room he found the general only half dressed and spluttering and swearing at one of his boots which was hurting his corns as he pulled it on his foot. Since he greeted Watson with good humor, the skipper knew that the food and drink he had sent had already arrived. Magruder's aide-de-camp had opened one of the bottles "and was preparing something which was known at that time by the name of 'gin cocktail.' He cast his eye towards me in a laughing way and by way of acknowledgment said, 'This is some of your importations, Captain.'

"I knew there was a penalty for bringing in spiritous liquors, and it was declared contraband, and I replied that it was part of my ship's stores, which I had sent ashore as a donation to the hospital, and I hoped in so doing I had committed no breach of law or regulations.

" 'Oh no,' was the reply, 'when it is understood to be for the use of the medical department; and the gift was a very valuable one and greatly appreciated;' and he added with a smile, that both he and the General 'were on the sick list at present.'

"Having taken their cocktails, the General got his boot on all right and the cocktail seemed to have quite allayed the pain of the corns. He then congratulated me on my safe arrival and having looked over the list of the cargo, he said it was most valuable and came most opportune, and he would like to get the arms delivered as soon as possible."

A few days later Watson was surprised to see the irrepressible Captain McLusky climb aboard the *Rob Roy*.

"I have come to claim that dozen of brandy from you," he told his friend.

Surprised, Watson denied ever wagering any brandy. McLusky finally admitted that he had not, but "you will give it to me all the same because I have lost all mine." He went on to say that he also wanted another *carte* of Watson's as well as the photographs of several other notorious blockade runners because the original pictures had "fallen into the hands of the Yankees with all my clothes, liquors and other valuables."

Captain McLusky then related his encounter with the Union Navy which is not only unquestionably true but has no known parallel in the history of the Civil War. That the affair was effectively hushed up by a choleric and mortified Union commodore is not to be wondered at in the light of what happened to his prize crew at the hands of McLusky and his men aboard his "seagoing cigar box."

Captain Dave was not much of a navigator. He knew how to get his latitude from a meridian altitude, but he never carried a chronometer and usually figured his position by dead reckoning. As the *Scow* lumbered across the Gulf in the general direction of Texas, the winds were light and easterly, just as he had predicted. Yet he had not made due allowance for the leeway that his flat, slab-sided ark was making. So instead of sighting St. Louis Pass as he intended, he made a landfall about ten miles westward of the Brazos River, his destination.

Soon a Federal gunboat hove in sight and Captain Dave hastily put his craft before the wind, took up his centerboard and pointed for the Texas coast, which was under his lee, hoping to escape by beaching. But his awkward ark was too slow and the gunboat (a steamer) easily overhauled him and he was made a prize. McLusky and his men offered no resistance, the former reckoning no doubt that smooth words and a well-peeled eye would do them all more good.

The commander of the gunboat allowed Captain Dave and his crew to stay on the *Scow*. A prize crew consisting of a Federal lieutenant and six seamen were detailed, with orders to follow the steamer which was going to rejoin the blockading squadron off Galveston. Thereupon the officer in charge of the *Scow* brought her into the wind. Watching closely, Captain Dave noted that the fellow did not put down the centerboard. It was obvious that he had had no experience with a craft of this kind and probably did not even realize that it possessed a centerboard, much less its importance. As for Captain Dave, he chuckled to himself, considering it no part of his duty to instruct the enemy. McLusky also knew from past experience that the first thing that a prize crew usually did was to ransack a captured vessel for liquor and anything else of value which they might appropriate for their own use.

So Captain Dave lost no time in making things easy for the Yankees. He set a large jar of rum on top of the cargo in the hold, making sure that the bulkhead between the hold and the forecastle could be broken down with little trouble, especially for thirsty men in search of a drink.

Meanwhile McLusky and his men sat on deck with their seabags, pretending to be tired and glad of a rest. In a whispered interchange with his mate, Captain Dave told him to look sharp for a chance to recapture the vessel and to so advise the others.

The prize crew had come aboard armed with cutlasses and the lieutenant carried a revolver. When the seamen set about working the vessel they stuck their weapons in the belaying rack at the mainmast, for it was awkward to haul on lines with cutlasses in their belts.

All this time the *Scow* was moving crabwise and making great leeway because her centerboard was not down. In attempting to correct this, the Federal lieutenant kept luffing and hauling aft the sheets. This merely checked the vessel's speed and did not stop her rapid drift to leeward. Captain Dave and his mate also noticed that the seamen were making more trips into the fore-castle than might be expected and it did not take much guessing what the attraction was. In an hour or so most of them were weaving about decks and it was not because the vessel was pitching and rolling, for she was not. The rum jar in the hold was doing its work for the Southern cause.

After a quick survey of the coast ahead, Captain Dave saw to his joy that the *Scow* had sailed and drifted abreast of the Brazos River and was not more than six miles from shore. As far as he could see, there was no Yankee vessel patrolling off the river mouth.

"Some of the lieutenant's men were now pretty reasonably drunk," Watson observed in recounting his friend McLusky's adventure. "The gunboat was a long way ahead. The lieuten-ant was getting uneasy; and he was looking after her as if he would signal, when Dave, making a sign to his men, sprang upon the lieutenant, pinned his hands to his sides, and got hold of his revolver, while his mate, with the rest of his crew, grappled with the prize crew and got hold of their cutlasses; others seized handspikes, and a desperate fight took place. While Dave was struggling with the lieutenant, one of the prize crew who was a Negro, drew a knife and rushed up to stab Dave in the back; but just as he raised his hand for the blow he was felled to the deck with a handspike by the mate. The fight lasted for some time, but the prize crew was overpowered, some badly wounded but none killed.

"The lieutenant struggled hard, but Dave held him down on the deck, while he threatened Dave with the awful consequences of the act. In the meantime some of Dave's men had put the helm hard up, and eased off the sheets and the vessel was put before the wind, heading for the shore. Suddenly a gun was heard from the gunboat which signified that she had observed that something was wrong.

" 'Do you hear that?' cried the lieutenant who was fairly over-powered. 'For God's sake heave to, or the captain will sink you.'

" 'Let him fire away,' said Dave; 'he is there and I am here.'

"The change in the vessel's course had been observed from the gunboat and as we were now off before the wind, heading towards shore, they knew something must be wrong, and they had put about, and were bearing down upon us. They were, however, about four miles distant and the schooner was before the wind, heading direct for the [Confederate] forts at the mouth of the Brazos River, now about five miles away."

Just when safety seemed in sight, the wind began to die away and McLusky was afraid that the gunboat would overhaul him before he could come within range of the guns of the forts. Soon the wind died altogether and in desperation Captain Dave ordered his men to use the long sweeps he had had made in Havana for just such an emergency. He knew that if he and his men were captured it would go very bad with them all, even to the possible extent of being hanged for "piracy."

Closer and closer steamed the gunboat. It looked to McLusky as if the jig was up. He quickly decided to escape with his crew in the small boat. In no time at all he had it launched and put into it his sea chest and all of his valuables including his boxes of precious brandy. Just then a shot from the gunboat spouted water near by and Captain Dave gave the order to abandon ship. At the same moment a dark shape leaped from the deck and landed on the thwart of the boat. It was the Negro who had tried to stab McLusky. An instant later he cut the painter and the boat started to drift astern. McLusky whipped out the lieutenant's revolver and ran to the taffrail and was about to fire at the black, who cowered on the floorboards. But Captain Dave saw that it was no use, for the small boat had drifted out of range, carrying with it all of McLusky's valuables.

As if in compensation, the breeze came to life again. The centerboard was quickly lowered and the *Scow* picked up speed. Thanks to this unexpected wind and the delay caused by the gunboat stopping to pick up the Negro, the *Scow* managed to move tortoiselike into shallow water where the Federal vessel dared not follow. A little later Captain Dave came within range of the fort's guns and knew he was safe.

After nudging the *Scow* over the bar at the river mouth, Mc-Lusky reported to the Confederate commander of the fort as follows: "I brought you only two Yankees last time. This time I'm doing better, for I have brought you a whole damned Yankee prize crew and one officer."

As a result of careful investigation and questioning, the men from the gunboat were declared lawful prisoners of war. The wounded were sent to the hospital and the others were paroled and sent to board at one of the hotels in Houston with the under-standing that they were to report to the Confederate Marine Department every day.

Some time later Captain Dave received permission from General Magruder to go out to the blockading squadron under a flag of truce in an effort to recover his belongings, most particularly his brandy. He was also going to ask for changes of clothing for the Federal men he had captured. Upon arrival on the quarterdeck of the flagship, McLusky explained his mission to the commodore. When this gentleman realized that he was talking with the very man who had captured the missing prize crew, he was enraged. His face became crimson and he shouted that he would not return any of McLusky's effects. Furthermore, according to Watson's account of the incident, the Union commander accused the blockade runner of piracy, and, if he fell into the hands of the United States authorities, he would be tried and hanged—but Dave was a character, and the commander's threats were lost on him.

"Oh! now Captain," said Dave, "don't put yourself in a passion. Don't you know that I hold a commission in the Confederate States Navy? And if you don't respect that now, you did, not very long ago, when you made a truce here one morning" [referring to the defeat of the Federals at Galveston on the morning of January 1, 1863], "therefore what I did was no piracy, but a lawful act of war; and you know I was very good to your men."

"A little too good, confound you," said the commander, "to make them drunk."

"Oh no, Captain," said Dave, "that is not true. I never offered them a drink; they broke through into the hold and stole it; and you know, Captain, when thieves break through and steal they are always sure to be punished. Such are the ways of Providence, you know. . . . That nigger of yours, who ran away with the boat, and my things in it, and who has told you the whole story about the men getting drunk, he will, no doubt, be lionized by the Abolitionists, and placed on the list for promotion. But I doubt very much if he has told you that he was the cause of the men getting drunk, and the whole trouble that followed."

"How do you make that out?" said the commander. "He did not drink; he was quite sober."

"No," said Dave, "but he was the one that first set about plundering."

Then McLusky related how the Negro had broken down the bulkhead and discovered the jar of rum. As he finished the story Dave remarked:

"So now, I think, for that bit of information you might give me back my things."

"I won't deliver anything to you," said the commander. "That story of yours may be inquired into, but I don't believe a word of it."

"Will you give me back one of my boxes of brandy? I am sure that neither you nor any of your officers have any use for such a thing," said Dave, with a smile of ironical simplicity.

The commander scowled, but made no reply.

"If you do," continued Dave, "I will give half of it to the poor lieutenant, as I know he cannot get a drop ashore."

"He doesn't want it; he doesn't require it," roared the commander. "Confound you and your liquor; it has done too much harm already." And the commodore stalked away.

The boat was still waiting for the captured lieutenant's chest, which was being packed up, when another officer, who had been standing by while Dave was reasoning with the commander, and who, Dave thought, seemed rather to enjoy the story of the Negro breaking into the hold . . . came and talked over the side to Dave in a sort of bantering way.

Dave still asked for his chest—if it was on the commodore's ship, and if they had opened it. The officer said the chest was on board their ship, and they had opened it and taken note of the contents.

"Then," said Dave, "I am sure you would not find anything that would be of any value to you, or afford you any information whatever."

"Oh, I beg your pardon," said the officer; "we have got some valuable information. We have got your *cartes de visite* and also the *figure-heads* [photographs] of some of your blockade-running friends, so that we will be able to identify them when we come across them."

"Oh, you ought not to keep them," said Dave; "they don't belong to me and these gentlemen will be annoyed."

"Oh, tell them to make themselves easy," returned the officer. "We will be very glad to recognize both you and them when we get hold of either of you, and these *cartes* will greatly assist us in tracing you. In the meantime, you can inform Captain M and Captain W that their *cartes*, along with yours, will be honored with a place in the Rogue's Gallery in New York."

The lieutenant's things were now in the boat, and McLusky shoved off. When at a certain distance from the fleet the white flags on the boat and on the ships were hauled down, and the truce was ended. Soon after, Dave came laughing to tell me about the honorable place where my *carte* was to be hung up.

In taking leave of plucky Captain Dave McLusky, it is fitting to quote a toast often given by him and his fellow blockade runners at some of their convivial gatherings:

"Here's to the Confederates that produce the cotton; to the Yankees that maintain the blockade and keep up the price of cotton; and to the Britishers who buy the cotton and pay the high price for it. So three cheers for all three—and a long continuance of the war and success to blockade runners!"

Early in the fall after an argument with his partner who had a half interest in the *Rob Roy*, Captain Watson reluctantly agreed to have his beloved schooner sold at auction. He tried to bid her in at $3,500 but was not successful.

The new owners retained the vessel under British registry but decided to shift her run from Galveston to the Suwanee River on the west coast of Florida. The Suwanee was supposed not to be closely blockaded and was considered an obscure place where there was an abundance of cotton.

The *Rob Roy* sailed from Havana for her new destination about ten days after she changed hands. Her life after that was tragically brief. Reaching the Florida coast, following a three-day run, the pilot could not find the entrance to the Suwanee. While the schooner was cruising up and down searching, the U.S. gunboat *Fox* bore down on her. In panic the pilot ran the *Rob Roy* onto the beach and set fire to the schooner. The crew made their getaway in the small boat. They landed safely down the beach, where George (one of Watson's original crew) stood in sorrow and saw his "good old craft," as he called her, burned to the water's edge.

Now that Captain Watson had no vessel of his own and being unwilling to risk his money on another, he accepted command of the blockade-running steamer *Phoenix*. She was a large, fast propeller-driven ship and he brought her through the Union fleet and into Galveston undamaged. Later he was captain of the steamer *Jeanette*.

General Lee's surrender in April 1865, followed by that of General Johnston, sounded the death knell of blockade running in the Gulf of Mexico. A large number of fast steamers from England and others from Bermuda and Nassau which had lately come to Havana to get into the lush trade were now idle; many never had a chance to make a single trip; others, especially built and fitted out in British ports at huge expense, arrived on the scene when all was over.

In casting up a balance sheet on his trips through the blockade aboard the *Rob Roy*, Captain Watson discovered that he came out just slightly better than when he started. "On my part," he remarks, ". . . I realized more from my wages and bonuses for my services as master than from any trade speculations." As to the business in general, Watson says that it is difficult to estimate what gains or lossses were experienced by those who invested in blockade running. Merchants and speculators who ventured on a large scale in steamers, received immense returns when they made safe voyages in and out of blockaded ports, thanks to the enormous price of cotton and Britain's hungry mills. "On the other hand," he points out, "leaving out altogether the risk of heavy loss in case of capture, the large amount of capital invested, and the great expense of working the ships was a considerable counterbalance. In the case of smaller ventures in schooners, there was less at stake, but the progress was slow, the voyages protracted and attended with more risk and danger."

All in all, he considered that the ones who had the best of the business were the commission merchants, who acted as consignees, agents and brokers, at both ends of the trip. It was they who bought and sold the inward and outward cargoes, furnished stores and did a general commission business without any risk or danger comparable to that of the men who ran the blockade.

Watson closes his narrative with a suggestion of nostalgia when he remarks that in spite of the privations, hazards and anxiety, blockade running in the Gulf was, "on the whole, a rather enjoyable occupation, with something of the zest of yacht-racing—a kind of exciting sport of the highest order."

Those who, like Watson, played the game, usually played it with skill, ingenuity and real courage. And over and beyond the satisfaction in outwitting the enemy was the excitement of the chase and the thrill of escape.

CHAPTER 9

Captain Maffitt,
Prince of Blockade Runners

FEBRUARY 22, 1819, was a gray, stormy day in mid-Atlantic. The British sailing ship rolled and pitched sickeningly but doggedly kept her bowsprit pointed toward the west. Below, in a stuffy cabin, Ann Maffitt, young wife of the Reverend John Newland Maffitt lay still and white; not from sea sickness but from the weariness of childbirth. She had just been delivered of a healthy boy whom she promptly named after his father. Years later this baby, grown to manhood remarked that "since I was born a son of old Neptune, I was duty-bound to offer my allegiance to the sea."

The baby's father, Reverend John Maffitt, was an Irishman— a Methodist minister who had preceded his wife to Connecticut. He was having a hard struggle to make ends meet. When John Newland, Jr., was five years old, he was taken to North Carolina by his uncle, Dr. William Maffitt, apparently to relieve the family of one hungry mouth to feed. Dr. William Maffitt was a prosperous physician who lived at "Ellerslie," a plantation near Fayetteville, North Carolina. Here young Maffitt lived happily and grew strong. Even in those early years he showed a capacity for leadership and displayed traits of character which were to make him the most courageous and successful blockade runner of the Confederacy.

When young Maffitt was thirteen years old, friends of his

father obtained a commission for him as midshipman in the United States Navy. He received his commission in February 1832. In those days, there was no Naval Academy,* and Maffitt was posted direct to the U.S. sloop-of-war *St. Louis* which was about to depart on a cruise to the West Indies. For several years Maffitt served aboard the *St. Louis*, patrolling West Indian waters and visiting the various islands. Early in 1835 he was ordered to the U.S. frigate *Constitution (Old Ironsides)*, at that time flagship of the squadron commanded by Commodore Elliot, which was on the eve of departure for a good-will cruise to the Mediterranean. During this tour of duty Maffitt sent back to his family and friends a series of graphic descriptions of his adventures and visits to the various Mediterranean countries under the title of *Nautilus, or Cruising Under Canvas*. Years later it was published in book form.

After three years on the Mediterranean station, midshipman Maffitt was ordered to the United States aboard the U.S. schooner *Shark*. During the passage home the crew was on the verge of mutiny, having broken into the spirit room and become drunk and aggressive. Young Maffitt, who was on deck at the time, promptly quelled the rioters and helped secure the ringleaders. When he reached the United States he stood for an examination to obtain the rank of Passed Midshipman. He successfully passed the examination and was ordered to the U.S. sloop-of-war *Vandalia* in November 1838. For the next four years, until early in 1842, John Newland Maffitt served aboard various naval vessels along the Atlantic Coast. Then he was transferred to the United States Coast Survey for duty in charting sections of the Atlantic Coast. At this time Professor F. R. Hassler was superintendent of the United States Coast Survey. Under his supervision the project made marked progress in charting the long and intricate coast line from Massachusetts to Louisiana.

Although he did not know it at that time, the then Lieutenant Maffitt was learning details of the coast (particularly North

---

* What is now the United States Naval Academy at Annapolis was founded in 1845 as the Naval School, later reorganized in 1850 as the United States Naval Academy.

Carolina) that were to stand him in good stead years later during the era of blockade running.

As lieutenant commanding the United States Coast Survey schooner *Gallatin*, Maffitt helped chart the shoals in the vicinity of Charleston and then transferred his headquarters to Smithville, North Carolina. This ancient fishing village at the mouth of the Cape Fear River was the site of Fort Johnson, garrisoned by United States troops. Upon arrival at Smithville aboard the *Gallatin* June 1851 he discovered that the village was a favorite summer resort for the society folk of Wilmington and the surrounding area. The officers and families of the Coast Survey were housed at the barracks at Fort Johnson and were heartily welcomed by the summer residents of Smithville.

Since Smithville had few outside interests, Lieutenant Maffitt organized a dramatic company. Under the tactful and energetic supervision of "Manager" Maffitt, a dozen or more plays were produced during the summer of 1852, among them the Gilbert and Sullivan opera "Box and Cox."

Orton plantation* was often the scene of dramatic festivities and lavish entertainment during those halcyon days before the war. Lieutenant Maffitt, in a letter to the Wilmington *Herald* of August 30, 1851, gives a colorful picture of one of these affairs:

About 8 o'clock I arrived at the mansion of my friend and found the house and grounds beautifully illuminated with varigated lights. The large balcony in front was decorated for the ballroom; and in the rear garden a miniature stage was erected, tastefully decorated. The whole forming a *coup d'oeil* calculated to entrance the senses and force upon the mind the conviction that our worthy host held in his possession the famous lamp of Aladdin.

As I was the only stranger present, mine host took some little trouble in escorting me from apartment to apartment and from romantic arbour to romantic retreat until my senses seemed lost in their magic charms. Soft and sweet music from concealed orchestras vibrated upon the atmosphere of the stilly night; the Chinese pagoda that fronted the stage proscenium sparkled with

* A showplace to this day.

a thousand lights that fully disclosed the lovely flowers which bloomed around, relieved by rich clusters of scuppernong grapes sparkling in their emerald garments. I returned again to the ball-room. The Lord of Orton had marshalled the dance. In truth the arrangements were perfect in all their parts. . . . This is a most healthy and delightful resort. It is time that the South should be true to her own interests, even in matters of this kind. Had the amount now spent in the North by citizens of our own and the neighboring state of South Carolina been expended at home in equally as healthy a place, it would be productive of a vast amount of benefit to a class of people that the wealthy are by every patriotic sentiment bound to succor.

After fourteen years of service on hydrographic duty, Maffitt was suddenly and unexpectedly retired in 1857 by a naval commission. The only charge on which his retirement was founded was that his continued service on the Coast Survey and lack of active duty aboard men-of-war rendered him unfit for advancement. He promptly protested and a hearing was ordered. It was a long-drawn-out affair during which many of Maffitt's service friends and acquaintances testified in his behalf. The case was finally settled by a decision of the board to retain Maffitt in the service. He was thereupon restored to duty and placed in command of the U.S. brig *Dolphin*. Part of the blame for Maffitt's difficulties should be placed on the shoulders of President Franklin Pierce and the then Secretary of the Navy, Mr. Dobbin, whose poor administration of the law resulted in 201 officers being stricken from the active service list and consigned to disgrace. Maffitt's case created general indignation throughout the country; so much so that Congress promptly passed remedial laws, and the action of the Naval Board was annulled as well as condemned.

While in command of the *Dolphin*, Lieutenant Maffitt gave chase and captured a sailing vessel which was smuggling African slaves. After the vessel was brought into port she was condemned and sold and the slaves given their freedom. The crew was tried, found guilty and sentenced to prison.

After some months of office duty in Washington during the winter of 1859, Lieutenant Maffitt assumed command of the U.S. steamer *Crusader* and took her to the Coast of Cuba to intercept and capture slavers and pirates. That he was successful in this enterprise is shown by the following newspaper clipping* dated May 27, 1860. It reads in part as follows:

As the U.S. steamer *Crusader* was cruising in the old Bahama Channel, not far from Nuevitas, on the 23d of May, a square-rigged vessel of moderate size was reported from aloft. We immediately stood for her, as no sail is allowed to pass us in these slaver-haunted waters, or even to come in sight, without having her character ascertained. As soon as she found herself an object of pursuit, the strange sail began to behave in such a manner as strongly excited our suspicions, and at length fairly put her helm up and ran in for the shore, thus taking the last and most desperate chance of escape. Unfortunately for her, the wind was so light that she was prevented from effecting her purpose, and we rapidly overhauled her, notwithstanding that she was carrying all her canvas.

The *Crusader* now hoisted English colors and fired a gun to windward, when, after some delay, the bark (for such she proved to be) finally displayed the French flag at the peak. By this time, however, we were so near that we were enabled to see that her hatches were all closely covered over, and as we continued to approach we could even distinguish at intervals the peculiarly loathsome odor of a crowded slave-ship. Under these circumstances it was determined to board her, and accordingly a boat and the English ensign were lowered at the same time, and the American colors were hoisted. No sooner did the *Crusader's* boat leave the side than the bark hauled down the French colors, and as we subsequently learned, threw them and her Portuguese papers overboard together; so that when she was boarded she had neither papers nor colors, and was confessedly without name or nationality.

For a little while there was dead silence on board both ships,

* Though this unsigned account perhaps deliberately avoids singling out the commander, it is very likely that Maffitt wrote it.

though the increasing strong ammoniacal African odor placed beyond all doubt the fact that the bark had under her hatches a cargo of Negroes. And now we began to hear a sort of suppressed moaning, which soon swelled into the unmistakable murmur of many human voices. As our boat reached the side of the bark, and the officer in charge sprang on deck, with a tremendous shout the hatches were forced open from below, and out burst hundreds of self-liberated slaves. As they caught sight of the Stars and Stripes floating so near—which no doubt seemed to these poor wretches like a bright rainbow of promise—they became perfectly frantic with joy. They climbed up all along the rail—they hung on the shrouds—they clustered like swarming bees in the rigging, while from sea to sky rose the wildest acclamations of delight. They danced, and leaped, and waved their arms in the air, and screamed and yelled in a discordant but pathetic concert. There was one thing, however, even more touching than all this outcry of barbaric rejoicing. My attention was attracted to a group consisting of somewhat more than a hundred women, withdrawn apart from the shouting and noisy men. Their behavior was in strong contrast with that of the others, and was characteristic of their sex. Entirely nude, but innocently unabashed, they sat or knelt in tearful and silent thankfulness. Several of them held infants in their arms, and through their tears, like sunshine behind a cloud, beamed an expression of the deepest gratitude and happiness. The men looked as though they had just been raised from despair to the most exultant gladness. The scene of confusion on board the bark, when the negroes found themselves released from the accustomed restraint, baffles all description. They had, of course, all been kept on a very small allowance of food and water during the passage. The first use they made of their liberty was to satisfy their hunger and thirst, which they did by breaking into the bread barrels and water-casks, and then running about eating, drinking, dancing and screaming, all at once.

By this time a detachment of marines arrived from the *Crusader*, and order was at once restored and an organization established. The Negroes were clothed with pieces of canvas, and the captain, supercargo and crew sent on board the *Crusader* as prisoners.

During a passage of 45 days from the Gulf of Guinea, only seven slaves died, which is certainly a very small number.

The passage from Cuba to Key West was made without any deaths among the Negroes, and without any incident of interest. Barracoons have been erected at Key West for the accommodation of recaptured slaves, and our cargo will be sent thither as soon as possible. The prisoners will remain in charge of the U.S. Marshal, to await the result of their trial.

During the summer of 1860 several other slavers were captured by Captain Maffitt's steamer including a pirate vessel called *Young Antonio.*

Meanwhile events further north were taking ominous shape. Secession was in the air. Uncertainty, suspicion and resentment churned across the land, stirring the dust of war.

Early in January 1861 Lieutenant Maffitt received orders from the Secretary of the Navy to bring the *Crusader* from Pensacola to Mobile. While there he was to cash a check on the Collector of the Port for the prize money due the officers and crew for their capture of the slaving vessels. When Maffitt arrived in Mobile he found the city very much agitated by Alabama's recently passed ordinance of secession. Certain elements of the city were so aroused by the presence of the U.S. war vessel that a band of ruffians organized to capture her.

When Maffitt heard the news he immediately made preparations for defense, got up steam and cleared for action. He also declared to the prominent citizens of the city that if any hostile act was committed he would immediately let go a broadside and sink any approaching vessels. Maffitt's firm stand resulted in the abandonment of the scheme; the money due the officers and crew of the *Crusader* was paid to them by the Collector of the Port and she left Mobile to resume her former cruising grounds. After a short stay in Havana, however, Maffitt was ordered to bring the vessel north to New York. Upon arrival he was told to settle his accounts and relinquish command. Then he went immediately to his home in Washington.

Maffitt's reactions to the events which followed are made clear by entries in his private journal:

Washington, April 13, 1861: At six p.m. the news of Fort Sumter's fall was circulated and the excitement was intense. All Southerners were jubilant; the Black Republicans gave in to the most excessive expressions of indignation—yet but few fancied that there would be war between the North and South—all seemed to think that a conference would take place, that unquestionably should put to rest all vexed questions, and the Union, through conservatism thus be saved.

April 28, 1861: I sent in my resignation this day. Found that I could not collect bonds due me or yet transfer my property, packed up and made ready for a Southern course. On the 18th I started my children to Charleston on a visit to my brother-in-law; from thence to proceed to "Ellerslie," near Fayetteville, North Carolina where their home would be in the family of my cousin. Washington was full of soldiers and the roll of artillery wagons could be heard day and night as battery after battery entered the city. Still, no one, even after the fall of Sumter seemed to anticipate that a great revolution was at hand. The abolitionists were vindictive and vented their sentiments right and left. Southern families were daily departing and resignations from the Army and Navy were daily announced in language of gall and bitterness.

April 29, 1861: The government has now commenced to taboo those suspected of Southern proclivities and secret arrests were being made. Being informed by a reliable friend that my name was on the list of those who were to be arrested, I concluded that my property had to take care of itself and I made arrangements to secretly depart.

May 2, 1861: I managed through the kindly feeling of a Federal officer to pass over the Long Bridge, which was carefully guarded by a battery and company of artillery. How 'twas done becomes me not to state even in a private journal—but this much I will say, the officer who befriended me did not imagine that hostilities would occur. In a brief time he lost his battery and was captured at Bull Run. I remained in Alexandria all night, and on the morning of the 3d of May I started for Richmond and arrived in Montgomery on the 7th. In an interview with

Mr. Jefferson Davis, in which I offered my services to the Confederacy, he informed me that the South did not contemplate creating a Navy, and on my asking the pertinent question why then were naval officers invited to resign their positions in the United States Navy and join the Confederacy, his answer was that they could join the Army. Mr. Davis said, "Our friends at the North assure us that there will be no war." I replied by giving him a description of the troops which I myself had seen pouring into Washington, and also informed him that the roll of artillery went on day and night. So unsatisfactory did this interview prove, and so discouraged was I, that I went to the hotel to pack my trunk for Europe. Upon this scene came with haste Robert Toombs, Ben Hill, and others, who came direct from seeing Mr. Davis, and who insisted that the Confederacy could not afford to lose my services. I finally received a lieutenant's commission, with orders to report to Commodore Tattnall at Savannah, Georgia.

General Beauregard had politely invited me to join his staff, but much to my regret the Secretary refused the permission. I was pained to find that the Cabinet was injudiciously selected. Mr. Walker, as Secretary of War, fell far short of the requirements of his important office. Of all positions that most required energy, knowledge, and promptness of conception, the office of Secretary of War surely was paramount. But not a member of the Government anticipated war—not one; hence there was short-sighted policy and a lack of action, that distressed those who, recently from the North, had witnessed the great gatherings and the tremendous exertions of the Navy Department for the occasion. Unfortunately for the Navy, Mr. Davis was not impressed with the necessity of building ships and preparing the South at a time when economy and success could have been secured. The Confederate Government was anxious for a peaceful separation, and the wish was father to the thought—consequently, but little energy was manifested for a struggle, while at the North all was activity and practical application of immense means.

Mr. Mallory was placed at the head of the Navy Department, in marked opposition to the sentiment of the people. The Senate—a provisional Congress—repeatedly rejected his nomination on the grounds of inability for the office; but Captains Rosseau,

Tattnall, and Ingraham indorsed him, and their judgment eventually biased the Congressional vote. The puerile attempt to improvise a Navy is a part of the melancholy history of our mistakes.

Many years later,* Captain Maffitt described what went on at Montgomery at this time:

As if by magic, the city became thronged with military aspirants; martial music resounded through the streets, as volunteer companies from adjacent towns and counties marched to the fairground, which was soon transformed into a field of Mars.

All arrangements connected with the military status of the Confederacy appeared to move in a smooth and even groove, propelled, as it were, by the natural proclivities of the people; but when the question of the inauguration of a Navy was propounded, the Government instantly seemed to be at sea without rudder, compass, or charts by which to steer upon the bewildering ocean of absolute necessity.

Many of the States, as they severally withdrew from the old Union, had established provisional State navies. The Governors of each State, by authority of their legislatures, purchased such small river steamers and tugboats as were obtainable, armed them with one gun each, and placed them in charge of such ex-naval officers as had resigned from the Federal Navy. When the Confederacy assumed its functions as an inaugurated government, the States transferred their troops and provisional navies to the same, and officers and vessels were enrolled upon the official Naval Register.

As an exclusively agricultural community, the South had hitherto depended upon the North for all her maritime necessities, and this commercial sectionality left her, as a natural consequence, without seamen, machine-shops, ship-yards, or any of those accessories upon which nautical enterprise depends. These serious obstacles, with the aid of intelligent naval officers, could, for general practical purposes, have been surmounted. The Confederacy called for the naval sons of the South, and promptly —with but few exceptions—the call was responded to by edu-

* In an article in the *United States Service Magazine*, October 1880.

cated and efficient gentlemen, who severed their connection with the Federal service at great personal as well as professional sacrifice.

Dire necessity soon coerced the Government into placing some force upon our threatened waters, and the Secretary of the Navy was under the necessity of obtaining such steamers as could be purchased in open market. The vessels thus obtained were of the most fragile character, generally consisting of old dilapidated tugboats and flimsy passenger steamers, sans speed, sans ability to support suitable ordnance. All were purchased at speculative prices, and at much exceeding the cost of constructing (at the favorable period) substantial and efficient gunboats. A brief experience, coupled with mortifications, convinced the Navy Department that steamers built for commercial purposes were not in the least calculated for the necessities of war. Contracts were accordingly entered into at New Orleans and other places for the construction of proper war vessels.

On May 9, 1861, Lieutenant Maffitt, Confederate States Navy, arrived in Savannah and was ordered to command the steamer *Savannah*, which until a short time before had plied as a passenger boat by the inland water route to Jacksonville, Florida. "A more absurd abortion for a man-of-war was rarely witnessed," wrote Maffitt. This vessel along with two old tugs, the *Samson* and *Resolute*, and the *Lady Davis*, an iron tug, were intended to act as a squadron for the protection of the Port of Savannah. The *Lady Davis* became the "flagship."

"When called upon for my opinion," recalled Maffitt, "I unhesitatingly condemned the whole squadron, save as provisional guard-boats and suggested that vessels of proper capacity should be at once built and purchased."

After returning from Norfolk with guns to mount on the "squadron," Maffitt visited Mobile, Alabama. Always observant, he noted in his journal local conditions:

Throughout the South a kind of desultory style of defense was in progress, but nothing commensurate to our necessities and the crisis that was evidently approaching. The Yankees were held too much in contempt—great stress was laid on the recognition of the Confederacy by the necessities of Europe, a delusive hope pregnant with misfortune. The moral sentiment of the world is against us on the question of slavery, and though cotton has its power, I very much fear that we will ere long become convinced that 'tis not regal—we must achieve our independence and alone.

I made various proposals: 1st, to destroy New York Navy Yard—not difficult at the period. (No favor shown it.) 2d, I suggested the importance of running in large quantities of arms, clothing, stores, shoes, provisions, etc., as the blockade was not as permanently established as it unquestionably would be. (No!) 3d, to purchase in England and France propellers with powerful engines, to be used as gunboats, to be built at once and adapted to our waters. (No.) 4th, to turn the ship *Thompson* (a prize), of 1,200 tons, into a floating ironclad battery for Port Royal and to separate the guns of the two forts, so as to spread them along the line of beach, that the enemy in the event of assault would not have so small a focus on which to concentrate their fire. (Agreed to when too late!)

During the summer much sickness prevailed in the squadron—mostly swamp fevers of the worst character.

The vessels made frequent inland cruises and always gave evidence of their total inability to meet the Federal gunboats with prospect of success.

By December 1861 Maffitt had become a naval aid to General Robert E. Lee and was busy with duties of a general character, surveying, erecting batteries and placing obstructions along the coast of South Carolina. A month later, on January 7, 1862, Lieutenant Maffitt received the orders that embarked him on his career as a blockade runner and gave him an opportunity to exercise all the experience, ability and courage which had been growing within him during his long years of naval service. The ship assigned to Maffitt was the *Cecile*, offered to the government by Fraser, Trenholm & Company of Charleston and Liverpool. She was said to be unusually fast and could stow to advantage about 700 bales of cotton.

Maffitt knew only too well of the North's determination to

dethrone "King Cotton." If Lincoln's government could cause this commodity to become less important as an aid to the Confederacy, then the Confederacy's credit abroad for the purchase of materials of war would suffer. But cotton prices were skyrocketing. Profits were fantastic for those who were willing to run major risks to bring that cotton safely eastward through the blockade. Even at this early date a steamer with the average capacity of 800 bales of cotton often netted about $420,000 on a round trip. Already the shipyards of England and Scotland were busy building steamers especially designed for the blockade-running trade. In later years Maffitt recalled that "in a brief time the harbors of Bermuda and Nassau swarmed with sky-colored vessels eagerly seeking pilots and adventurous seamen to assist in transporting desirable cargoes into Dixie. Thus was blockade running established as an instrument of war.

"In the hands of foreigners it proved in some respects injurious. Cargoes landed in the Confederacy were usually paid for with Confederate currency. The blockaders then changed this currency into gold at an enormous discount, thereby producing a perceptible depreciation in the status of Confederate money. Many adventurous speculators made fortunes, while others came to grief. Notwithstanding the difficulties and extreme hazards attending these ventures, cotton, with its magnetic power, attracted constant supplies for the war, and enabled our armies to maintain a bold and oft successful opposition to the splendidly equipped men of the North."

The *Cecile* lay at the wharf in Wilmington, North Carolina, and across her gangplank marched a steady procession of Negro stevedores trundling bales of cotton which were carefully stowed in her hold. Late in the afternoon the *Cecile* dropped down the Cape Fear River and anchored before sunset off the village of Smithville. During the twilight hour Lieutenant Maffitt carefully reconnoitered the enemy. He saw that the blockading squadron had moved into such a position as to seal the channel for the night. The prospects did not look promising. Another thing that worried Maffitt was the reluctance of the moon to go behind a bank of clouds on the horizon. At last the moonlight faded into darkness and Maffitt quietly gave orders to hoist the anchor and get under way.

The captain of the *Cecile* was not only an intrepid blockade runner, but also possessed a flair for description as may be seen from the following account which was later published in the *United States Service Magazine* for June and July, 1882:

In silence Fort Caswell is passed, and a dim glimpse of Fort Campbell affords a farewell view of Dixie, as the steamer's head is turned seaward through the channel. The swelling greetings of the Atlantic billows announce that the bar is passed; over the cresting waves the good craft swiftly dashes, as if impatient to promptly face her trials of the night. Through the settled darkness all eyes on board are peering, eagerly straining to catch a view of the dreaded sentinels who sternly guard the tabooed channel. Nothing white is exposed to view; every light is extinguished, save those that are hooded in the binnacle and engine-room. No sound disturbs the solemn silence of the moment but the dismal moaning of the northeast wind and unwelcome, but unavoidable, dashing of our paddles.

Night-glasses scan the bleared horizon for a time in vain; suddenly an officer with bated breath announces several steamers. Eagerly pointing he reports two at anchor and others slowly cruising. Instantly out of the gloom and spindrift emerges the somber phantom form of the blockading fleet. The moment of trial is at hand; firmness and decision are essential for the emergency. Dashing between the two at anchor, we pass so near as to excite astonishment at our non-discovery; but this resulted from the color of our hull, which, under certain stages of the atmosphere, blended so perfectly with the haze as to render the steamer nearly invisible.

How keenly the grim hulls of the enemy are watched! How taut, like harp-strings, every nerve is strung, anxiously vibrating with each pulsation of the throbbing heart! We emerge to windward from between the two at anchor.

"Captain," whispered the pilot, "according to my chop logic them chaps aren't going to squint us this blessed night."

Ere a response could be uttered a broad-spread flash of intense light blazed from the flag's Drummond [light] for in passing to windward the noise of our paddles betrayed the proximity of a blockade runner. "Full speed!" I shouted to the engineer. Instantly the increased revolutions responded to the order. Then came the roar of heavy guns, the howl of shot, and scream of bursting shells. Around, above, and through the severed rigging the iron demons howled, as if pandemonium had discharged its infernal spirits into the air.

Under the influence of a terrible shock the steamer quivers with aspen vibrations. An explosion follows; she is struck!

"What is the damage?" I ask.

"A shell, sir, has knocked overboard several bales of cotton and wounded two of the crew," was the response of the boatswain.

By the sheen of the Drummond lights the sea is so clearly illuminated as to exhibit the perils of our position, and show the grouping around us of the fleet, as their batteries belched forth a hailstorm of angry missiles, threatening instant annihilation.

In the turmoil of excitement a frightened passenger, contrary to orders, invaded the bridge. Wringing his hands in agony, he implored me to surrender and save his life and the lives of all on board. Much provoked, I directed one of our quartermasters stationed near me to take the lubber below. Without ceremony he seized the unhappy individual, and as he hurried him to the cabin, menacingly exclaimed, "Shut up your fly-trap, or by the powers of Moll Kelly I'll hould ye up as a target for the divarsion of them Yankee gunners!"

As perils multiplied, our Mazeppa speed increased and gradually withdrew us from the circle of danger. At last we distance the party. Spontaneously the crew give three hearty cheers as a relief to their pent-up anxiety, and everyone began to breathe more naturally.

During the night we were subjected to occasional trials of speed, to avoid suspicious strangers whose characters could not be determined. In fact, nothing in the shape of a steamer was to be trusted, as we entertained the belief that Confederates were Ismaelites upon the broad ocean—the recipients of no man's courtesy.

Day dawned upon one of ocean's most beautiful mornings; the soft blue sky circled the bluer horizon, and over the broad expanse a profound calm settled upon the sleeping waters. It seemed difficult to realize that such serenity was ever tortured into the most wild and terrific commotion by the rude storms and hurricanes that often held high revelry, where now not a ruffled wave appeared or a gentle ripple bleared the mirrored surface.

On the inbound voyage there were gloomy predictions of disaster by water-front authorities at Nassau, for the Federal cruisers had increased their vigilance greatly over the past few months.

Nevertheless the little *Cecile* set out in the dark of the night and by daybreak was approaching Abaco Light. This was a point where the blockade runners shifted course and came out from the shelter of the Bahamas. As the light grew stronger, three Federal cruisers were sighted bearing down. Maffitt ordered full steam ahead but not before several shells splintered her spars and bulwarks. "This," recalled Maffitt, "warned us of the urgent necessity for travelling, particularly as 900 barrels of gunpowder constituted a portion of our cargo. A chance shell exploding in the hold would have consigned steamer and all hands to Tophet. We were in capital running condition, and soon passed out of range."

The *Cecile* had scarcely escaped pursuit when the cry of "Sail Ho" again came winging from the crow's-nest and the lookout announced two steamers ahead and standing in toward them. Maffitt ordered a zigzag course and succeeded in out-maneuvering the enemy vessels. By this time he thought that his troubles were over and was about to take a nap after being up all night when the mate reported, "Captain, a burning vessel is reported from aloft, sir."

Sure enough, through his glass Maffitt could distinctly see, some four miles ahead, a vessel enveloped in smoke. Relates Maffitt:

Increasing our speed, we quickly ran quite near the burning vessel. She proved to be a Spanish bark, with ensign at half-mast.

Out of her fore hatch arose a dense smoke. Abaft were clustered a panic-stricken group of passengers and crew. Among them several ladies were observed. An ineffectual effort had been made to hoist out the long-boat, which was still suspended by the yard and stay-tackles.

Sending an officer aloft to keep a sharp lookout that we might not be surprised by the enemy while engaged in succoring the unfortunate, the chief mate was dispatched in the cutter to render such assistance as his professional intelligence might suggest. He found the few passengers, among whom were four ladies, much calmer than the officers and crew; the latter, in place of endeavoring to extinguish the fire, which had broken out in the forecastle apartment, were confusedly hauling upon the stay-tackle in a vain effort to launch the long-boat. Our mate, with his boat's crew, passed the jabbering, panic-stricken Spaniards, and proceeded at once to the forecastle, which he instantly del-uged with water, and, to the astonishment of all hands, speedily subdued the trifling conflagration, which proved to have resulted from the burning of a quantity of lamp rags that had probably been set on fire by one of the crew who carelessly emptied his pipe when about to repair on deck. The quantity of old duds that lay scattered about Jack's luxuriously furnished apartment supplied abundant materials for raising a dense smoke, but the rough construction of the vessel in this locality fortunately offered nothing inflammable, and the great sensation, under the influence of a cool head, soon subsided into a farce.

The mate, who was much of a wag, enjoyed the general per-turbation of the passengers, particularly on learning that three of the ladies hailed from Marblehead, and were returning from a visit made to an uncle who owned a well-stocked sugar plantation near Sagua Le Grand, in Cuba. A Spanish vessel bound to Hali-fax had been selected to convey them to a British port conveni-ent for transportation to New York or Boston, without the risk of being captured by Confederate "buccaneers," who, according to Cuban rumors, swarmed over the ocean. . . .

A hail from the steamer caused our mate to make his adieu, but not before announcing himself as one of the awful Southern slaveholders they had in conversation anathematized. They would not believe that so kind and polite a gentleman could possibly be a wicked "rebel." "But I am, ladies, and also a slave-

owner, as is your uncle. Farewell." Instead of manifesting anger
at the retort, they laughed heartily, and waved their handkerchiefs in kind adieu, utterly unsuspicious of having received
kindness and courtesy from a blockade-runner. We made the
best of speed on our way to Wilmington.

When 60 miles off the Carolina coast, Maffitt decided to run
down toward the mouth of the Cape Fear at full speed and then
proceed more cautiously through the blockading fleet. He was
well aware of the difficulties that lay ahead. There were no
lighthouses or beacons to guide him and his success in eluding
his pursuers depended upon a fearless approach, exact navigation
and complete knowledge of soundings and currents.

Again Maffitt's long familiarity with the coast line stood him
in good stead, for after a close brush with the enemy and an
almost miraculous escape at sixteen knots, and pursued by exploding shells, the *Cecile* safely negotiated the channel and came to
anchor at one o'clock in the morning off of Smithville.

During February, March and part of April, 1862, Captain
Maffitt continued to run the blockade bringing in arms, ammunition, clothing and other necessities for the Confederacy. On
April 11 he transferred his command to the steamer *Nassau*
(formerly the steamer *Gordon*) and continued in the blockade-
running business for several weeks.

During this period of the war, it was a common practice to
carry passengers aboard blockade runners plying between Bermuda or Nassau and the Southern mainland. Maffitt notes in his
journal that on his arrival at Nassau on May 4, he landed several
passengers including a Mr. and Mrs. De Leon, his own daughter
Florie and another lady.

Late that same evening Maffitt received a visitor whose information transformed his blockade-running activities into something new and even more exciting. The man who visited Maffitt
was Mr. Low, a provisional master of the Confederate States
Navy. In low tones he told Maffitt that he had come to Nassau
secretly aboard the Confederate gunboat *Oreto* and delivered

Ruins of Fort Fisher.

The Lillian running into Wilmington

a letter from Commander J. D. Bulloch requesting that Maffitt at once assume command of this vessel. The letter also instructed him to take the *Oreto* quickly to sea before the government authorities at Nassau became suspicious as to her character and ultimate occupation.

"Where is she lying now?" asked Maffitt.

"At Cockran's anchorage, nine miles east of Nassau," answered Mr. Low. "She must leave just as soon as possible or she may be confiscated," he added.

Maffitt realized at once that he could not possibly take the *Oreto* to sea unless he had an efficient crew. So he immediately wrote to Secretary Mallory asking him to send without delay experienced lieutenants and other necessary officers; also funds so as to get the *Oreto* out of Nassau with promptness and dispatch.

The answer to Maffitt's letter brought three inexperienced young officers who knew nothing about the sea, together with instructions to embark immediately on a cruise as a Confederate man-of-war.

Disturbing news now reached Maffitt about his daughter. He had sent her back to Wilmington aboard the blockade runner *Nassau*. But due to the captain's bad management and lack of blockade-running experience, the *Nassau* fell into the hands of a Federal cruiser commanded by Captain George Walker. The capture was accompanied by lively shellfire, but Florie Maffitt sat on the open deck unperturbed until the captain warned her of the danger and advised that she go to her cabin. Even when below she insisted on looking out of the porthole to watch the engagement. The fact that the *Nassau* had tons of powder on board did not seem to unnerve the young lady. According to the story told later by the pilot and crew of the *Nassau*, Florie urged the captain not to surrender. On being reminded of the danger from the cargo of powder and his duty to her father to see that she came to no harm, she exclaimed with tears in her eyes that her father would prefer her being blown up rather than have the steamer fall into Yankee hands. After being captured, Florie was taken to New York and later returned unharmed to her family, thanks to the influence of Captain Walker who was an old shipmate of her father's during ante bellum days.

Meanwhile the *Oreto* had been rechristened the *Florida*. Her objective was to cruise the Southern Atlantic as a commerce destroyer or engage in any advantageous action against Federal men-of-war. At the same time the vessel was to regard strictly the rights of neutrals. However, the British Government at Nassau had refused to permit the *Florida* to put to sea and Maffitt was anxiously waiting a final court decision. The situation did not look promising even if the authorities released the vessel, for twelve Federal men-of-war were cruising outside, awaiting the exit of the *Florida*. Seamen, firemen and engineers were hard to obtain. Certain necessary equipment and armament could not be removed from the bonded warehouse because Maffitt had no invoice.

At last on August 7 the Vice Admiralty Court arrived at a decision. According to their verdict it had been clearly proven that the *Oreto* had left England unarmed and unequipped and had continued so during her stay at Nassau. Therefore, Judge Lee decreed that she was to be released. On the following day Maffitt and his officers and crew took possession of the *Florida* and brought her out of the harbor. Late the following day the vessel arrived at a desolate, uninhabited island called Green Key ninety miles southward of New Providence Island. Here commenced a task more difficult and laborious than anything in Maffitt's previous experience. The *Florida's* crew consisted of twenty-five men all told. This pitifully small force had to hoist aboard two 7-inch rifled guns and six 6-inch guns, together with their carriages, powder, shot, shell and general equipment and stores. Officers and men stripped to the waist and went doggedly to work under the broiling tropical sun. The next day one of the crew sickened and within eight hours was dead. Maffitt noted the yellow appearance of the corpse.

After eight days of back-breaking work the guns had been mounted and everything seemed ready for sea. Yet not one gun could be fired, because in the haste and secrecy of loading, all the rammers, sponges, sights, locks, beds and quoins had been left at Nassau. Nevertheless, the *Florida* got under way. The weather was calm and beautiful and all hands enjoyed a well-earned rest. Next day two men were reported sick and soon the vessel was engulfed in an epidemic of yellow fever. No physician was aboard. Medical supplies were sketchy. Not knowing the cause of yellow fever, Maffitt noted in his journal that as the trade wind freshened, the hope was indulged that the pure ocean air would disinfect the *Florida* and relieve her from the malaria of the fell disease. "Alas!" wrote Maffitt, "there was no balm in Gilead. By sundown more than half the crew, with two officers, were added to the sick list."

By this time the *Florida* was approaching the coast of Cuba. In desperation Maffitt decided to shape his course for Cárdenas. When he finally anchored in the harbor the ship's working force had been reduced by the epidemic to one fireman and two seamen. Nurses were obtained from Havana and the ship became a floating hospital. Maffitt was on his feet day and night helping tend the delirious men. Weakened by fatigue and anxiety, Maffitt himself soon came down with the disease and was ill for more than a week. After coming out of his coma, Maffitt overheard the Spanish doctor remark, "It is now twenty minutes after nine o'clock in the morning. I am convinced, from careful investigation, that Captain Maffitt cannot survive beyond meridian." Maffitt recalls exclaiming, "You're a liar, sir; I have too much to do and cannot afford to die!" And he did not. Within the next few days he managed to get on his feet although terribly emaciated and in a weak condition. It was only then that he learned that his beloved son, Laurens, who had accompanied him aboard the *Florida*, had died of yellow fever. This loss weighed heavily on Maffitt, although he said no word to his mates.

On September 1 the *Florida* arrived in the harbor of Havana and was met by sympathetic Cubans and Confederate residents. In giving thought to his situation, Maffitt clearly realized that the *Florida* could never perform her duties as a man-of-war unless she was properly officered and equipped. "This conviction determined me to sail for Mobile," recalled Maffitt, "which I learned had a smaller blockading force on duty than any other Southern port. So at 9 P.M. we sailed, avoiding the enemy's fleet gathered off the Moro, by running some distance close to the shore."

By three in the afternoon of the fourth of September 1862 the *Florida* fetched Fort Morgan on Mobile Bay. This was a pleasant sight although marred somewhat by two Federal cruisers on hand as a "welcoming committee."

Maffitt was still weak from yellow fever but insisted on keeping the bridge. Lieutenant Stribling, executive officer, suggested that because of the poor condition of the crew and the inability of the *Florida* to offer resistance to the enemy it would be advisable to stand off again and postpone the attempt to enter the harbor until nightfall. Maffitt vetoed this suggestion because it would be impossible to find the channel in the blackness of the night. Consequently, he determined to run boldly in and take the chance of being shelled by the blockading fleet. "We will hoist English colors as a ruse and boldly stand for the commanding officer's ship," he remarked. "The remembrance of the delicate *Trent* affair may perhaps cause some deliberation and care before the [enemy] batteries are set loose upon us; four minutes of hesitation on their part may save us."

Thereupon the English colors were hoisted to the gaff and the *Florida* plunged full steam ahead for the Federal flagship. This vessel was the ten-gun *Oneida*, Captain Preble commanding. Seeing the strange vessel approach, the *Oneida* attempted to cut her off but Maffitt sheered toward her. Preble ordered the *Oneida* full speed astern to avoid a collision. Then she fired a warning gun and ordered the stranger to heave to. Apparently the *Oneida* was still under the impression that the *Florida* was an English vessel because of her general appearance and bold approach. Maffitt ignored the command to heave to and continued his course. A second angry shot whistled across the *Florida's* bow, followed almost immediately by a broadside. This blast carried away some of the blockade runner's hammock nettings and much of her standing and running rigging. What

saved the *Florida* from complete annihilation was the fact that
the *Oneida's* guns were aimed too high and some of the shot
passed overhead. Had they been depressed, the career of the
Florida would have ended right there. Two other ships of the
Federal squadron immediately joined the *Oneida* in a fierce
fusillade. They were bent on completely destroying this bold
Confederate.

For the first time Maffitt began to lose hope. The firing
was so intense he did not feel that his boat could live through it.
The two other Federal vessels were now in position on each side
of his bow and Maffitt shouted to his quartermaster to starboard
the helm so as to bring the gunboats in line and escape the fire
of one of them. At the same time an 11-inch shell from the
Oneida pierced the *Florida* and penetrated her coal bunkers on
the port side, struck the port forward boiler and exploded in the
berth deck, wounding nine men and decapitating a tenth. Fortunately the shell did not explode. If it had, the whole vessel
would have been blown to bits and probably no man would have
lived to tell the tale.

One of the Federal vessels, the *Winona*, landed a shell in the
cabin. It passed through the pantry. At the same time an 11-
inch shell from the *Oneida* exploded close to the port gangway
and seriously injured the vessel.

In desperation Maffitt ordered his men aloft to loose the topsails and topgallant sails. But the moment the *Florida's* men were
seen on the yards, all the Federal gunboats loaded their twenty-
four pound cannon with shrapnel and shot away the standing
rigging. A number of men were wounded and the crew only
succeeded in letting fall the topsails.

All this time the *Florida* had been flying English colors. Now
Maffitt hauled them down and hoisted the Confederate flag. But
the man who was trying to follow this order had his fingers shot
off and a moment later the halliards were severed by shrapnel
so that it was some minutes before the Dixie flag floated from the
gaff.

It is easy to understand how frustrated Maffitt must have
been, in command of a vessel mounting cannon which could not

be fired because of their lack of rammers, sponges, sights and other equipment. Maffitt recalled that "the loud explosions, roar of shots and shell, crashing spars and rigging, mingled with the moans of our sick and wounded, instead of intimidating, only increased our determination to enter the distant harbor."

Another 11-inch shell from the *Oneida* passed along the berth deck three inches above the water line, but failed to explode. Miraculously the *Florida* had not been mortally wounded and managed to limp painfully and slowly away from the pursuing enemy vessels. They in turn fed resin and other combustible materials into their boilers in an effort to overhaul the blockade runner. But gradually the *Florida* increased her distance and, after a while the Federal shot and shell began to fall short. Continuing her desperate push toward the channel the *Florida* finally made it and anchored safely close to the Confederate Fort Morgan, whose garrison cheered her wildly.

As a result of his courageous run through the Federal blockade Maffitt became a hero. He was officially thanked by Admiral Franklin Buchanan, C.S.N., and received a congratulatory letter from S. R. Mallory, Secretary of the Navy. Mallory closed his letter with these words, "The escape of your defenseless vessel from an overwhelming force with liberty to choose its ground and mode of attack was alone due to the handsome manner in which she was handled, and I do not remember that the union of thorough professional skill, coolness and daring have ever been better exhibited in a naval dash of a single ship."

Maffitt was weak and exhausted from his ordeal mainly because he had not completely recovered from his severe bout with yellow fever. But the excellent treatment he received ashore at Mobile quickly restored him to health. Some weeks later he was ordered by the Secretary of the Navy to fit out his vessel for a cruise against the enemy, this time provided with ample funds. Mallory emphasized the necessity for capturing or destroying as many enemy vessels as possible. As the Secretary's parting remarks pointed out: "The *Florida* will have the honor of making the third naval cruiser under the flag of the Confederate States and the Department relies with confidence upon the abilities and conduct of yourself, officers and men for its success; and with my earnest wishes for the prosperity of your cruise and your triumphant return to your country, I am respectfully your obedient servant etc. . . ."

It was nearly the middle of January 1863 before the *Florida* was properly fitted out for her dash back through the blockade and out into the Atlantic. Meanwhile Maffitt had received no promotion. Although Mallory spoke in high terms of Maffitt's accomplishments, his excuse for not promoting Maffitt seems flimsy. He stated that it had been his intention at first to promote Maffitt, but as the service was "civil" rather than military (the *Florida* not having her guns mounted!) Mallory had concluded to await a suitable occasion when he might promote Maffitt in a "legitimate" performance of his duty.

January 16 dawned with a cold rain and high wind. By midnight Maffitt had full steam up on the *Florida* and was anxiously waiting for the opinion of the pilot as to whether it was too dark to see Lighthouse Island, but he said that the night was too black and the departure was put off for some hours. By two o'clock in the morning the wind had moderated and the stars were out. A light mist covered the surface of the water. Maffitt ordered the vessel to get under way. Double reefs were taken in her topsails and trysails. Everything was secured for bad weather. A double watch was set and the crew piped to quarters.

Maffitt had banked on the bitter cold and the darkness to dull the alertness of the Federal lookouts. That he had guessed right was demonstrated a few minutes later when to Maffitt's astonishment he was able to pass without being discovered quite near to a blockader lying inside the bar. Soon the alarm was given by another ship, whose drums beat the call. Lights flashed and a general commotion ensued as cables were slipped and the chase was on.

Pursued by six rampant Federal gunboats, the *Florida* clapped on all canvas and opened the steam valve wide. All day long the chase kept up and by dusk it looked as if safety was in sight. But the heavy pitching had sprung the *Florida*'s fore topsail yard. Repairs were quickly made. Nevertheless the reduction of canvas cut down her speed and the leading Federal cruiser began to creep dangerously close. Fortunately the freshening breeze caught the repaired topsail and the *Florida* surged ahead once more and safely made her escape.

By daylight next morning there was nothing in sight but a foamy sea and black clouds with the *Florida* fleeing ahead of the wind. She ran at a top speed of fourteen and a half knots, wet but riding like a pilot boat. So ended the daring round trip of the *Florida* through the Federal blockade, a little ship that managed to bluff her way past some of the most powerful vessels of the United States Navy.

Once at sea the *Florida* embarked on a long cruise that left a trail of captured vessels and burned hulks in her wake. Most of the ships were burned because there was no port on the Atlantic Coast into which it was safe to bring the prizes.

On February 25, 1863, the *Florida* arrived at Bridgetown, Barbados. She was the first Confederate States man-of-war to visit this British island. When Maffitt called on Governor Walker he found him to be quite a pleasant gentleman though much troubled with a nervous disease. The Governor seemed in doubt as to his power to permit Maffitt to coal ship. But when Maffitt told him that he had been in a severe storm which had done considerable damage and that the vessel's fuel had been used up in escaping it, the Governor allowed the *Florida* to take on coal and stores.

Continuing her cruise of destruction, the *Florida* reached the coast of South America and steamed as far south as Brazil. Finally, in May, came the long-awaited letter from Secretary Mallory informing Maffitt that the President had promoted him to the rank of commander "for gallant and meritorious conduct in command of the steam sloop *Florida* in running the blockade in and out of the Port of Mobile against an overwhelming force of the enemy and under his fire and since in actively cruising against and destroying the enemy's commerce."

By the middle of July Maffitt had captured between twenty and thirty vessels, mostly clipper ships. The majority of them he burned. Turning north again, Maffitt stopped briefly at Bermuda. Finally late in the summer, it was found that the *Florida's* shaft required re-laying and her machinery overhauling. Maffitt then determined to run her across the Atlantic to France and apply for permission to dock and repair at Brest. After much delay and red tape on the part of the French authorities, permission was granted.

According to a French writer of the time, "The presence of the Confederate vessel in French waters has created a sensation which is extending rapidly all over the empire and resounding in Paris as a thunderstorm . . . the most astounding rumors are going the rounds and strange to say are fast obtaining credence among the people." These rumors claimed that the *Florida's* hull was filled with gold captured from the enemy. Commander Maffitt was called a sea wolf whose thirst for blood could not be quenched; his officers were termed the most desperate pirates that ever roamed over the ocean; his crew the refuse of the earth, a set of desperadoes and cutthroats. Before entering Brest harbor, the *Florida* was said to have been seen with several corpses hanging from her masts. To offset these lies, an article based on the *Florida's* log book was shortly published in the newspaper *l'Ocean de Brest* (apparently at Maffitt's instigation). This completely demolished the false rumors allegedly spread by enemies of the Confederacy. Now for the first time in many months the young officers and crew of the *Florida* had a chance to amuse themselves, purchase new uniforms and be entertained by enthusiastic French well-wishers. Shortly before the *Florida* was refitted and ready to go to sea, Captain Maffitt suffered a severe heart attack. Upon advice of French doctors he applied for leave of absence from the Confederate States Navy. This was readily granted and he was relieved by Captain Barney.

About this time a correspondent for the London *Times* visited the *Florida* as she lay in the harbor of Brest and gave the following description of Captain Maffitt: "He is a slight, middle-sized, well-knit man of about 42, a merry looking man with a ready, determined air, full of life and business—apparently the sort of man who is equally ready for a fight or a jollification, and whose preference for the latter would by no means interfere with his creditable conduct of the former."

During the Britisher's interview with Captain Maffitt, the latter told him: "We have taken, all together, 72 prizes and estimated the value at 15 million dollars. The *Jacob Bell* alone was worth two million." The word "we" as used by Captain Maffitt included the three other Confederate raiders, the *Clarence*, *Tacony* and *Alabama*. Captain Maffitt also pointed out to this correspondent that when the *Florida* came into Brest she had been to sea for eight months without spending four days in port. Before entering the French harbor she had not been more than twenty-four hours in any one port, although she visited Nassau, Bermuda, Pernambuco and Ceará, Brazil. In all this time they had lost only fifteen men, including those who were killed and wounded at Mobile, a paymaster who died of consumption and one officer who was drowned.

After spending some time in travel on the Scandinavian Peninsula in an effort to recover his health, Captain Maffitt returned to the Confederacy aboard the blockade runner *Florie*. Although there is no evidence to support the supposition, it is likely that this blockade runner was named in honor of Maffitt's daughter of the same name. Apparently Captain Maffitt was on leave from active duty from the end of September 1863 until the spring of 1864, for the next thing we hear of him he is in command of the blockade runner *Lillian*, running between Bermuda and Wilmington. A graphic account of the voyage aboard this beautiful, fast and specially designed craft, is given us by the Honorable Francis C. Lawley, a relation of Gladstone who later became editor of the famous London *Telegraph* and a member of Parliament. En route to General Lee's headquarters as a war correspondent for the London *Times*, Mr. Lawley found himself at Bermuda and faced with the decision of running the blockade aboard either the *Florie* or the *Lillian*. They were both new vessels built by Messrs. Thompson of Glasgow and credited with being excellent sea boats. The time was May 1864 and Wilmington the destination of both.

By this time the Federal blockade had become very tight, with a great many more ships on duty than before. Captures and destruction of blockade runners had increased month by month. As Lawley noted: "From the moment that a blockade runner left Bermuda or Nassau, she was liable to be sighted by the U.S.S. *Vanderbilt* or by the U.S.S. *James Adger* or some other 14 or 15-knot boat which allowed her to get some hundreds miles out to sea so that she could not double back and take shelter in a British port and then went for her." He describes the *Lillian* and the *Florie* as "light, gossamer craft, with three funnels apiece." Their big tubular boilers capable of standing a tremendous pressure of steam were the only strong and heavy articles aboard. These ships were built for speed because, lacking armament, they depended entirely on their ability to outrun Federal cruisers. Lying there quietly at anchor the two vessels seemed more like beautiful steam yachts about to start a transatlantic race. Painted a dull lead-gray color, they had practically no rigging. Crow's-nests were fixed on foremasts and mainmasts. The vessels were supplied with plentiful amounts of Welsh coal (anthracite) especially brought out from England.

Mr. Lawley's choice of the *Lillian* was influenced principally by her master, Captain John Newland Maffitt. Lawley describes him as "a favorite of General Lee, who was always glad to relieve the strain upon his mind by listening to his old friends' sea yarns, and one glance of his resolute, straightforward face made me determine that I would go with him. He was in truth a fine specimen of a sailor and the more I saw of him during our short three days and four nights voyage, the more I liked him." Lawley had good reason to write as he did. The *Lillian* and the *Florie* were rivals and there was much talk and betting as to which of the sleek blockade runners would be the first to arrive safely off Fort Fisher.

The *Lillian* left port on the evening of June 1 steaming almost abreast of the *Florie*, with which she kept company until darkness fell. The sea was as calm as a mill dam. Aboard the *Lillian* were eight passengers, Englishmen and Americans who apparently enjoyed themselves with plentiful supplies of spiritous beverages spiced with the flavor of danger and adventure. After the hot atmosphere of Bermuda, the cool sea breeze was delightfully welcome. The first night everyone slept well and when morning dawned there was not a vessel in sight. The *Florie* had disappeared. Sunshine flooded the blue sea, while schools of flying fish darted like silver arrows from wave to wave. A little later, the lookout reported smoke on the horizon and for a while it seemed that the unknown vessel was burning. On closer approach she proved to be a Federal cruiser, emitting a dense white cloud of Cumberland coal smoke and beating rapidly eastward, apparently in pursuit of another outward-bound blockade runner. As soon as this discovery was made, Maffitt ordered the wheel put over and the *Lillian* resumed her original course. By noon of the third day the weather had changed to a dull overcast, so thick that Captain Maffitt was unable to take an observation of the sun with his sextant. But he estimated that by dawn of the next day they might possibly make the run into Wilmington. So the *Lillian* was pushed for all she was worth and, as Lawley described it, her "sharp bow seemed to cleave the waves like a razor, and the exhilaration of flying through the water at a speed which defied pursuit, raised our spirits to such a pitch that the famous old song, 'There's A Good Time Coming Boys!' burst in a chorus from our lips, followed by such familiar Confederate war strains as

> 'Then let the big guns roar as they will,
>   We'll be gay and happy still;
>
> 'Gay and happy, free and easy,
>   We'll be gay and happy still.' "

When darkness fell, strict orders were issued that not a single light was to be shown on deck. No one was allowed to smoke. The slightest pinpoint of light would quickly be seen by prowling Federal cruisers with the inevitable result of pursuit and shellfire. The *Lillian* blew off her steam under water; not a wisp of smoke showed from her stack, thanks to the good Welsh coal.

On she went through the gloaming like a ghost. Lawley's description of her bow as cleaving the water like a razor is apt, for the *Lillian's* forward deck was constructed in the form of a turtle-back so that she could pass quickly through a turbulent sea.

Tension began to mount among the *Lillian's* passengers. Two o'clock, three o'clock and three-thirty came and went, but still there was no evidence of land or a glimpse of the dim light that was kept shining on the Mound, one of the batteries of Fort Fisher. It must be kept in mind that Captain Maffitt was operating under dead reckoning, always a difficult form of navigation in thick weather, with unruly tides and winds that must be taken into account.

By four o'clock in the morning the *Lillian* found herself well off shore between the inside and outside squadrons of blockading men-of-war. Maffitt was well aware of his danger, yet from four o'clock in the morning until one-thirty in the afternoon the little vessel was unmolested. Then a big steamer hove in sight and the *Lillian* frantically got up steam. The blockade runner was carrying a large number of mailbags consigned to the Confederate government and to make sure that these would not fall into the hands of the enemy, Captain Maffitt had them brought on deck. Orders were given for heaving them overboard (properly weighted with lead) if capture seemed likely.

After what seemed hours (but in reality was only a matter of a few minutes) the little *Lillian* began to answer to the wide open throttle and her driving power pushed her through the waves like a thoroughbred horse responding to the spur of his rider. The steam pressure mounted steadily until the vessel was making over fourteen knots, her bow pointing eastward again away from the Federal cruisers. After speeding out of danger for more than two and a half hours, Maffitt ordered the helm put over and her bowsprit was again pointed toward Wilmington.

Once more the blockade runner approached the grim squadron of Federal vessels. "It is in such moments that you realize how paramount is the influence of a dauntless chief upon all around him," wrote Mr. Lawley. "And it is felt more in so confined a space as the deck of a ship than it is in a great battle on land.

Nevertheless we could not but proceed—indeed Captain Maffitt's anxious face told us so—that our position was far from comfortable, pursued as we were by vessels a few miles off to the rear, which clearly saw us, and swiftly approaching a powerful squadron of heavily armed blockaders, which had not yet caught sight of the *Lillian's* two masts, but which might do so at any moment."

Fortunately for all aboard the *Lillian*, night fell before they came too close to the second Federal squadron. Whether it was because many of the Federal sailors were having their supper or due to a mist hovering over the sea, the fact remains that the *Lillian* crept in cautiously, passing blockader after blockader, so close that at every moment they expected a flash of light and a thunderous cannonading. To everyone's amazement only a few shots were fired and soon the *Lillian* was within range of the great guns of Fort Fisher which kept the pursuers at a respectable distance.

But the danger was not over. Dead ahead was a small Federal launch groping for the channel or perhaps intent on sinking rocks and other obstructions into the channel near Fort Fisher. Lawley felt sure that if the launch had not sheered away at the last moment Maffitt would have coolly run her down. As matters turned out the launch escaped without the crew even firing their muskets at the fast-moving blockade runner.

"Another moment," wrote Lawley with evident relief, "we lay safe and sound below the Mound, eagerly asking for news from within the Confederacy, and as eagerly questioned in our turn for news from without."

After this one voyage, Captain Maffitt was detailed to take command of the gunboat *Albemarle*. He served aboard this vessel until September 9, 1864, when he was detached and ordered to Wilmington to take command of the government-owned blockade runner *Owl*. She was the first of several steamers built for, and on account of, the Confederate government and which were run under the direction of Secretary of the Navy Mallory. Only experienced naval officers were detailed to command government-owned blockade runners and Maffitt was considered the prince of them all.

In studying the official documents of the period, it is interesting to note one written to Commander Maffitt by Secretary Mallory dated September 19, 1864. This deals with instructions for the disposition of the vessel before capture. Mallory made it very plain that Confederate steamers should not fall into the enemy's hands. Apart from the specific loss sustained by the Confederacy in the capture of such blockade runners they were also considered extremely important as the fastest and most efficient part of the blockade-running operation. Maffitt was therefore instructed to devise and adopt thorough and efficient means for saving the lives of his officers and crew or passengers (if any), and then destroying the vessel and cargo. As regards passengers, Mallory had recently issued orders prohibiting their passage aboard blockade runners unless they were government officials or civilians of importance. Although Mallory did not specify the means for the destruction of the vessels, Maffitt and others easily devised them. They took a number of barrels of powder, laid fuses and got everything in readiness so that within moments after capture seemed imminent, the vessel could be blown to smithereens.

It was not until December 21, 1864, that the *Owl* was able to set out from Wilmington to breach the blockade. Aboard were 780 bales of cotton. With three other blockade runners she successfully avoided the Federal cruisers. Upon arrival at Saint George's, Bermuda, Maffitt noticed a number of steamers loaded and impatiently waiting to travel eastward but delayed because of the lack of news of the outcome of the Federal expedition against Fort Fisher under General Butler. When the news came through everyone in Bermuda was delighted, for this first assault on the great fort was unsuccessful and it was called a Confederate victory. Thereupon six blockade runners joyfully departed for Dixie. They were destined never to meet again.

Maffitt did not sail with the others and when he finally arrived off the mouth of the Cape Fear River he noticed a large fire burning at Bald Head and was disturbed at the lack of response to his signals. Since Fort Caswell looked quiet and peaceful Maffitt decided to venture in and tied up at the fort's wharf. He was immediately boarded by Captain E. S. Martin, Confederate Chief of Ordnance, who told him the sad news that Fort Fisher had surrendered to General Terry and Admiral Porter following the second and successful Federal assault by land and sea. Also that a train of powder had been laid to blow up Fort Caswell "before the Yankees arrived." Maffitt was quick to realize the danger of his position. Federal gunboats were approaching to investigate him. He was told that it would only be a matter of hours before Fort Caswell would be attacked. Since his home port was completely blocked by the enemy, Maffitt felt it his duty to try and land his cargo somewhere else, preferably Charleston. So he immediately set out.

Back and forth in front of Charleston's harbor mouth crept the *Owl*, watching, waiting for a chance to sneak in. In order to make certain that precious government mail would not be captured by the enemy, the mailbags were slung over the quarter by a stout line. The quartermaster was ordered to stand by the line with a hatchet. The moment capture seemed inevitable he was ordered to cut the line and let the bags fall and sink to the bottom of the sea. Meanwhile a heavy mist had spread like a woolly blanket across the harbor and Maffitt saw to his horror a cruiser dead ahead. He scarcely had more than fifteen or twenty feet between him and the enemy before he was able to sheer off. At the same time he received a full broadside that cut away the *Owl's* turtleback, perforated the forecastle and tore up the bulwarks in front of the engine room. Twelve men were wounded. The quartermaster was so convinced that capture was unavoidable he swung his hatchet and sent the mailbags to the bottom. But swift action by Maffitt enabled the *Owl* to escape further damage and she picked her way out of the melee and fled out to sea.

Maffitt was completely discouraged. His phenomenal luck seemed to have abandoned him and he felt like a waif of the ocean with no friendly port willing to receive him. Yet he reasoned that it was his sacred duty to land the precious cargo of war materials at some Southern port with the hope that perhaps they would reach Lee's struggling armies in time to be of use. The only other port that seemed to hold a possibility for entrance was Galveston, Texas.

Upon arrival there he saw sixteen Federal cruisers patrolling up and down; also there was the problem of the great reaches of mud flats which if not negotiated at the proper turn of the tide would catch and hold his vessel in a trap. This is exactly what happened. The *Owl* became grounded on Bird Island shoals at the entrance to Galveston Harbor. It was a most exposed point and within the range of the enemy's guns. They promptly rained shot and shell around the stranded vessel. To the rescue came Captain James H. MacGarvey, who steamed out to the stranded vessel in the little *Diana* and succeeded in assisting the *Owl* to refloat herself.

At this point the record becomes obscure as to how Maffitt succeeded in reaching safety within Galveston Harbor. But this undoubtedly took place since the record shows a receipt from the surveyor of the Port of Galveston for $222.15 for duties on clearance of goods imported into the port on the steamer *Owl*.

After discharging his cargo Maffitt wormed his way out of Galveston and pointed the *Owl* to Nassau. Meanwhile Lee surrendered and the war appeared to be over. But by this time Maffitt had received orders from the Confederate States Navy Department (sent weeks earlier) to proceed to England with his cargo.

Upon arrival in England Captain Maffitt sadly delivered the *Owl* to Fraser, Trenholm & Company. From a letter to one of his cousins dated September 12, 1865, it is apparent that Maffitt did not intend to go home, but planned to remain in England after relinquishing command of the *Owl*. His comments are illuminating:

"I cannot tell you how angered I was to hear of the infamous conduct of Sherman's army as they passed through Fayetteville—but it was in many places even worse than what you experienced.

"Well, the war is over and I am truly glad of it—though deeply depressed by the unexpected *total* failure. I hoped for at least success enough to give us the power of claiming just and liberal terms. As it is, we are entirely at the mercy of despotism of the meanest qualifications and sentiments the most base. God help the South—for the people require his grace and divine assistance in their time of sorrow and humiliation." Maffitt then goes on to say that he had decided to remain in England rather than "take the nauseous dose, or 'pardon-asking pill.'" He was intent on preparing himself for an examination that would make him a captain of vessels flying the British flag.

Soon afterward he passed this examination and was put in command of the British merchant steamer *Widgeon,* trading between Liverpool and South American ports. A letter from Captain Maffitt to his family, written from South America, indicates that his main reason in taking this job was to earn money to support his family, "which I would not be permitted to do in the U.S. I shall return as soon as my engagement terminates and see what I can do for the recovery of my property. It would not be wise for me to give up a good position for the present and I presume the ill feeling at the North will fade in time."

Finally in 1867 Maffitt decided that it was safe to return to the United States. Upon arrival in New York he decided to look up some of his old naval friends in the Brooklyn Navy Yard. To his pleasure and surprise he was welcomed cordially by his ante bellum shipmates.

Then began an attempt by Captain Maffitt to secure restitution of his confiscated property which he valued at $75,000. After a long, discouraging period he finally concluded that he would be unsuccessful, so he decided to return to Wilmington, North Carolina, and live with his daughter Florie. Soon afterward he purchased a farm of 212 acres on the sound near Wrightsville Beach. He named his place "The Moorings" and here he spent the rest of his life.

One of those who visited Captain Maffitt shortly after his second marriage in 1870 was David McRae of Scotland. This gentleman wrote a book narrating the incidents of his visit to America and referred to Captain Maffitt "as perhaps the ablest naval officer who had lent his sword to the Confederacy. It was said by more than one that if he had stood by the North he would have been in Admiral Farragut's place today. He held, however, strong Southern views . . ." In describing Captain Maffitt at this time, Mr. McRae observed him to be "a cultivated and gentlemanly man, small-sized and spare in figure, but with a fine cast head, a dark, keen eye, a strong tuft of black whiskers on his chin and a firm little mouth that seemed to express the energy and determination of his character. I remember very well his dignified appearance as he stepped about in his short military cloak, and with his keen and somewhat stern look. He was in reduced circumstances, having staked his whole fortune and position upon the Lost Cause; but like so many of his old military and naval associates he was trying his hand at business and striving to reconcile himself to the new order of things."

In talking to McRae about the war, Maffitt commented, "The Northern navy contributed materially to the successful issue of the war. The grand mistake of the South was neglecting her navy. All our army movements out West were baffled by the armed Federal steamers which swarmed on western waters, and which our government provided nothing to meet. Before the capture of New Orleans, the South ought to have had a navy strong enough to prevent the capture of that city, and hold firmly the Mississippi and its tributaries. This would have prevented many disastrous battles; it would have made Sherman's march through the country impossible and Lee would still have been master of his lines. Yes sir, the errors of our government were numerous but her neglect of the navy proved irremediable and fatal."

Captain Maffitt attempted to make a living by becoming a practical farmer, was reasonably successful, at least in raising enough food to feed his family. At this time he also published his book of reminiscences of life aboard the U.S.S. *Constitution* entitled *Nautilus, or Cruising Under Canvas*. Maffitt conducted an active correspondence with many of his old shipmates of wartime days and also met and talked with a number of them.

When Grover Cleveland was elected to the presidency in

1884, friends of Captain Maffitt recommended him for a position in the Customhouse at Wilmington. Cleveland refused to confirm the nomination. The news was a severe shock to the intrepid blockade-running captain. His repudiation so worked on his mind that he was ill for three months and never recovered. He died on May 15, 1886.

Thus passed a courageous sailor of the South, without doubt the most skillful blockade runner of all that band of seafarers who repeatedly pierced strong Federal flotillas blocking Southern ports. He was a man who remained steadfast to his principles and did what he felt was right. He was an accomplished seaman and navigator and never lacked the will or courage to take his vessels safely through the danger zone.

Captain Maffitt's obituary notice in a Wilmington newspaper, although couched in the flowery terms of the period, well describes that gentleman:

Thus, one by one, the leaves of the flowers that fade and fall, these reminders of the lost cause pass from the stage of action to join the silent majority; and of all brave, daring men who so gloriously illustrated, on land and sea for the liberty loving people can accomplish when contending for the right, none was braver and truer than the gallant gentleman who was yesterday laid to rest in beautiful Oakdale and whom we admired living and mourn dead.

CHAPTER 10

Pursuits, Escapes and Captures

THE ORDERS issued by the Confederate government regarding destruction of westbound blockade-running vessels in case of pursuit and threatened capture also applied to eastbound voyages, for it was well known that the Federals were hungry for cotton. In most cases these orders were complied with by the commanders of blockade runners to the best of their ability. Every effort was of course made to avoid capture before a vessel was destroyed by its own officers and crew. All sorts of dodges were resorted to, such as smoke screens, feeding the boilers with cotton soaked in turpentine to increase steam pressure, zigzag maneuvering and daring runs along the surf close to shore.

By the end of the war, the beaches north and south of the Cape Fear River were strewn with the wreckage of blockade runners which had been beached after being boxed in and shelled by Union cruisers. The commanders of forts Fisher and Caswell were alert day and night to protect blockade runners who were being pursued. If a blockade runner could come within range of the guns of these friendly forts he knew he was safe, for Federal cruisers would not venture within striking distance of those heavy shore batteries.

Not a few blockade-running steamers went ashore because of the unfamiliarity of their pilots with the coast and depth of water. Others came to grief because the pilots panicked and drove the vessels onto the sand when a little more persistence and courage would have enabled them to escape.

During the whole course of the war there were numerous actions along the beaches, particularly north of Fort Fisher. Colonel Lamb, the commandant, kept a mobile force of infantry, cavalry and field artillery ready to sally forth from the fort and

277

render assistance to any blockade runner that had gone ashore and might be the object of salvage attempts by the Federal Navy.

One of the earliest blockade runners to come to grief was the *Modern Greece*, a large British propeller steamer of about one thousand tons. She was one of those early vessels sent by British interests to run the blockade before small, light-draught steamers were put into service. According to the records, she was one of the largest blockade runners of the war.

On the morning of June 27, 1862, the *Modern Greece* had safely eluded the line of Federal cruisers guarding the eastern entrance to the Cape Fear River. But by the time she had crept to within three miles of Fort Fisher and was headed for New Inlet, she was spied by the U.S.S. *Cambridge*. This cruiser immediately gave chase and pelted the *Modern Greece* with shells. Soon the Federal cruiser *Stars and Stripes* joined in the chase and also opened fire.

There was no choice but for the *Modern Greece* to run ashore to avoid capture. Her crew made their escape to the beach in boats and Fort Fisher joined in the affair with several warning shots to the Federal cruisers which had drawn in close in an attempt to haul off the stranded vessel. Meanwhile, the crew of the *Modern Greece*, who had returned to the vessel in an effort to salvage part of her cargo, were in immediate danger because apparently the officers of Fort Fisher had decided to blow the vessel to bits to prevent her falling into enemy hands. When Fisher's shells began dropping, the crew received warning and abandoned the vessel. Minutes later it was blown to smithereens by a well-placed shell from the fort. It was a grand explosion, for she was carrying 1,000 tons of gunpowder for the Confederate Army.

Before her destruction, however, fast work by the crew resulted in salvaging a large amount of clothing and a number of barrels of brandy. These were conveyed to the fort and according to a contempory report "spirits flowed like water for several weeks to the scandal of the fort and its defenders."

The fast little steamer *Venus* was nearly torn apart by Union Navy gunfire while attempting to reach shore. The *Venus* was only 365 tons. Her master was Charles Murray. On this fateful voyage her cargo consisted of 600 cases of rifles, 300 boxes of cartridges, one puncheon of rum (100 gallons) and a large quantity of luxury merchandise.

Early in the morning of October 21, 1863, the lookout aboard the U.S.S. *Niphon* sighted the small vessel speeding toward Old Inlet. Almost the first shot fired by a bowchaser of the *Niphon* shot away the foremast of the *Venus*. A few moments later another shot entered and exploded in the wardroom, injuring several passengers. The third shot passed through the forecastle killing one man. The pilot headed the *Venus* straight toward the beach but not before a fourth shell struck the steamer under the guardrail near the waterline. It bent her plates so badly that water poured into her hold. Shortly after, her stem ground into the sand. The *Niphon* followed up her victory by quickly putting an armed boat over the side. It reached the *Venus* before she could be destroyed by her own people. Captain Murray and his entire crew of twenty-one were captured. Ordinarily the officers and crew of a captured blockade runner were confined in a Northern prison for only a short length of time and then paroled on their promise not to engage again in blockade running. However, if a notorious pilot was involved, his prison term could be extended. On the very same day that the U.S.S. *Niphon* captured the *Venus*, this Federal cruiser added a second runner to her long list of vessels run ashore. This was the fast Crenshaw steamer *Hebe*, capable of a speed of fourteen knots. She was intercepted by the *Niphon* nine miles from Fort Fisher. Her pilot discovered that escape was impossible, and promptly ran her ashore. The *Hebe's* crew left her in small boats and reached the beach safely. Apparently the *Niphon* concluded that the *Hebe* was not so hard aground that she could not be pulled off. But when the salvage crew attempted to haul her, they were swamped by the heavy seas. Although their boat capsized the crew managed to swim ashore. This was observed by the alert personnel at Fort Fisher and a detachment of cavalry was immediately dispatched by Colonel Lamb. The Confederate horsemen rounded up all the Federal sailors. The

Niphon moved in closer and began shelling the beach. A mobile battery of Whitworth guns under the command of Captain Munn of the fort opened fire on the *Niphon* and drove her off. (Whitworth guns were fast firing and modern for that day, with a range of five to six miles.) A second boatload of Federal sailors who were attempting to land and rescue their captured comrades was shelled and destroyed.

Shortly after the foregoing action, the *Niphon* was joined by another Federal cruiser, the *Minnesota,* which opened heavy fire on Captain Munn and his guns. Although the battery's horses were killed, Munn continued to serve his guns and move them to a new position, by hand. However, the heavy cannon fire from the *Minnesota* was too much for the small, Confederate battery. Having fired his last round and with two of his guns disabled, one gunner killed, and a lieutenant and four men wounded, Captain Munn fell back with the survivors, protected by heavy, enfilade fire from Fort Fisher.

In the end, the Federals failed in their attempt to salvage the *Hebe,* for she was burned to the waterline by the Confederates the same night. During the last year of the war, Colonel Lamb and his Whitworth guns were responsible for saving dozens of blockade runners and millions of dollars' worth of cargo. General W. H. C. Whiting in a letter to the Honorable James A. Sedden, Confederate Secretary of War, begged to have a larger force of artillerymen detailed to the fort and additional horses to draw the field guns, for he felt that the mobile Whitworth battery was extremely valuable in assisting stranded blockade runners.

From Union Navy records comes a description of the destruction of the blockade runner *Wild Darrell* at Stump Inlet, February 1, 1864. Lieutenant Commander F. A. Row, in charge of the U.S. cruiser *Sassacus,* reported to Admiral S. P. Lee:

We sighted the blockade runner about 11:00 A.M. on the morning of February 1. Evidently her pilot either became confused or was fearful of capture, for he ran his vessel ashore. As we headed for the beached steamer, we observed the crew busily throwing the cargo overboard. A shot across her bow failed to stop this procedure so I sent an armed boat and boarded the vessel which proved to be the *Wild Darrell*. We discovered, however, that the engine room force had filled the furnaces and were trying to burn out the boilers. I immediately ordered the fires hauled and fortunately found the machinery in perfect order. That part of the cargo which still remained aboard was general merchandise for civilian use.

After several hours of work, we got out hawsers and attempted to pull her off the beach. Being unsuccessful, we enlisted the aid of the U.S.S. *Florida*, Commander Crosby. But her assistance was of no avail.

During this operation, Confederate forces appeared on the beach and opened fire, with musketry. Several of our boats coming from the prize were struck by the bullets.

Both the *Sassacus* and the *Florida* opened fire and forced the Confederate infantrymen to retreat. After due consultation, it was decided to destroy the *Wild Darrell*, since it appeared impossible to haul her off. Thereupon we set her on fire with shells and riddled her to the waterline. She burned fiercely and was a total loss.

The *Georgiana McCaw* was a little steamer of 700 tons which came to grief at 3:30 on the morning of June 2, 1864. Stranded on the Western Bar, she was shelled by the U.S.S. *Victoria*, which straddled her with eight-inch shells and rounds of grape. Part of the crew managed to escape in two boats to the shore, but the cruiser, standing in close and sending a boat aboard, captured twenty-nine of the crew including the captain, most of the officers, and three passengers. The Union boarding parties set fire to the vessel and she continued to burn until 10:00 in the morning. The *Georgiana* was a total loss. Meanwhile Fort Caswell opened up on the small boats of the Federal boarding party and forced them to return to the *Victoria*.

Sometimes a blockade runner made scarcely more than one or two trips before she fell prey to Union cruisers. This was especially true during the last two years of the war. The *Ella* was a smart little paddle-wheel steamer of 404 tons, C. J. Barkley, master. She was owned by the Bee Company of Charleston, South Carolina. Her first trip, in August 1864, had been extremely successful and she had brought a mixed cargo of war supplies and civilian merchandise safely into Charleston. On her second trip to Wilmington, however, things were different. This time 50 per cent of her valuable cargo was war supplies and the balance consisted of luxury items owned by private parties and speculators. The record does not say which Union vessel chased her ashore, but when she grounded she was immediately abandoned by her officers and crew. The latter profanely refused to return and try to save the cargo. The Union cruiser shelled her methodically, but again, as in so many other cases, the Confederate forces at Fort Fisher made a gallant attempt to prevent her falling into enemy hands. Captain Badham and his battery of light field artillery bombarded the vessel and wrecked her completely, after removing her cargo. According to contemporary accounts, six Federal shells from the cruiser passed completely through the *Ella* while the Confederates were carrying her cargo ashore. Part of this consisted of London dock and Holland's gin. A member of the garrison at Fort Fisher recalled that when the cases of liquor floated ashore, "they were immediately sampled by the entire garrison, officers and men. The fort was one great bar room that night. Even the holy man of a chaplin got a snoot full and said a very queer grace at the headquarters mess table next morning."

If a blockade runner approaching the Carolina coast was able to pass the outer squadron of U.S. war vessels and arrive near the mainland, she would either lie off at a distance or run in close to the land north or south of the port and wait for darkness. Vessels frequently remained unnoticed for a whole day. Or they might lie hidden in one of the many inlets near by. Masonboro Inlet to the north of the Cape Fear was a favorite hiding place. When darkness came the steamers would sneak out and made a dash for New Inlet. A blockade runner's trip through the inshore Federal squadron was exciting, but not so dangerous as it looked. The runner could make no armed resistance, for her captain and crew could have been posted as pirates and treated accordingly.

One of the difficulties of running the blockade was the absence of lights along the coast. In coming close to, or steaming along the shore, the flames from Confederate salt works were often used as guides. At Charleston there was a light on Fort Sumter. At Wilmington, in the first year of the war, the Frying Pan Shoals light ship was taken inside Old Inlet and anchored near Fort Caswell, where she was raided and burned by armed boats from the U.S.S. *Mount Vernon*. At New Inlet, a light had been placed on the Mound early in the war, extinguished at the beginning of 1863 and later replaced, together with other dim range lights along the coast. It was found that these lights combined with a system of secret signals constituted less danger to the blockade runners than trying to make port in utter darkness. The signaling—lights at night and flags by day—was done by the Confederate States Signal Corps who accompanied the vessels. Captain Wilkinson was in charge of installing the lights and detailing pilots and signal officers to the various boats.

From the standpoint of Union naval officers, life aboard the blockading squadron was often frustrating. It was not an easy matter to hit a small, fast-moving target speeding at from fourteen to eighteen knots an hour through the pitch-black night. A great deal of powder and shot was expended in trying to sink runners. The naval ordnance of that period was highly inaccurate, with no scientific range-finding system. With this primitive equipment it was difficult to make direct hits on a low-lying vessel from a cruiser whose decks were heaving up and down in the heavy seas common to that coast. To aid in locating blockade runners on dark nights, the United States Navy developed calcium flares or rockets which gave brief but brilliant illumination over a wide area. These enabled the Federals to locate the enemy, get the range and open fire. Late in the war, some Union cruisers were equipped with powerful searchlights taken from locomotives.

The chances were mostly in favor of the blockade runner.

Her commander had only to head for a port and run in and he could choose time and weather and all other circumstances most favorable to him. He could even choose his destination. If, for example, conditions were rough at Charleston, he could change course and head for Wilmington. Once through the blockade, officers and crew of the runner had time for rest and rollicking ashore.

Not so with the men of the blockading squadrons. They suffered from a number of disadvantages. They never knew when a blockade runner might try to steal through their lines. Each war vessel had to operate quickly and take whatever measures seemed feasible at the time. Service aboard a cruiser was monotonous and uncomfortable, peppered only occasionally by periods of action and shooting. Eternal vigilance was the watchword. A solitary moment of napping might let the quarry slip through.

Fog was another nuisance. "There is one obstruction to a constantly efficient blockade, that can neither be removed or overcome," wrote Admiral du Pont to Secretary Gideon Welles, "and that is fog. Vessels that lie in wait to run the blockade, having skillful pilots, and being desperate in their attempts, cannot but sometimes succeed under the favor of fog or darkness."

The officers of the blockading squadrons attempted to keep up the morale of their crews by providing them with books, periodicals, music and entertainment, recruited from those in the forecastles who had talent. Great attention was also given to prompt delivery of mail from home, brought down from the North by special fast dispatch boats.

Aboard one U.S. cruiser operating off Masonboro Inlet, however, the lack of a piano in the wardroom was sorely felt, especially since several of the officers could play. So a group of the younger ones secretly decided to fill the need by a raid ashore. On a brilliant moonlight night they rowed ashore in a lifeboat and entered one of the estuaries upon whose banks were several handsome plantation houses. Selecting the largest, they swept noiselessly up to the landing and walked to the mansion. Peering through the tall French doors of the drawing room they saw, at one end, bathed in moonlight, a handsome grand piano. One of the daredevils was all for sitting down and playing the "Moonlight Sonata" on the spot but was hushed by his comrades. Although they tried to be very quiet in forcing the door, a slight noise was made which awoke the mistress of the mansion. Since her husband was fighting in Virginia and the slaves were too far away to summon, the resolute lady decided to investigate. When she looked out of the window and saw the shadowy figures of men apparently trying to break in, she went into action. Rushing to the closet she secured her husband's loaded shotgun and returned to the window. By this time the young naval officers were carrying the piano out of the front door. The Southern lady, adept at bird shooting, swung the gun to her shoulder and fired both barrels. A high pitched *ping-g-g* resounded from the piano, for her shot had severed several strings, including high C! The Yankees merely laughed and hurried toward their boat with their musical burden, shouting "Thank you, Lady Rebel!" to the irate female.

Among the Union Naval officers who served aboard the various blockading squadrons was Captain (later Rear Admiral) John J. Almy. For fourteen months he was in command of the U.S. Steamer *Connecticut*, operating off Wilmington. During this time his vessel captured and sent north four steamers: *Juno, Scotia, Minnie* and *Greyhound*, with cargoes worth $1,063,-352.49. In addition, Captain Almy's record included the forcing ashore and destroying four more famous runners: *Phantom, Herald, Ceres* and *Diamond*.

The capture of the *Juno* was accompanied by a humorous exchange between Captain Almy and her disgruntled skipper. When the latter came aboard, Almy said politely, "Good morning sir, glad to see you."

To which the Southerner replied, "Damned if I'm glad to see *you!*"

A week before, the *Juno* had safely run into Wilmington and discharged her English cargo of war materials. She was outward-bound with a load of cotton, tobacco and turpentine when overhauled by the *Connecticut*. Among the papers found aboard was an unfinished letter by the captain addressed to the ship's

owners in England, in which he described his run into Wilmington through ". . . sleepy-headed Yankees at night." He said he
expected to be lucky enough to make his exit from Wilmington
with the same ease with which he entered.

Aboard Federal naval vessels, instead of the usual cry of the
lookout, "Sail ho!" it was common practice for a seaman to yell
"Black snake!" when a blockade runner was sighted. Immediately all would be commotion. As the chase commenced,
everyone on board would rush to his post and strain to see the
fleeing steamer.

One of the pursuits by the *Connecticut* lasted 15 hours. As
she approached her quarry her crew saw the blockade runner's
men throw nearly all her cargo overboard. It consisted of a
variety of British merchandise, for the steamer was inbound.
Bales, boxes and barrels covered the sea in the wake of the fleeing
runner, which had opened her steam throttle wide. She hoped
that her sacrificed cargo would enable her to add perhaps a knot
or two to her speed. The markings on some of the boxes could
be plainly seen by the Union sailors, especially several marked
"Shoes." This caused a waggish tar to remark, "Perhaps if we
could get and put on some of those shoes we could run faster
and catch those Rebs!"

According to Captain Almy's log, the blockade runner's sacrifice of her cargo paid off, for she managed to put on just enough
speed to escape. She arrived safely in Nassau, loaded another
cargo and returned without incident to Wilmington.

It was rare that a vessel carrying contraband succeeded in
breaking free, once it was in Union hands. But such was the
case of the *Emily St. Pierre*. To make matters more remarkable,
she was a full-rigged sailing vessel of 1,000 tons, owned by a
citizen of Charleston, South Carolina. On March 18, 1862, when
homeward-bound from Calcutta with a cargo of 2,173 bales of
gunny cloth (used for baling cotton) she was overhauled and
captured near the Carolina coast by the U.S.S. *Florida*, J. R.
Goldsborough commanding. A prize crew was put aboard and
she was ordered north to Philadelphia in charge of Acting Master
Josiah Stone.

The weather was mild and calm and by the twenty-first the
Emily St. Pierre was about thirty miles east of Cape Hatteras.
Then things began to happen.

Here is how Josiah Stone described what took place in his
report to Admiral du Pont:

"Captain Wilson [of the *Emily St. Pierre*] came on deck . . .
spoke to me in a pleasant manner . . . spoke of the nice wind
we had all night." After chatting for ten or fifteen minutes Wilson asked Stone if he would take him to the cabin and "show
him the position of the ship on the chart. I walked in with
him . . . he grabbed me by my collar and drew a belaying pin
from under his vest. At that moment Wilson's cook and steward
sprang out of a stateroom, put two revolvers at my head, threatened my life, put me in irons, put me in a small room and locked
me in, and then told me that he had taken Mr. Hornsby, the
master's mate and Mr. John S. Smith the same way.

"He [Wilson] went into these officers' rooms while they were
asleep, put them in irons and put gags in their mouths: after this
he went on deck. Six of my men being asleep in the forecastle,
he locked them in. He then got three of my men who were on
deck to go down in a scuttle and pass up a coil of heavy rope;
told the men that I wanted it. When the men were down there,
he put the hatches on, and thus had all the crew fastened up except three. He then got some of the crew to help him work the
ship to Liverpool."

Captain Wilson's intrepid recapture of his ship is reminiscent
of the privateering days of the War of 1812. His exploit was
not without casualties, however. One man fell from the foreyard
and died. Another, who had tried to resist being put in irons,
was shot by Wilson and wounded, but not seriously.

Acting Master Stone, on his return from his involuntary voyage to Liverpool, was severely reprimanded by Admiral du Pont
for not confining the prisoners aboard the *Emily St. Pierre*, thus
inviting a counterattack. Perhaps some allowance should be made
for slow-witted Stone, who was a volunteer from the merchant
service.

Yachtsmen of today who cruise up and down the Carolina

coast may be interested to know that the very waters upon which they sail were once plowed by the historic schooner-yacht, *America,* which after winning a series of international races, became a notorious blockade runner during the early days of the Civil War. The *America* was schooner rigged, an almost exact duplicate of a New York pilot boat of the period. After winning the celebrated America Cup at the international yacht races off Cowes in 1851, she was bought by a wealthy British army officer by the name of Lord John de Blaquiers. Since he was more interested in cruising than racing, he cut down her spars and also strengthened her hull with iron braces. The changes reduced the *America's* speed but on several occasions during 1851 and 1852 Lord de Blaquiers entered her in English races and she won several of them. The following year the *America* was bought by Lord Templetown. He soon tired of her and she was laid up for five years, from 1854 to 1859. This long period of inactivity caused her hull to be riddled with dry rot, but apparently she was thought to be worth rebuilding. She was given new oak frames and teak planking and sold to an Englishman, Captain H. E. Decie, who renamed her *Camilla* and spent the winter of 1860 aboard her cruising through the West Indies. Whether this was an excuse for blockade running, is unknown, but the fact remains that early in 1861 the distinguished yacht made several blockade-running trips and brought in a quantity of valuable medicines, including morphine, quinine, surgical instruments, ammunition and clothing.

Later on that year, while at Savannah, Captain Decie sold her to the Confederate government. Since Messrs. Mason and Slidell were about to depart for Europe, it was planned to use the *America* to take them to Havana or Nassau where they could board a steamer for England. It is not clear as to why the Confederate government abandoned this idea but we do know that the *America* again resumed blockade running. By this time however, her good luck was fast running out and to avoid capture by a Federal cruiser her captain ran her ashore and scuttled her at Haw Creek at the head of Dunn's Lake, St. Johns River, Florida.

A month or two later while the U.S.S. *Ottawa* was scouting

Wreck of a blockade runner off Sullivan's Island, S.C.

From PICTORIAL and HISTORICAL NEW HANOVER COUNTY,
by William Lord deRosset

Wilmington's Front Street after Union capture. Released prisoners are marching to the transports.

up the river, her commander, Lieutenant T. H. Stevens, investigated what appeared to him to be the hull of a yacht. He recognized her as the *America* and determined to salvage her if possible. At this time she was a sad-looking spectacle, without ground tackle or sails. Her tall shapely top masts were gone as well as some of her other spars. After a deal of trouble, Lieutenant Stevens raised the *America,* patched her up and made her ready to be moved. Along with the steamer *St. Marys* which Stevens had also raised, the *Ottawa* towed the two vessels north. After undergoing extensive repairs the *America* joined the South Atlantic Blockading Squadron and was used as a dispatch boat. On two occasions her fine sailing qualities enabled her to overhaul and capture a couple of Confederate vessels.

Meanwhile the Naval Academy, which had been temporarily moved from Annapolis to Rhode Island, was in need of a practice ship for midshipmen. The *America* was considered ideal for the purpose and was detached from war duty on May 5, 1863, and sent to Newport. There she remained until 1870 when the government sold her to the notorious Union ex-general, Benjamin F. Butler. He and his family sailed her for many years until at last he sold her to a group representing the Eastern Yacht Club of Massachusetts. They in turn made a present of the *America* to the Navy Department with the understanding that she was to be placed on exhibit at the United States Naval Academy in Annapolis as a floating marine museum.

Of all the many blockade runners that braved the hazards of attack from Union war vessels, the steamers *Siren* and *Kate* chalked up outstanding records for themselves. The *Kate* made forty-one round trips between the British West Indies before she came to grief at the hands of the Federals. The *Siren* made sixty-four trips and millions of dollars for her owners. The little *Kate* was so well known that her activities were the subject of an editorial in the September 30, 1863, issue of the Richmond *Dispatch,* which must have nettled the Union Navy. The editorial read as follows:

"The steamer *Kate* from Nassau successfully ran the blockade into Wilmington on Thursday. She ran into Savannah early in August. Then she ran out of Savannah and went to Wilmington. From Wilmington she started for Nassau about the middle of August and now she comes back to Wilmington with an assorted cargo of arms and ammunition. In other words, the *Kate* is a regular packet, performing her trips with regularity and dispatch. Her successful voyages do not, indeed, tend to exalt our estimate of the officers of the blockading squadron. Let us console ourselves therefore, like Mr. Disraeli, by allowing them to increase our respect for the energy of human nature!"

The *General Beauregard* was a smart little steamer which was boxed in by a Union cruiser and stranded just north of Fort Fisher in December 1863. Next morning two Federal gunboats, the *Howquah* and *Tuscarora*, steamed in toward her and, throwing discretion to the winds, attempted to make her a prize. Apparently they underestimated the vigilance of Colonel Lamb, commandant of Fort Fisher, two miles away. During the night he had received news of the *Beauregard*, and by morning had placed a small battery of Whitworth guns in a natural sand dune bastion a few hundred yards from the stranded vessel.

Colonel Lamb must have been a good poker player, for he held his hand until the Federal steamer had come in close to the *Beauregard*. Bedlam broke loose when shells from the accurate Whitworths started tearing the Federal gunboats to pieces. The *Tuscarora* was out of service fourteen months. The *Howquah* limped out to sea a few miles and sank. There was great rejoicing in Wilmington at the news of this victory over the blockaders.

As might be expected, there were heroes and cowards among the pilots and captains of vessels running the blockade. These men either showed their metal or a yellow streak when danger crowded close. One of the most heroic men was Pilot John William Anderson of the *Mary Celeste*. In August 1863 while inbound for Wilmington with holds crammed with war supplies, Pilot Anderson was stricken with yellow fever. As the *Mary Celeste* neared the North Carolina coast it was plain to all aboard that Anderson was near death. At the critical hour of dawn the vessel found herself fleeing from a Union cruiser. Like a fast greyhound the *Mary Celeste* dashed for New Inlet. Anderson was dying in his cabin. Ahead lay the treacherous bar, over which the vessel must pass before safety was assured. No one on board except Anderson knew how to negotiate this short but dangerous stretch of water. Although he was nearly delirious, he knew from the cannon shots close at hand that his vessel was about to be captured. He also knew what that meant in terms of loss, not only to the owners but to the Confederate States of America. Too weak to get up unaided, he demanded to be taken to the bridge. Two seamen brought him to the wheelhouse and there supported him while he conned the ship over the bar to safety under the friendly guns of Fort Fisher. A few moments later, those on the bridge saw Anderson bend his head as if to cough, but were horrified to see him in the throes of the black vomit, sure sign of imminent death. He was dead less than a minute later.

An amusing dialogue took place between the pilot of the blockade runner *Atlanta* while she was in a dangerous position off Fort Caswell. It was in July 1864. Before leaving Bermuda the captain received reports that several of the fastest blockade runners had been forced to return to port after unsuccessful attempts to enter Charleston and Wilmington. It was said that the ocean and coast were alive with Federal ships.

The *Atlanta* approached Old Inlet bar in the middle of the night and sailed boldly between two ships of the fleet. Their lookouts must have been dozing, for only a few shots were fired. The *Atlanta* skipped safely through. It was fortunate that she did, for she had aboard 400 tons of meat for Lee's hungry fighters.

In recalling the incident later, the pilot said: "The chief officer was a Virginia man named Charles Nelson. I ordered him to find out the depth of the water, for the *Atlanta* was getting into shoal water fast. Nelson went to the leadsman, found out the soundings but reported so slowly that I reproached him for it.

"Said I, 'Can't even a shell make you move faster?' (Two of them had exploded between us a moment before.)

"His answer was, 'What's the use, sir? I might go just fast enough to get in the way of one of those d——d shells.'"

If a Federal cruiser got the range of a blockade runner in

reasonably good weather the latter could receive an unmerciful pounding. An example of this was the damage inflicted on the steamer *Armstrong* just before her capture. She received 195 shot and shells from the Federal cruiser *R. R. Cuyler*, a fast screw steamer. The chase lasted seven hours. Damage included: paddle box shot away; cabin set afire by explosive shells. The crew managed to quench the flames as the plucky *Armstrong* staggered toward shore. In a last-minute effort to increase speed, all her anchor chain was jettisoned, her masts cut away and 400 precious bales of cotton, representing a loss of approximately $125,000, thrown overboard. Miraculously, no one was killed or even scratched. The vessel was stranded, a total loss. Since the *Armstrong* was beached on a section out of range of Confederate shore batteries, the crew of the *Cuyler* was able to salvage many of the bales which floated ashore and thus made themselves some tidy prize money.

This prize money was the one big hope of every officer and man aboard the blockading squadrons. An article on this subject in the December 1870 issue of *Harper's Monthly Magazine*, described the situation as follows: "What a life of adventure and watchfulness there was aboard the blockading squadron! What hopes of prize money! What eager chases of a flying enemy! The chase of a blockade runner was always a scene of intense excitement to every person aboard the Federal cruiser. Pride, patriotism and pocket were all appealed to. Blockade runners were richly laden, and their capture put half their value of vessel and cargo into the pockets of their captors. England was very unpopular with the Union sailors, for that nation had built and manned many of these illegal traders. It gave Union seamen pleasure to know that their capture touched the purses of English merchants."

When the capture was made the vessel was sent with a prize crew to a Northern port. When the condemnation proceedings commenced, the lawyers for the captured vessel always tried to delay the sale so that the expenses would be so heavy that neither the United States government nor the captors would realize any money out of it. They wanted their ill wind should blow no good to any Yankee. The laws that regulated the condemnation of prizes provided that all who joined in the capture should share in the proceeds; the captors generally got half the value of the property, both ship and cargo. The United States government got the other half. The proceeds, after payment of expenses, were divided among the captors according to their pay and rank The commanding officer of the squadron received 5 per cent; the fleet captain, 1 per cent. But if the capture was made by a single vessel, her commander got 10 per cent. When the *Hope* was captured by the little tug *Eolus* off Wilmington on October 22, 1864, the acting master of the latter won $13,164.85 for his day's work. The assistant engineer received from the same prize $6,657, or more than four years' pay. The seamen were awarded over $1,000 apiece, while the cabin boy, whose pay was less than two dollars and a half a week, received $532.60 for his share.

The *Eolus* was a lucky ship, because nine days later she assisted in the capture of the big steamer *Lady Sterling*. Her cargo sold for more than $500,000. In this case the seamen each received $2,000 in addition to the $1,000 they had pocketed from the *Hope*.

Earlier in the war, in July 1862, the U.S.S. *Magnolia* captured the contraband steamer *Memphis*. Her cotton and resin were valued at more than half a million dollars so that a lieutenant from the *Magnolia* received $38,318.55 for his single share.

"Out of sixteen hundred captures of blockade runners claimed by the Federal Navy, fewer than eight hundred were condemned and the proceeds paid over. Yet these eight hundred vessels brought more than $25,000,000 at auction. As much property was destroyed as captured, of course, so that it is safe to say that the losses to the owners and shareholders in blockade running enterprises was over $50,000,000."*

One of the most responsible positions aboard a blockade runner was that of leadsmen. This work required great physical endurance, for the leadsman had to keep swinging the heavy lead attached to the line, casting it ahead of the moving vessel and

* *Harper's New Monthly Magazine*, December 1870, p. 108.

allowing it to sink to the bottom. Then he had to haul the lead back on deck, read the fathoms correctly and report the soundings to the bridge. When shoal water was reached, the safety of the ship and cargo and lives of all on board depended on the leadsman's skill and faithfulness. If he was treacherous he could easily deliver the ship into the hands of the enemy by calling off false soundings, or allowing her to run ashore.

One of the most skillful leadsmen was a slave owned by the pilot of a blockade runner. Under fire and with the ship going fast into shoal water the pilot said to his slave, "You can't get correct soundings, the ship is going too fast. I'll slow her down for you."

The Negro leadsman answered with a grin, "This is no time to slow down sir. You let her go. I'll give you the bottom!" And he did so until he was near exhaustion and the ship was safely over the Charleston bar.

This man often stood in the forechains for hours in cold weather, with the spray flying over him. Yet he never made a mistake or gave an incorrect cast of the lead. Once, when the vessel was approaching Nassau, the master said to the slave as he pointed shoreward, "Every man on that island is as free as I am, so will *you* be when we get there."

The slave answered, "I did not want to come here to be free, sir. I could have gone with the Yankees long ago if I had wished."

He was referring to what the Union General Butler called "Intelligent Contrabands." They were Negroes who managed to reach the Federal blockading squadrons in small boats and rafts and who asked to be freed. These Contrabands often supplied naval officers with valuable information about what was going on ashore, movements of blockade runners and conditions along the coast.

Another tale of courage is related by the master of another blockade runner. It concerns his quartermaster, William Cuthbert. Once, when the vessel was being shelled by a Union cruiser, the captain asked Cuthbert if he was hurt. Cuthbert replied, "I am all right, sir, but I do not know how much wheel there is left or the compass: give me a star to steer by."

The astonished captain saw that a Federal shell had passed between the quartermaster and his mate as they stood on either side of the six-foot wheel, taking out two spokes, destroying the compass and burying itself in the deck. Yet Cuthbert was steering the ship as if nothing had happened.

Until Hurricane Hazel scoured the North Carolina coast in August 1955, it was possible to see, at low tide near Wrightsville Beach, the rusting remains of the notorious contraband steamer *Fanny and Jenny*. The thick gray iron of her hull withstood the batterings of the Atlantic for ninety years and this ancient piece of wreckage was a well-known sight to the summer visitors of this popular resort.

She was once a sleek and daring vessel, manned by young North Carolinians who lacked nothing in courage and audacity. On the night of February 9, 1864, the *Fanny and Jenny*, a fore-and-aft side-wheeler, almost new and considered queen of the blockade runners, was plunging through rough seas in the direction of New Inlet. It was an unusually black night and as the *Fanny and Jenny* plowed along, she was suddenly hailed with the shout, "Heave to!" from the U.S.S. *Florida*.

Instead of obeying, the runner opened up with every ounce of steam and lunged forward on a zigzag escape course. By now another Federal cruiser had joined the chase and both opened fire with grape and canister.

The skipper of the *Fanny and Jenny*, realizing that the jig was up, ordered the wheel hard over and headed straight for shore. Another burst of fire from the pursuing men-of-war carried away a paddle wheel and the foremast. Again the guns roared and the runner's smokestack rolled on the deck pierced by scores of holes from deadly canister. Still other shots punctured her hull and the water poured into her holds. Caught between two fires, the crew scrambled into the two lifeboats and tried to make shore through the pounding surf. One of the boats capsized and the captain and purser were drowned. The survivors were headed off by an armed boat from the *Florida*.

The *Fanny and Jenny* was a mass of flames, ignited by bomb-shells from the other Union cruiser. Soon a great explosion tore the blockade runner to pieces, for she was loaded with tons of gunpowder. In addition to that cargo, the *Fanny and Jenny* carried a handsome solid gold, jewel-studded sword with the inscription: "To General Robert E. Lee, from his British Sympathizers." It was also rumored that the vessel carried a sizable amount of gold subscribed by British people who sided with the South. Whether or not this is true is hard to say. At least, as far as is known, no gold pieces have washed up on Wrightsville Beach since the *Fanny and Jenny* was lost and somewhere among those shifting sands lies buried the handsome British sword that never reached General Robert E. Lee.

CHAPTER 11

The Two Battles of Fort Fisher

BUTLER'S DUD

M<small>R</small>. A. P. S<small>MITH</small> stood in the pilothouse of the steamer *Swallow*, hands thrust deep in his trousers pockets. An unlighted cheroot was clamped between his teeth. Dourly he scanned the darkening Cape Fear River, then turned and faced Pilot Roy D. Cluett, a native of Smithville.

"Please be extremely careful on this voyage, Mr. Cluett," Smith said. "The owners are counting heavily on the profits and the risk is all theirs since the marine insurance companies have had so many losses lately they've refused to insure blockade runners any more."

"Stop worrying," Cluett advised him. "If the *Swallow* is lost, I'm responsible, not you. You are merely the company's agent."

"I know that," Smith retorted testily, "but I don't like the look of things. I tried to persuade the company to wait until we know definitely whether or not the Yankees intend to attack Fort Fisher. But they shrugged and told me not to listen to rumors. Nevertheless I think this voyage is risky, very risky."

This conversation, recorded in letters of Pilot Cluett, took place during the evening of December 23, 1864. Shortly afterward the *Swallow* dropped downriver, following the dim range lights to Fort Fisher landing, where she anchored. The hook had scarcely been dropped when a picket boat came alongside and the coxswain climbed to the bridge with a message for Pilot Cluett and Captain Tayton. He told them that something was brewing seaward. Strange lights had been seen to northward, far out at sea. The Confederate naval authorities advised Pilot Cluett to make his run through Old Inlet and head due east, for

297

the Union cruisers had hauled unusually far offshore that night.

It was well past midnight when the low silhouette of Fort Caswell showed above the skyline of the western shore. During his years at sea, Cluett had kept watch on many a black night, but none had been like this. It seemed to him as if he "could reach out and gather the darkness by handfulls. The north-easter which had swept the coast a few days ago had blown itself out, yet the sea was still troubled and the swells, marching shoreward, row on row, made the *Swallow* labor and pitch. A frigid wind caught the tops of the waves and blew them in slanting sheets of spray across the bridge. Astern was a broad wake of yeasty foam, churned by the steamer's paddle wheels. Not a light showed from the fort. Yet I knew that many a look-out and sentry was wide awake, watching us as we slipped swiftly through Old Inlet and into the open sea."

When the fort had merged with the shadow line of the shore, Cluett took his station on the starboard wing of the bridge. Captain Tayton posted himself at the opposite wing. Both stared straight ahead, trying to pierce the inky blackness. It was no use. They might as well have been blind men groping their way through a tunnel. All they knew was that their steamer was heading toward Bermuda and that she was safely clear of the land and breasting the long rollers like a thoroughbred. The lash of them against the *Swallow's* stem made a dull, booming sound and Captain Tayton took up the engine-room speaking tube and spoke to the chief engineer, telling him to reduce speed to ten knots. There was always a chance that the top-heavy deck cargo of cotton bales might shift, with disastrous results.

A half-hour later the lookout reported lights ahead: "A whole string of 'em on the horizon, broad on the port bow."

Cluett's narrative describes how he raised his telescope and verified the lookout's report, saying that "it looked like the whole d——d Union Navy was off there!"

Captain Tayton remarked that they could not be part of the blockading squadron for there were too many vessels and the blockaders never showed lights.

For a long time both officers studied the line of lights through their spy glasses. They looked like a distant row of street lamps. Captain Tayton guessed that the Union fleet, if such it was, was steaming slowly out of the north, about twenty-five miles due east of Fort Fisher. After the *Swallow* had changed to a more southeasterly course, the lights of the enemy vessels gradually winked out, one by one, lost under the rim of the sea. Yet the question still remained: what did those lights mean?

By now, the middle of December in the fourth year of the war, the fortunes of the Confederacy and her armies were at an all-time low. More than at any other period was Wilmington of vital importance to the Southern cause. Food supplies and cattle from across the Mississippi had been cut off by Union army victories. The fall of Atlanta and Sherman's devastating march across Georgia to Savannah had wrecked that state's railroad system. Lee, with his back to the wall at Petersburg, could no longer count on supplies or any assistance from the Deep South.

What other resource was left? Charleston was now so tightly blockaded that it had virtually lost contact with the outside world. Wilmington alone remained, the South's last port of entry for munitions from Europe. Unless Fort Fisher held, and the Cape Fear kept open to blockade runners, Lee would not be able to supply his armies or feed them.

Did those lights out there mean that Lincoln had decided to try and sever this last life line of the Confederacy? Or were those men-of-war merely making a reconnaissance in force? It was even possible that that line of vesels indicated a thrust further south, perhaps an attempt to batter through Charleston's strong forts and capture the city from the sea instead of from the land.

If a real battle was in the making at Fort Fisher and the Federals won, Wilmington was doomed. Fort Caswell alone could not protect the southern mouth of the Cape Fear. Once the Union men-of-war got past Fort Fisher, they could blast their way upriver. Their troops could move up both sides and converge on the poorly defended city.

Fort Fisher was the key to the whole area and if it could withstand attack, the South could still lock the North out of Wilmington and maintain her overseas supply line. Fort Fisher must not fall! It could not fall. Had not Colonel Lamb, the commandant, declared it to be impregnable? Yes, and that was not only his considered opinion, but that of the best engineering brains of the Confederate army. They had embodied in Fort Fisher all the lessons learned by the British at Sevastopol and by Beauregard when he bombarded Fort Sumter. The forts defending Sevastopol during the Crimean War had been constructed of heavy blocks of granite. The British found out after the surrender that more Russian artillerymen had been killed by flying hunks and splinters of stone than from shells. During the engagement against brick-built Sumter, the air was filled with flying debris, lethal in its effect.

With these examples in mind, Confederate engineers had set to work to make Fort Fisher different—and different it was indeed. It embodied the most modern concepts of defense against attack, both from land and sea. The shape of the fort was like the inverted letter L. The vertical arm of the L was the sea face. The horizontal arm was the land face, extending directly across Confederate Point and practically fencing it in. Instead of constructing a single fortification of masonry (like Sumter and Sevastopol) the Confederate engineers built a long series of batteries guarded by earthworks. The guns were protected by a system of heavy traverses made of sand and earth and sodded with coarse marsh grass. A solid shot could only plow into them harmlessly. If a shell exploded, the only danger was from flying shell fragments, not from stone and bricks. There were also bombproofs, similar to dugouts in modern warfare, where the gun crews could take shelter during heavy bombardments. Magazines deep in the earth protected against powder explosions.

Actually Fort Fisher was not one fort, but a series of them—various parts of the fort were referred to by different names. On the tip of Confederate Point stood Battery Buchanan, the outgrowth of the original Battery Bolles. Buchanan and a number of other batteries commanded New Inlet, where the narrow, winding channel made it necessary for every vessel that entered to come under the guns. Further north was Mound Battery, a favorite landmark for blockade runners. All the way from the Mound to the Northeast Bastion was one long series of gun emplacements, thirteen hundred yards long. Each of the batteries was connected with a strong infantry parapet. The same type of heavy traverses were used to guard the guns on the land face, together with bombproofs and magazines. Altogether there were thirty, containing fourteen thousand, five hundred square feet of floor space. The traverses afforded excellent protection to the gunners against enfilading gunfire from enemy vessels.

The construction of Fort Fisher had taken nearly four years from the time the first gun was emplaced on Confederate Point. Its size had doubled within the past two years. Hundreds of slaves and mules had been drafted from the neighboring plantations for this work. It was undoubtedly the largest and strongest earthwork fort in the world at the time. People called it the Gibraltar of the South.

The fort's total armament consisted of forty-seven guns and three mortars, including Columbiads of 11-inch caliber. Twenty-three cannon protected the fort's sea face, while twenty-four were mounted on the land face. The heaviest of the guns were those that pointed out to sea.

What the captain and pilot of the blockade runner *Swallow* had seen on the night of December 23, 1864, was indeed a Union armada. Late that fall Acting Rear Admiral Sam Phillips Lee, commander of the North Atlantic Blockading Squadron, had reported to Gideon Welles that he needed more and speedier vessels if he was expected to bottle up the Cape Fear. Ample proof that his request was urgent was the fact that his entire squadron had captured or destroyed only forty-four blockade runners off Wilmington in a whole year. Southern newspapers jibed that he had stopped only ten per cent of all runners through the blockade. It was even broadly hinted by the Northern press that some Union officers were "in cahoots" with the blockade runners.

These things spurred Welles to act on a long-contemplated

plan for slamming the back door to Richmond once and for all. In a letter to President Lincoln he said, ". . . blockade running has been systematized into a business, and the ingenuity and skill of Englishmen and the resources of English capital are used without stint in assisting the Rebels."

After long and patient negotiations with General Halleck and Secretary of War Stanton, Welles finally received their approval for a joint Army-Navy expedition against Wilmington. What was to follow had a considerably more important bearing on the outcome of the war than some of our earlier historians were willing to admit. Now, however, from the vantage point of nearly a hundred years it becomes clear that if Fort Fisher had been allowed to stand much longer, the life of the Confederacy would have been lengthened by months or even a year or more. Perhaps one of the reasons why the two battles of Fort Fisher have received less than their deserved degree of study and evaluation is that a great deal was going on in a number of places at the same time. December 1864 and January 1865 were dramatic months. The siege of Petersburg had dragged on for half a year by December. In the same month Hood attacked and captured Nashville. Other stirring events included the engagement at Murfreesboro and Sherman's siege and capture of Savannah. In January the stalemate at Petersburg continued, with alarms and excursions on both sides which focused the attention of the military and civilians alike.

Not only were the battles of Fort Fisher notable for their effect on the outcome of the war, but for two other unique reasons. During the first battle the Federal forces exploded what in that day was the equivalent of the H-bomb. In the second battle the Union forces used amphibious tactics that were the forerunners of those employed during World War II against Japanese-held islands in the South Pacific.

The thing that actually clinched the proposition to attack Fort Fisher was Grant's somewhat reluctant approval. He was not keen on opening up another campaign that might drag on, but in the end he agreed, with one condition, that Admiral Lee should not head the expedition. He was not sufficiently energetic, Grant opined. A more daring man was needed. The most logical choice was David Porter, whose Mississippi River gunboats had blasted the road to Vicksburg. He had vitality and he was always eager for a fight. On September 22, Porter was detached from the Mississippi Squadron, conferred with Grant and then came east to relieve Admiral Lee.

Plans and preparations for the Wilmington expedition were delayed by red tape and a dispute between the Army and Navy over the exchange of naval prisoners. By the time this was ironed out, a month or more had slipped by. In the meantime there was the question as to who should command the Army forces. If Grant and Halleck had scoured the list of army generals they could not have chosen a man more calculated to infuriate Southerners than the one they chose: Butler, "Beast" Butler, dictator of occupied New Orleans and "insulter of Southern womanhood"; alias "Spoons" Butler for his alleged stealing of silver spoons during the occupation; Butler, slippery politician, puffed with pride, bulging with bombast; "Old Cock-Eye" who had decreed that runaway slaves were legitimate prizes of war because they were "contraband." Butler, crafty character who was said to exert a strange and evil hold over General Grant—an influence that has never been satisfactorily explained.

Nor were the chances of success of the proposed expedition enhanced by the fact that Porter and Butler thoroughly disliked each other. It started at the surrender of forts Jackson and St. Phillip on the Mississippi. Porter had accepted the capitulation of the Confederate defenders before General Butler, in charge of land forces, had a chance to get there.

Ignoring these drawbacks, Welles went ahead with characteristic energy to gather men, ships and arms for the assault on Fisher. He took the best ships from the various blockading squadrons, marshaled his monitors and repaired as many other vessels as the overworked yards of the North could handle. The majority of the men had little or no seafaring experience. Many of them were Army draftees who rushed to enlist in the Navy for fear of being shot down in front of Petersburg's trenches. Welles had hoped to send his armada southward during October, the best month for the purpose, but the month went by and preparations were far from complete. The men-of-war and transports lay idle at Hampton Roads and Beaufort, waiting to be loaded.

Just then came the Big Idea and it sprang from the bulbous brow of none other than the "Beast" himself, Butler. During a short stopover in Washington, Butler went to see Lincoln and told him about reading a newspaper story concerning the explosion of a great ammunition dump somewhere near London. Many tenement houses were leveled and the windows within a twenty-mile radius shattered. If a great explosion could wreak such extensive damage, Butler pointed out to the President, why not set off a ship full of powder close to Fort Fisher in advance of the Army-Navy assault. The terrific detonation would dismount every gun in the fort and render the garrison so stunned and helpless that Union forces could practically walk into the place without firing a shot. In fact, Butler declared, it would not be surprising if most of the garrison would be killed by the concussion. For the second time during the blockade, here was an Idea that looked as if it might be a quick and easy short cut to success. Number One was the Stone Fleet. It remained to be seen whether or not Fort Fisher could be invested by the blowing up of a powder ship.

Lincoln apparently was noncommittal. But Butler buttonholed Assistant Secretary of the Navy G. V. Fox and gave him the Big Idea. Fox then told Welles. At first he was inclined to shrug the thing off as being a harebrained scheme, but agreed to take it under advisement.

This was right at the time of Lincoln's second term election, which added further delays to the Wilmington expedition. Some of the pessimists in the government said that the Navy's obviously large preparations had tipped off the Confederates in North Carolina. Meanwhile, Porter's assumption of command over the blockading squadrons had whipped them into action and within the surprisingly short space of three weeks had captured or run ashore blockade runners valued, with their cargoes, at more than two million dollars.

The delays in getting the expedition started actually helped Butler sell his idea of the powder ship. It seems that he came to see Porter aboard the U.S.S. *Malvern* with a great show of secrecy and a long preamble. What did Porter think of Butler and his Ideas? Here is what he sarcastically wrote in his book, *Incidents and Anecdotes of the Civil War:*

"Perhaps, thought I, he plans to introduce rattlesnakes into Fort Fisher on the sly; but this idea I at once dismissed; there is nothing in the Constitution which would authorize such a proceeding.

"I whispered to Captain Breeze, 'The General is going to propose his Petroleum Bath, such as he has already proposed to use on James River. He is going to attack Fort Fisher from seaward by setting afloat tons of petroleum when the wind is on the shore, and, by igniting it, knock the rebs out of their boots!' I thought the absurdity of such an idea would be a great recommendation, especially as it would cost a great deal of money, for at that time there was great competition in Washington as to which department could make the largest expenditure."

Finally Butler got down to the details of his powder boat scheme. "He argued the subject with so much eloquence and showed such a knowledge of pyrotechnics, that no one could controvert his opinions.

"When the matter of the proposed powder boat had been submitted, I saw at once that here was something to simplify matters very much, requiring no act of Congress or interference of the Committee on the Conduct of the War! The army and navy had plenty of bad powder and worthless vessels—in fact, material for half a dozen powder-boats if necessary."

In spite of this flippant remark, Porter was impressed by Butler's plan. He admitted as much in his memoirs: In a short speech he "accepted the general's plan, at the same time eulogizing the head that could conceive such a brilliant idea. The navy and the powder boat would be all-sufficient, and I rather liked the notion, as the expedition would be entirely a naval affair, and

I was not anxious to repeat my Red River experience on the Atlantic Coast.*

"I think I stood higher in General Butler's estimation at that moment than I have ever done, before or since, for, on the whole, he didn't seem to fancy me, as I had an unpleasant way of speaking my mind and not permitting anyone to interfere with my business.

"I don't hesitate to say that I encouraged this scheme of a powder-boat, for in it I saw the road to success, and I was pleased to see that, notwithstanding General Butler's enthusiasm at the idea of blowing up Fort Fisher, he was not at all disinclined to have the navy go along, and *also the contingent of troops that had been originally proposed!*" [The italics are Admiral Porter's.]

At this point in his memoirs the Admiral does a bit of backwatering, pointing out that although many persons ridiculed Butler's idea, he himself felt that it would be "worth while to try everything, and some of our most scientific minds in Washington were so much impressed with the idea of the powder-boat that they carefully investigated the subject. The results of their calculations went to show that if a hundred and fifty tons of powder, confined in an enclosed space, could be *at once* exploded at a short distance from Fort Fisher, the concussion would displace so much air and so rapidly that it would kill every living thing in the vicinity, and wipe the sand fort out of existence."

Basically, the theory was correct, as proved by bombing casualties in World War II, particularly the effect of the atom bomb on the people of Hiroshima and Nagasaki. But of course the immensity of the concussion required to kill human life was grossly miscalculated.

Porter admits that he must have been "somewhat excited, as I telegraphed Captain Wise, Chief of the Bureau of Ordnance,

---

* The Red River expedition was an attempt to capture the defenses of Vicksburg in reverse by sending a fleet of gunboats from the Mississippi into the Yazoo. Twice Porter tried to force his armored vessels and transports through shallow bayous, streams and channels, coming close to disaster on both occasions.

Navy Department, that I wanted fifteen thousand pounds of powder to blow up Fort Fisher, instead of one hundred and fifty tons, the amount asked for by General Butler. I was vexed at Wise's answer, 'Why don't you make a requisition for Niagara Falls and Mount Vesuvius? They will do the job for you.'

"This little mistake of two ciphers would indicate that I was not so phlegmatic as usual, so I really think I must have believed in the scheme.

"After General Butler and his staff had departed, Captain Breeze said to me: 'Admiral, you certainly don't believe in that idea of a powder-boat. It has about as much chance of blowing up the fort as I have of flying!'

" 'And who knows,' I said, 'whether a machine may not soon be perfected to enable us all to fly,* as it only requires forty horsepower in a cubic foot of space, and a propeller that will make such a vacuum that the air will rush in and drive the thing along.'

"Breeze looked disappointed that I should lend myself to such a project. I directed him to make signal to the powder-magazine and inquire how much powder they had on hand.

"Breeze sighed as he walked out of the cabin, and I thought I heard him say, 'All bosh!'—but one has to be a little deaf occasionally."

Porter went right ahead and got hold of an old steamer, *Louisiana*, tore out her insides and made her ready to receive a bellyful of gunpowder. An intricate firing mechanism was designed so that the entire charge would be detonated at once.

By December 10, General Butler had all his troops aboard the transports, but Admiral Porter was far from sanguine about the rough-and-ready general's ability to capture Fort Fisher. On the same day he wrote Fox that Butler and General Weitzel "seem to have a vague idea of what they are going to do . . . depending on the explosion to do all the work . . . Grant, though, has nothing to say, and Butler has it all his own fashion."

At last, on December 13, the armada set sail for a rendezvous twenty-five miles east of Fort Fisher. From the moment the fleet

* Prophetic words!

got under way, everything went wrong. To begin with, a long article in the Philadelphia *Press* a day or so after the fleet sailed gave the Confederates ample warning of Federal intentions. Next, storms scattered the ships and the transports were days late at the rendezvous. But the most mortifying thing of all was the dismal failure of Butler's vaunted powder ship.

For a first-hand account of what happened, we will cross over to the Confederate side and hear about it from Lieutenant Roby of the Confederate cruiser *Chicamauga*, who with a number of seamen and two midshipmen had been detailed to go to Fort Fisher and serve two Brooke 8-inch banded rifles that had been transferred there to augment the fort's armament: "Soon we were tramping over the long stretches of sand to Fort Fisher. Those lads had no idea of what they were in for. Neither had I. Everyone was joking and laughing as if they were on a picnic.

"My bluejackets were quartered in the fort. No one at headquarters had arranged for accommodations for me and my midshipmen. So we had to shift for ourselves. As every other place was crowded, we bedded ourselves down for the night in an abandoned hut outside the fort and a little to the north of it among the dunes back of the beach. That's how the three of us happened to be so close to the Yankee's powder ship when she exploded the following night. We were asleep on the floor of the hut in that uneasy, half-consciousness which men have when they know that a battle is in the offing. All at once we were jarred awake by a terrific concussion; then another and another. We thought at first that the big guns of the fort had fired a sudden salvo. We ran outside just as the last charge of powder and most of the Yankee ship went sky-high. Great sections of deck planking hurtled high in the air and spun into the sea like pinwheels. From the stern, burning powder bags shot in all directions. A great pillar of smoke hung over the wreck. Gradually the fire in the hold died down. Darkness closed in again and all was silent. We went back to the hut and tried to finish our sleep. It was impossible, so we talked till dawn."

Butler's dud. The execution was worse than the conception.

In the darkness the *Louisiana* had been run too far north of the fort and grounded too far off the beach. Then something went wrong with the fuses that were going to set off the charge. The entire cargo of powder was supposed to go off at once. Instead, there was a series of explosions and a lot of noise and smoke. The whole thing was a flop.*

To be sure, Porter started bombarding Fort Fisher. But Butler, thinking that he had demolished the fort, rushed toward shore in his steamer, only to turn tail hastily when Fisher's big guns hurled their shells around him. Disgruntled, he began making preparations for moving his troops ashore to the north of the fort with the intention of storming the land face.

The navy began firing at 11:30 in the morning and the ironclads moved in, led by *Ironsides*, and followed by *Monadnock*, *Canonicus* and *Mahopac*. The other vessels in the fleet, forty-three in all, not counting transports, followed suit. Fort Fisher replied only occasionally to the steady rain of shells. The Confederates seemed to be conserving their powder. Hits from the fleet exploded two of the underground magazines and some of the outbuildings caught fire.

Several of Fort Fisher's guns centered their fire on a number of old-fashioned wooden frigates among the Federal fleet. As a round shot hit them, splinters flew in all directions. The frigates were quick to reply. They were armed with a wide variety of ordnance, from huge 15-inch shell guns to 100-pound Parrot rifles.

About two o'clock in the afternoon the Federal fire increased in tempo. Once in a while, after a spherical shell struck a Confederate battery, nearly spent, it exploded with its base toward the gunners. This caused the bottom end of the shell to fall among the men. One young fellow, full of bravado, was just

---

* That night a boat came to Porter's flagship from shore. It contained four Confederate deserters. When Porter talked with them he asked about the effect of the explosion. "It was dreadful," one of them replied, "it woke up everybody in Fort Fisher." Confederate officers thought that a boiler had burst aboard one of the large frigates.

raising a bottle of whisky to his lips when one of the spent shell ends shattered the bottle. He yelled bloody murder, but got no sympathy from his comrades who cursed him for wasting their liquor.

"By God!" he gasped, wiping his torn fingers on his shirt, "I swear I'll never touch another drop as long as I live." He made good his promise, for a half-hour later he was decapitated by a round shot.

The afternoon dragged on, filled with enormous detonations, blood, dust and sweat. At three o'clock a young courier ran at top speed across the open space between two of the batteries. Just before he reached safety a large shell exploded directly above him. When the smoke cleared, the lad had disappeared. Only a few fragments of flesh and bone spattered the ground.

Toward sunset, one of the Brooke rifles burst. It was like a thunder clap. The explosion was so fierce that it split the huge gun from the jaws of the cascabel horizontally through the trunnions and then sliced perpendicularly through the chase. Half of the breech was blown back over the heads of the gun crew. The other half smashed through the carriage to the ground. At the same time the heavy iron bands around the breech sprang apart and thrashed viciously among the terrified men. Most of them were injured. Two were killed by the iron bands.

The captain of the remaining Brooke ordered a reduction in the charge of powder. It would decrease the range, but he did not want another explosion. He rigged an extra lanyard and ordered the crew to lie prone in a shallow trench when the piece was fired. Nevertheless, in about an hour, Number Two blew up. The casualties were less severe than when Number One let go. Only one was killed, two badly hurt and six had minor wounds. Explosions of this kind were common on both sides. Admiral Porter had all his Parrot guns explode during the second battle of Fort Fisher, caused, no doubt, by overheating and heavy powder charges. Tough steels had not been perfected at that time and many iron castings were imperfect.

Since several of Butler's transports had not yet arrived from

Beaufort as expected, he postponed his landing operations until the next day which was Christmas. The men-of-war renewed their bombardment as Butler's troops came ashore in small boats.

Officers of the fleet, watching these operations through their spyglasses, saw about three thousand infantrymen land on the beach and begin to advance toward the strongly fortified land face which was protected by palisades of sharpened logs and a high parapet, behind which Confederate soldiers waited with cocked muskets. The Union troops halted out of musket range and there was much scurrying about and reconnoitering and a bit of firing from skirmishers and sharpshooters on both sides. General Weitzel could be seen in person, making observations, about six hundred yards off. Then suddenly the Federal troops turned their backs on the enemy, marched up the beach and reimbarked. Says a contemporary naval account: "We drew off at sunset, leaving the ironclads to fire through the night, expecting the troops would attack in the morning when we would fire again. I received word from General Weitzel that it was impractical to assault."

Actually it was Butler who made that decision. In a letter written to Porter on that very day, December 25, he excused his failure to attack by saying that after "making a thorough reconnaissance of Fort Fisher, both General Weitzel and myself are full of the opinion that the place could not be carried by assault, as it was left substantially uninjured as a defensive work by the way of navy fire . . . I shall therefore sail for Hampton Roads as soon as the transport fleet can be got in order."

One can imagine how Admiral Porter seethed when he got this message. Obviously he could do nothing to subdue Fisher without troop support. So he had no choice but to follow Butler north. The fleet anchored off Beaufort and awaited further orders.

Soon after arrival, Porter wrote to Grant: "Send me the same soldiers with another general, and we will have the fort." So ended the first battle of Fort Fisher. To Welles, Porter wrote: "It was . . . nothing more than I expected when General Butler mixed himself up in this expedition . . . General Butler only came . . . to reap credit for the affair, supposing the explosion would sweep the works off the face of the earth."*

PORTER'S PUNCH

The Federal authorities were far from through with the project. On December 29 Welles wrote Grant a letter that clearly implied that a better job could have been done: "Ships can approach nearer the enemy's works at New Inlet than was anticipated.** Their fire can keep the enemy away from their guns. A landing can easily be effected upon the beach north of Fort Fisher, not only of troops, but all their supplies. . . . The Navy can assist in the siege . . . precisely as it covered the operations which resulted in the capture of Wagner." This refers to the heavy bombardment of Fort Wagner in Charleston Harbor, the silencing of its guns and its final capture by troops under General Gillmore.

"Under these circumstances," Welles wrote in the same letter, "I invite you to such military co-operation as will ensure the fall of Fort Fisher, the importance of which has already received your careful consideration."

Right after the first of January 1865 things began to hum again at Beaufort. Porter was busy loading his ships with coal, food and ammunition. It was not an easy job, for the vessels had no harbor and it was the season of gales. There was one compensation however. General Terry had replaced Butler as com-

---

* A slightly more successful explosion aimed at destroying Confederate defensive works occurred on July 30, 1864, when a great mine, which had been dug under Elliott's Salient at Petersburg, went off in an eruption of smoke, flame and dirt. It made a crater one hundred and seventy feet long, sixty feet wide and thirty feet deep. Guns and men were blown high in the air. Union troops attempting to exploit the Confederate confusion advanced into the resultant gap but bungled the attack and permitted the Confederates to regroup and fight them off. The net result was a huge hole and four thousand Union casualties.

** It is surprising that the Union Navy did not know or take the trouble to report the unusual depth of water close to the beach for several miles north of Fort Fisher. Blockade runners had long used this approach and by running almost within the first line of breakers were able to escape pursuing cruisers more often than not.

mander of the troops. And Porter had faith in Terry's ability. Grimly the transports and men-of-war rode out the succession of storms and by January 12 were under way, headed south in three majestic columns. By nightfall the armada was within sight of Fort Fisher and Porter sent a signal to all vessels to ride out the darkness at anchor.

The same night a group of serious-faced officers met at Colonel Lamb's headquarters at Fort Fisher. The Union fleet had been sighted and everyone knew they meant business this time. Lamb explained that in spite of hurried work on the fortifications since the first battle, comparatively little had been accomplished. He had sent an urgent telegram to the Confederate War Department asking for more cannon. None was received. His requisitions for more ammunition, especially hand grenades for use against assaulting troops, remained unfilled. A cargo of shells from England had been lost on a blockade runner two days before. Lamb had been especially anxious to place marine torpedoes offshore where the Federal ironclads would anchor prior to opening the bombardment. These also were not forthcoming. Aside from written regrets, all he got was some useless bolts for his Armstrong guns. It was most necessary, he told his battery commanders, to conserve ammunition. Orders were given that once the attack began each gun was to be fired only once every half-hour until disabled or destroyed, unless orders were given to concentrate on a specific target. If enemy men-of-war attempted to cross New Inlet Bar and run into the river, every gun in working order was to be immediately brought to bear to prevent their passage. At this time the total garrison of Fort Fisher numbered eight hundred men of the 36th North Carolina. Of these, a hundred or more were sick and unfit for duty. Lamb had telegraphed General Braxton Bragg, urgently asking as many men as he could possibly send. No reply came that night. Bragg was encamped with his supporting army at Sugar Loaf several miles north of the fort. A rumor had reached Lamb that Bragg was about to shift camp to another site sixteen miles beyond Wilmington.

Nevertheless, Lamb confidently told his officers that he expected reinforcements in the morning. Meanwhile, he said it was each man's duty to fight with what they had as long as God gave them strength and courage.

Shortly after dawn next morning, Colonel Lamb and his staff made a thorough inspection of the works to make sure they were in order and ready for action. As they stood on top of the traverse of the Pulpit Battery, which jutted out from the sea face, a cold breeze whipped against their long, gray overcoats. They gazed steadily out over the slate-colored sea.

Scattered at intervals among the offshore breakers were the wrecks of blockade runners. One was the *Ann Marie*; another the famous *Beauregard*. Others, wrecked earlier, were rusted and unrecognizable hulks. Further out, the Confederate officers counted fifty-three Federal vessels. The fleet had now weighed anchor and was steaming majestically in three parallel columns, scarcely four miles away. On the wings of the freshening wind the smoke from more than sixty funnels drifted to windward like a rain cloud. It was an awesome sight, for it was the largest assemblage of armored war vessels the world had known up to that time—numbering a total of six hundred guns of all calibers.

In the van, closest to shore, steamed the monitors. They were low, ugly and powerful. From their round turrets, which looked like cheeseboxes, protruded the snouts of massive guns. In the lead of the second line was the *New Ironsides*, capable of throwing a greater weight of metal than any of the others: fourteen 11-inch shell guns, two 150-pounders and two 60-pounders. She could inflict fearful damage with her eleven-hundred-pound broadsides. The largest of the monitors was the twin-turreted *Monadnock*, mounting four 15-inch shell guns.

In Fisher's traverses gray-uniformed gunners stood silent and alert at their pieces; others were bringing up shells and ammunition. Overhead the Stars and Bars and regimental flags made bright patches of color against the pale, cold sky. Toward the land face of the fort was the wooden line of the palisades, sharpened logs to ward off infantry. Except for the wash of the surf along the beach and the screams of the circling gulls, a strange, tremulous silence hovered over the vast fortification.

Then the starboard broadside of the *New Ironsides* spouted thunder and flame. The air shrilled with iron. Two guns from the Confederate bastion answered with a deep-throated roar. The second battle of Fort Fisher was joined. Spherical shells exploded high in the air, their metal fragments kicking up lumps of sod on the slopes of the traverses.

Colonel Lamb's attractive wife and two small children had occupied a rustic cottage among the dunes back of the fort until the previous evening, when her husband arranged for evacuation across the river to Orton plantation. Mrs. Lamb had been happy at the cottage, for there had been gay social life: dinners and interesting evenings with her husband's friends, famous block-ade runners, correspondents from English and Southern news-papers and magazines and notables from Wilmington. There had been fox hunting too, and swimming on the beach when the surf was mild. The evening that the Union fleet had been sighted, Colonel Lamb sent his wife a message, advising her of the enemy approach and telling her to pack up and be ready to embark in a boat he had ordered made ready at the wharf. Later, to make sure that everything was all right, Lamb mounted his horse and galloped to the cottage to say good-by. To his amazement he found his wife sound asleep in a chair, with her two children cuddled in her arms. Apparently she had grown weary waiting for someone to come and tell her that the boat was ready. The colonel tenderly awoke his family and shep-herded them to the landing, then stood silently watching the boat disappear in the darkness.

Continuously during January 13 and 14 the United States Navy poured a steady fire on Fort Fisher. It was so heavy that it was im-possible for the Confederates to repair the damage to their works during the night, for the *New Ironsides* and the monitors "bowled their eleven and fifteen inch shells along the parapet, scattering shrapnel in the darkness. We could scarcely gather up and bury our dead without fresh casualties."

Meanwhile reinforcements had arrived, seven hundred North Carolina artillerymen, sent down from Wilmington by General Whiting. After a hasty noontime meal on the fourteenth, Colonel Lamb and his staff made another inspection of the works on the land face. The firing was heavier now. Acrid powder smoke swirled upward and drifted off as if the whole fort were afire. From the assembled fleet came crashing thunder, followed by the ripping rush of shells and the nearer answering fire of the Confederate guns. As the group of officers approached the bastion along the sheltered footwalk they could see men hurrying through the haze carrying loaded stretchers to the hospital bombproof.

A young lieutenant hurried up to Colonel Lamb. "There's a big flotilla of small boats carrying Yankee troops from the transports to the beach about two miles north," he reported. "Some have already landed and are moving inland. We think they are digging earthworks."

Colonel Lamb nodded and told the officer to return to his post. This was what Lamb had been expecting all along. It had become obvious to even an unmilitary eye that the enemy was using better strategy than during their first attempt to win the fort. The ironclads were anchored close in, as Welles had ordered, only seven hundred to a thousand yards away. From this short range they were pouring concentrated fire on the salient of the land face, trying to reduce the high parapet to a slope that could be scaled by Federal troops. The thirteen ships of Squadron Two now lay within three quarters of a mile of the beach north of the fort. They were raking the land face also, clear up to the river. On this side also, their objective was to level the traverses, knock out the guns, scatter the palisades and batter down the twenty-foot embankment. This would enable the blue-clad columns deploying across the neck of the peninsula to carry Fisher by storm without being decimated by Confederate fire. The powerful frigates *Wabash* and *Minnesota* now took position less than a mile from the sea face, so that their line of fire extended south from the salient. Shell bursts all along the traverses gave grim evidence of their intent to disable the fort's big guns.

Still further south and at a greater distance from the beach lay the fourteen ships of Squadron Three. Their long-range rifles and shell guns were delivering a heavy load of destruction all the way down to Mound Battery.

As Colonel Lamb conferred briefly with each battery commander, the gunners yelled above the din that they would hold the fort against a hundred thousand Yankees. When Lamb reached the extreme western end of the land face he stopped and looked down the road that led up from Battery Buchanan. Half a dozen officers were trudging along the rutted track. Recognizing them, Lamb hurried down the steps of the nearest gun chamber to meet them.

As the two groups of officers came toward each other, the contrast between them was marked: tall, blond Colonel Lamb in a rumpled, dirt-spattered overcoat; his staff were equally dirty and unshaven. But the approaching officers were immaculate, with well-polished boots and bright epaulets. At their head walked a slight, soldierly man with the stars of a major general on his collar.

"General Whiting!" Lamb saluted and held out his hand.

Whiting removed his gauntlet and clasped the proffered palm.

"How did you get here, sir?" the colonel asked. "If I had known you were coming . . ."

"I commandeered a picket boat. We landed fifteen minutes ago."

"I appreciate your coming, sir. The command of the fort is yours."

"No," Whiting replied. "I came here entirely on my own initiative and without orders. Officially, I have no business here. I shall give you whatever counsel I can. But you are in supreme command to conduct the defense." General Whiting then drew Lamb aside and said quietly, "Lamb, I have come to share your fate. You and your garrison are to be sacrificed."

Lamb's strong, bearded chin thrust forward resolutely. "Don't say so, General! We shall certainly whip the enemy!"

"If you do, it will be without outside help. When I left Wilmington, General Bragg was hurriedly removing his stores and ammunition from Sugar Loaf and looking for a place to fall back on."

This news came as a shock to the commander of Fort Fisher. He had telegraphed Bragg several times, begging him to send Hagood's South Carolina Brigade. They were veteran troops. They would be of immense help in fighting off the coming assault by Federal infantry. He had also requested three brigades from Hoke's division to be deployed along the beach to prevent the Federals from landing.

The refusal of General Bragg to come to the rescue at Fort Fisher has never been satisfactorily explained. There had been friction between him and General Whiting at Drewry's Bluff. Whether that had anything to do with his refusal to reinforce Colonel Lamb is doubtful. Probably Bragg felt that he must conserve all his forces for an attempt to stop Sherman's oblique march across the state, feeling that Fisher was doomed by an overwhelming superiority of guns and men.

During the afternoon the bombardment of all parts of the fort continued with sustained violence. Reports from Lamb's scouts made it certain that, in spite of the heavy surf, the Federals had completed the debarkation of their troops, together with several batteries of light field pieces. Lamb and Whiting knew that an attack against the land face was imminent, probably the next day.

Actually, six thousand well-equipped Union soldiers had landed and now straddled the neck of the peninsula, from river to sea. Shells hurled by Squadron One into the dense growth of scrub pine and oak back of the beach caused a wild stampede of cattle belonging to the garrison. The Federals promptly rounded them up, shot and butchered them. There was plenty of beef in the Union lines that night.

As the sun went down, shadows from the battered Confederate works crept slowly across the beach and out into the tumbling waves. From north to south, as far as the eye could see, lay the enemy men-of-war, their masts, spars and funnels black against the evening sky. Spurts of flame winked rapidly up and down the line, piercing the low-hung smoke like sharp, red knives. Shells bursting above and beyond the fort's parapet were like lightning flashes, tinting the clouds with brief splashes of crimson.

Next morning at sunrise the Union fleet again steamed into position. With the sound of a thunderclap the *New Ironsides* let loose her first broadside. All day the fleet pounded the fort. Confederate officers estimated that a hundred shells a minute were bursting among the guns and traverses. As each big shell struck, there was an eruption of sand, sod, timbers and sometimes scraps of human beings. The crash and roar of these detonations beat on the ears of the beleaguered garrison like hammer strokes as they huddled in their bombproofs, deafening them so that they could scarcely hear anything but a shout. The earth trembled as mammoth 9-inch sphericals ricocheted along the parapets and rolled down behind the guns, disintegrating with shattering impact. It was inviting death now for any man to remain exposed above ground. Yet occasionally a Confederate gun still spoke. It was a sullen and slow response and frightfully costly in dead and wounded. No other fortification in the world's history up to that time, not even excepting those of the Russians at Sevastopol, had ever been subjected to such prolonged, powerful and shocking fire. Up and down the long defense line the Confederate guns were being knocked out, one by one.

Both Lamb and Whiting were bitter over Bragg's refusal of help. They knew that he knew of their desperate situation. With steamers at his command, he could have crossed the river the previous day to Smithville and from there, with a spyglass, watch every movement of the Federal forces. He could also have seen the hell that his comrades-in-arms were taking. He could also have sent a steamer down that night with perfect safety to the landing near Battery Buchanan. But he did not. The grim fact of the matter was that Bragg had washed his hands of Fisher and all it contained. Whiting and Lamb had planned to make a sally from the fort that night to forestall the attack of the Federal infantry. But only reinforcements from Bragg would have given the plan any chance of success, considering that only four of Fisher's guns were serviceable.

Daylight was but half an hour old when the guns of the fleet began bellowing again. It was plain that Porter wanted to knock out the last of the defender's ordnance before General Terry attacked. From the number of men arrayed against him, Lamb figured that his soldiers were badly outnumbered. He emphasized to his officers that it was most important to keep in close touch with all sections of the line and rush reinforcements wherever they were needed.

The Northeast Bastion, which was close to the beach, was now a shapeless pile of sand. Torn bodies lay among the debris. Great gaps showed along the traverses where Federal 15-inch shells had plowed and exploded. One of the 8-inch Confederate guns had received a direct hit so powerful that the cannon had been blown into three pieces. The butt had been hurled fifteen feet to the side and half buried in the traverse.

Only one gun remained in action at the Northeast Bastion. It was the 8-inch Blakely facing the sea. The crew crouched behind the traverse waiting to load and fire. When the order came they rushed through the smoke of bursting shells, aimed and fired the gun, then ran again for shelter.

At the lookout post a young lieutenant lay on his stomach and swept the beach north of the fort with his field glasses. The air was mild that morning and the sun shone brightly. The wind had dropped to a whisper. Off on the horizon the Federal transports rode like a flock of fat geese. Closer in were the three squadrons, spouting a seemingly endless stream of hot iron. The ironclads were so near that the lieutenant could see tongues of fire spurt from their gun muzzles and watch the vessels shiver from the recoil. Turning his glasses along the land face of the fort, the lookout noticed that the Federal ground troops had begun to deploy and were spreading out in a long skirmish line. Forward elements were digging rifle pits close to the palisades. Far to the left, near the Cape Fear River, tightly bunched patches of blue showed that even heavier forces were massing for an attack over there. Now and then a rifle cracked as Federal sharpshooters fired at any Confederate head that showed above the parapet.

The lieutenant scribbled a report and sent it back to Colonel Lamb. Fifteen minutes later the messenger returned with a note instructing the lieutenant to notify him the moment the Federals began to move en masse.

From the direction of Fisher's central sally port came the bark of two guns, fired in rapid succession. They were Confederate Napoleons, firing grape and canister into Federal forces that had now begun to press forward against the land face, rank upon rank. The young lieutenant sent these words back to Lamb: "They're coming."

Shortly after, more boats were seen approaching the shore. They were bluejackets and marines, sent to reinforce the Federal infantry. A half-hour later the first naval contingent landed on the beach, a mile and a half north of the fort. Colonel Lamb sent instructions to the captain of the Blakely 8-inch to fire on the other boats that had not yet landed. The first shot struck between two of them. A geyser of water spouted, but when it subsided the boats were still there. The gun captain decided to shift his fire to the sailors who were already on shore.

When the Blakely boomed again the shell struck in the midst of the company of sailors lined up on the beach. As the smoke drifted off, the watchers saw that a dozen bluejackets were lying on the sand.

Meanwhile two companies of Wilmington Home Guards had been sent to the land face to reinforce the thin line of defense. They were mostly old men and boys who had scarcely ever fired an army musket. They were further supported by three hundred men from Hagood's brigade who had managed to get ashore at the partly wrecked landing. Apparently the captain of the steamer became frightened at so much shot and shell going over his vessel; he backed out and went upriver again with the remaining troops still aboard.

Now the columns of bluejackets had begun to move down the beach, headed for the parapet. They began slowly, then moved faster and faster. Their officers had drawn their swords and were shouting and urging their men on, jogging awkwardly through the loose sand toward the salient. The Confederate defenders, standing tensely behind the parapet with rifles cocked saw, to their amazement, that the Federal sailors carried no rifles. They were armed only with cutlasses and revolvers!

The Blakely's crew hastily rammed case shot into its maw. Case shot, or canister, was deadly at close range. The effect was like that of a great shotgun, spewing hundreds of musket balls over a wide area. More than a score of sailors died from the single shot.

All at once the thunder of the fleet stopped. The silence came like an unexpected pain in the ears. On the parapet the Confederates glanced at one another, wondering why the firing had ceased. Then, a moment later, a new sound came from the sea, a medley of hoots and shrieks. Spurts of steam came from every enemy funnel. They were blowing their whistles in a vast, discordant chorus, signaling the ground forces to attack.

Along the beach a company of marines was making a dash for the rifle pits. Behind were the massed columns of the sailors who had unsheathed their cutlasses and were running forward. As the marines came within range, a line of blue light flashed from the Confederate parapet as the Home Guards and Hagood's men sent their first volley crashing down on the marines before they could reach the rifle pits. An instant later the second fusillade swept down on them. Running men pitched headlong into the sand, thrashing and screaming. Others, coming behind, stumbled over the bodies or stepped over them, hesitating to push on in the face of the deadly blast of lead. At the third burst from the parapet, the marines halted, then broke in panic and ran back toward the advancing column of sailors, merging with them in a confused mass. This was the first and only time that the United States Marines ever turned tail from the enemy.* Most of them were Irish recruits, with little if any battle training.

On the bloodstained beach the sailors had advanced another costly hundred yards and were lying flat on their bellies to escape the galling Confederate fire. Their officers shouted to the men to keep their heads down. A moment later a bugle blared and

---

* "A succession of rifle pits were most promptly occupied by a line of skirmishers composed of marines under Lieutenant Fagan. . . . The navy columns were ordered to advance by the flank along the beach, with the hope of forming them for the assault under cover of the marines; but exposed to a galling fire of musketry . . . threw a portion of the marines into the first line and the rest of them did not take position as they should." Captain Breeze's report, quoted by Daniel Ammen in *The Navy in the Civil War: The Atlantic Coast.*

the whole contingent leaped to its feet and sprinted forward. In their midst streamed the Stars and Stripes and Admiral Porter's flag. At the same instant the big Blakely belched a full load of canister, its muzzle depressed as far as it could go. As the blast of musket balls struck the massed bluejackets it was as if a huge flail had swept among them, raising a cloud of sand and dust, through which men writhed and lay still. Both Federal flags were down.

A cheer went up from the parapet and Colonel Lamb leaped to the top of a traverse and circled his sword over his head. "Hold fast for North Carolina and the Confederacy!" he shouted. A bullet tore through his coat and he jumped down.

From the sally port came a burst of musketry and the crack of the little Napoleons, enfilading the confused and disorganized sailors. Only scattered pistol fire came from a few in their ranks. It was hard to tell the dead from the living, for all of them were flat on the sand.

Once more the Blakely roared, adding horribly to the slaughter. Union naval officers were trying frantically to rally their men for a charge up the slope. Two officers and about twenty bluejackets, ignoring the hesitancy of the others, made a desperate dash. They had scarcely started up to the parapet when a scorching fire from above cut them down. Some of them lay where they fell. Others pitched back down the slope. This was too much for the survivors. They turned and began to run.

Once more the parapet flashed blue flame, cutting gaps into the mass of fleeing and panic-stricken sailors. Within a quarter of an hour the whole force of sailors and marines had withdrawn out of range, leaving between two and threee hundred of their dead and dying on the torn, red beach.

Among the wounded lying in the sand was a young ensign named Robley D. Evans who came very near dying that day, but, thanks to the courage of a marine, lived on for many years to become captain of the U.S.S. *Iowa* during the battle of Santiago in the Spanish-American war, retiring as a rear admiral. But on that day at Fort Fisher, young Evans was not thinking of the future. His mind was entirely concerned with the attack on the enemy palisades. His eyewitness report* gives a graphic description of the battle:

"At three o'clock the order to charge was given and we started for our long run of twelve hundred yards over the loose sand. The fleet kept up a hot fire until we approached within about six hundreds yards of the fort, and then ceased firing. The rebels seemed to understand our signals, and almost before the last gun was fired, manned the parapet and opened on us with twenty-six hundred muskets.** The army had not yet assaulted, so the whole garrison concentrated its fire on us. Under the shower of bullets the marines broke before reaching the rifle pits that had been dug for them, and did not appear again as an organization in the assault. Most of the men and many of the officers (marines) mixed with the column of sailors, and went on with them. About five hundred yards from the fort the head of the column suddenly stopped and, as if by magic, the whole mass of men went down like falling bricks." The survivors crawled forward "under a perfect hail of lead." They were so close that they could hear the Confederates' voices. "The [Union] officers were pulling their caps down over their eyes, for it was almost impossible to look at the deadly flashing blue line of parapet, and we all felt that in a few minutes we should get our cutlasses to work and make up the fearful loss we had suffered.

"At this moment I saw Colonel Lamb, the Confederate commander, gallantly standing on the parapet and calling on his men to get up and shoot the Yankees. I considered him within range of my revolver, so took a deliberate shot at him. As I fired, a bullet ripped through the front of my coat across my breast, turning me completely around. I felt a burning sensation, like a hot iron over my heart, and saw something red coming out of the hole in my coat which I took for blood . . . but that was no place to stop, so I went on at the head of my company."

A Confederate sharpshooter drew a bead on Evans and hit him in the left leg, a few inches below the knee. He fell to the

* From *A Sailor's Log,* by Robley D. Evans, Rear Admiral, U.S.N. New York, 1901, pp. 88-95.
** An obvious error. Fort Fisher's defenders were less than 2,000.

sand. Using a silk pocket handkerchief, he bound up the wound and hobbled to the front. With seven others he managed to penetrate the stockade but was again felled by the same sharp-shooter. This time the wound was in the right knee. He was bleeding dreadfully and could not get up from the ground. Soon he heard someone shout, "They are retreating!" and saw the naval contingents break and run to the rear. "Two minutes more and we should have been on the parapet," Evans wrote in his memoirs, "and then—nobody can ever guess what would have happened, but surely a dreadful loss of life."

The young ensign tried desperately to stanch the flow of blood from his wounds with the half-dozen silk handkerchiefs he had brought along in case of need. Meanwhile the sharpshooter who had twice hit him was lying only thirty-five yards away, wait-ing for a chance to finish him off. He continued to shoot at Evans, "at the same time addressing me in very forcible and uncomplimentary language." The Confederate's fifth shot struck Evans in the foot, tearing off the sole of his shoe, slicing off the tip of one of his toes and wrenching his ankle painfully.

This last was too much for the young Northerner. Anger stifled his pain. He rolled over and faced his enemy. Steadying himself, he leaned on his elbow, aimed and fired. The bullet caught the Confederate in the throat and passed out at the back of his neck. "He staggered around, after dropping his gun, and finally pitched over the parapet and rolled down near me, where he lay dead. I could see his feet as they projected over a pile of sand, and from their position knew he had fought his last fight."

A marine from the U.S.S. *Powhatan*, at the risk of his life, dragged Evans away from the stockade, only to be killed mo-ments later by a bullet in the neck. As night fell the tide came in and drowned many of the badly wounded Union sailors and marines who had fallen on the beach. Evans was still lying in the hole where the marine had dragged him and he felt the water trickling in. He was afraid he would be "drowned like a rat." After much pain and difficulty he managed to roll himself out of the hole. Bullets were still singing overhead and with the aid of another marine, Evans was pulled to safety behind a pile of sand. All around him men were being killed or wounded: "The scene on the beach at this time was a pitiful one—dead and wounded officers and men as far as one could see. As a rule they lay quiet on the sand and took their punishment like the brave lads they were, but occasionally the thirst brought on by loss of blood was more than they could bear, and a sound-wave would drift along, 'Water, water, water!' and then all would be quiet again. . . . Just as the sun went down and it did seem to go very slowly that afternoon, I saw an officer coming up the beach." He proved to be Dr. Longstreet, who gave Evans a drink of water and supervised his removal. After a long period in the Naval Hospital at Norfolk, during which he steadfastly refused to allow the doctors to amputate one of his legs, he arrived home in Philadelphia for a long convalescence.

Back at Fort Fisher, the Union infantry under General Terry had been able to penetrate the works on the extreme western end of the land face. Slowly and savagely the Federals fought their way from one gun chamber to another. The diversion staged by the naval brigade had enabled the Union infantry to break through. Knotted masses of men fought hand-to-hand. Union battle flags swayed in their midst, now down, now up, then moving on to the next gun chamber. New Federal forces kept pouring in from the western opening. The Confederates were fighting like madmen, but were forced relentlessly eastward along the land face. And there had been no word from General Bragg, nor reinforcements.

Here is what Colonel Lamb had to say at this point: "My men, led by Whiting, had driven the [Union] standard bearer from the top of the [fourth] traverse and the enemy from the parapet in front. They had recovered the gun chamber with great slaughter and on the parapet and on the long traverse of the next gun chamber the contestants were savagely firing into each other's faces, and in some cases clubbing their guns, being too close to load and fire. Whiting had been quickly wounded by two shots and had been carried to the hospital bombproof." The gallant general died of his wounds on March 10, 1865.

Lamb himself was wounded by a bullet in the thigh, but it was not fatal. He recovered and lived until 1909.

When the Federals had fought their way clear across the land face and were mopping up, the ironclads of the fleet opened up again. The destruction was even worse than before, "indescribably horrible," according to Lamb's account. "Great cannons were broken in two and over their ruins were lying the dead; others were partly buried in graves dug by the shells which had slain them."

After several gallant but futile counterattacks by the Confederate survivors, including all sick or wounded who could hold a musket, the weary defenders retreated south along the peninsula. Many of them escaped across the river in whatever boats they could find, in the face of galling fire from the fleet. "None of the guns of Fort Fisher were spiked," wrote Lamb in his report, "the men firing them until they were killed, wounded or driven out of the batteries by overwhelming numbers. The enemy threw out a heavy skirmish line and sent their fourth brigade to Battery Buchanan where it arrived about 10 P.M. and received the surrender of the garrison from Major James H. Hill and Lieutenant George D. Parker." So ended the second battle of Fort Fisher. Its capture was the result of overwhelming fire power, good ground tactics and man power far in excess of what the Confederates could muster.

In celebration of the victory each vessel in the fleet tied down its whistle and shot off every rocket they possessed. It was, even in Lamb's opinion, a "grand pyrotechnic display."

An even greater powder-burning, far exceeding the pyrotechnics of the previous night, took place just after sunrise the next morning. Thirteen thousand pounds of powder stored in Fisher's reserve magazine exploded with a terrific roar, erupting high in the air along with dirt, timbers, sod and scores of Federal soldiers and sailors, together with a few Confederate wounded. The conquerors blamed Colonel Lamb for causing the explosion, saying that he had electric wires* running from Fort Lamb on

---

* Colonel Lamb stated that these were *telegraph* wires.

the opposite side of the river to the magazine and had purposely set off the giant charge. Lamb angrily refuted this accusation, rightly saying that the underground magazine "made an artificial mound most inviting to a wearied soldier, and after the fight was occupied for the night by Colonel Alden's 169th New York and by some of my suffering soldiers. Two sailors, from the fleet, stupefied by liquors which they had found in the hospital and looking for the booty, were seen to enter the structure with lights and a moment after the green mound blew up."

The same morning small boats from the fleet were busy surveying the New Inlet channel and placing buoys for the guidance of vessels entering the Cape Fear River. Then the gunboats began feeling their way cautiously over the bar.

Although United States Army reports stated that Fort Fisher was defended by 2,500 men, there were actually less than 2,000 in the fort at the time of the attack. On the basis of 10,000 soldiers, sailors and marines in the attacking forces, the Confederates were outnumbered five to one. They were outgunned by more than thirteen to one. According to one Federal account of casualties, their army lost 700 killed and severely wounded. No figures are given for those lightly wounded or casualty statistics covering sailors and marines. Another Federal report gives total killed, wounded and missing as 1,445. No figures were given covering Confederate losses, except that 112 officers and 1,971 enlisted men were taken prisoners. The accuracy of these figures is open to question, since the total number of prisoners claimed by Federal forces is more than actually were in the fort! Also this claimed total of 2,083 Confederate officers and men made prisoners does not, of course, include those killed, wounded or missing. A correspondent of the New York *Tribune* set the number of prisoners at 2,300!

The forty-eight-hour bombardment of Fort Fisher was the greatest and most sustained artillery engagement of the entire Civil War and involved the largest number of shells and shot in the history of the world up to that time. The Union fleet fired 50,000 shot and shell of all calibers during the engagement. As many as twenty-five 11-inch shells were in the air at the same instant throughout most of the bombardment. Admiral Porter reported that there was scarcely a foot of ground in the main part of the fort that was not churned up by shells. He also made some significant comments on the effect of the capture of Fort Fisher on the outcome of the war: "The capture of the defenses of Wilmington closed the last door through which the Southern Confederacy received their supplies of clothing, arms and ammunition; therefore when Fort Fisher fell, it was only a matter of a short time when the rebellion would collapse. No matter how brave an enemy may be, or how well commanded, he must have provisions and military stores; and at this time General Lee had not enough materiel of war to last him three months!"

In describing the latter phases of the battle, Porter gave credit to both sides for behaving like heroes, for "there never was harder fighting anywhere by soldiers than on this memorable occasion." He then quotes General Badeau as saying that the importance of the victory was instantly recognized "by the rebels and loyal people alike. Lee knew its significance as well as Grant and the rejoicing of the North was not more heartfelt than the despondency of the Confederates."

Nowhere was this despondency more acute than in Wilmington and along the reaches of the Cape Fear. Confederate forces evacuated Fort Caswell, commanding Old Inlet—blew it up, knowing full well that it would be suicide to invite more cannonading from the Union fleet. The Confederate garrison made their way to Fort Anderson on the banks of the river near the site of Old Brunswick. By January 19, 1865, Admiral Porter had taken possession of Smithville. But the Federal forces were in no hurry to fight their way into Wilmington. They rested and waited for General Schofield's forces to arrive and support them. Meanwhile Confederate General Hoke remained warily at Sugar Loaf, for he had only a small force of 4,500 men under his command. At length on February 11, General Terry joined forces with Schofield and they moved forward. Surprisingly, they were checked by Hoke. After three days of skirmishing, the Union generals tried to turn Hoke's left and failed. Then Schofield tried another plan. He threw Cox's Division across to the western side of the Cape Fear with the idea that it would be easier to approach Wilmington from that direction. At the same time Porter obligingly bombarded Fort Anderson with his ironclads and made a shambles of the place. Instead of attacking the fort with his infantry, from the flank, Cox moved behind it and around Orton Pond. It looked to him as if the road to Wilmington was now clear. But General Hagood's men thought differently. They evacuated Fort Anderson like a swarm of angry bees and took up battle stations behind Town Creek. But again those Federal gunboats went into action and shelled Hoke's exposed right and rear. This forced him to fall back. He fought a gallant delaying action, but he lacked the men and munitions to defeat the strong Federal forces. On February 22, General Terry marched victoriously into Wilmington.

The water front on both sides of the river flamed with burning cotton bales and all manner of supplies that had been unloaded from blockade runners and awaited rail shipment to beleaguered Petersburg. A dozen or more slim steamers lay silently at anchor in the stream, their crews lining the rails and staring glumly at the long files of blue-clad troops marching along Water Street. They knew that the lush days of blockade running were over.

The Federals found themselves in possession of an unresisting city which tried to shut itself away from its conquerors. The homes of the citizens were shuttered. Business establishments were closed and shades drawn. Few citizens were to be seen on the streets. Only the colored folk capered and shouted and followed the troops to their camps, wide-eyed and eager to know all about "bein' free."

General Joseph R. Hawley was appointed Provost Marshal General in charge of the occupation. He had an eye for comfortable living and lost no time in appropriating for his headquarters the residence of leading citizen Dr. John D. Bellamy. This handsome mansion still stands at the corner of Fifth and Market streets. Hoke had headed for Goldsboro and Terry took most of the Union forces and went after him. Schofield did likewise.

Contemporary accounts of the occupation of Wilmington say that the soldiery respected the citizens, "but made free to request the household cooks to furnish them samples of their Southern dishes; among them corn bread, sweetened with molasses, which was a great delicacy for them."

One of the few citizens of the city to incur the wrath of General Hawley was Reverend (afterward Bishop) A. A. Watson. Hawley's wrath was caused because the rector of St. James Episcopal Church flatly refused to offer prayers for the President of the United States. Hawley promptly confiscated the keys to the church, ordered a band of Negroes to rip out all the pews and throw them into the street and to convert the building into a military hospital. Years later, the Federal government reimbursed St. James Church for the damage.

Businessmen were required to swear an oath of allegiance to the United States if they hoped to continue in business. Practically all of them did. Comments a contemporary writer, "There was naturally more or less confusion in household and business arrangements, owing to the new status of the Negroes, who were now free. Many faithful servants reluctantly took the position of those freed from their masters, but many of them still clung to the homes of those who had always cared for them, and to whom they were warmly attached. The presence of the Northern soldiers, and the new regime, however, filled some of the colored men with grand ideas as to the men from the North, and they endeavored to attach themselves to them."

Looking back over the four years of war when the entire resources of the United States Navy were directed toward enforcing the blockade, it becomes quite evident that the blockade was never fully effective. Like wars that were to be fought generations later, the Civil War was also a war of attrition in many respects. Along the Atlantic coast and the Gulf it was a matter of slow, steady strangulation. Month by month, year by year the pressure became greater until, with the fall of Fort Fisher, the Confederacy started its death gasps.

Only about half the blockade runners that glided through the night past watchful cruisers ever got caught. According to a report by Gideon Welles in December 1865, the Union Navy had captured or destroyed 295 blockade-running steamers, 44 sailing ships and 683 schooners making a total of 1,022 vessels. The adjudicated value of the captured ships and cargoes was placed at $24,500,000. This did not include an estimated additional amount of $7,000,000 worth of ships and cargoes run ashore and destroyed, making a total of $31,500,000. Southern authorities figured a higher total, at least $2,000,000 more. The total value of the blockade-running business, including ships and cargoes, can be conservatively estimated at $150,000,000, gold standard.

What happened to the gallant little ships that had risked death and destruction to succor the Confederacy? Most of them lived out their time in drab and uneventful voyages as cargo or passenger vesels. Their post-war lives were short for the most part, for they were frightfully expensive to operate and more often than not lost money for their new owners because of their limited cargo space and high-powered machinery. The rusty bones of two dozen or more of the unlucky ones still lie buried in the sands of the Carolina coast north and south of Fort Fisher.

The last blockade runners to enter the Cape Fear were three sleek beauties, *Blenheim, Charlotte* and *Stag*. They had left Bermuda before news of the fall of Fort Fisher had reached Georgetown and were cleverly decoyed into a trap by Admiral Porter. He detailed the indefatigable Lieutenant Cushing, hero of a dozen hairbreadth escapes and exploits, to establish decoy signals and range lights. Cushing soon accomplished his mission with the aid of a couple of "Intelligent Contrabands" who knew the signal code of the blockade runners.

On the night of January 19, the *Stag* and *Charlotte* steamed into Cape Fear as if all were at peace and anchored in the lee of Fort Fisher. They had hardly dropped their anchors before they were boarded by bluejackets and ordered to surrender.

Aboard the *Charlotte* the officers and passengers were just sitting down to a luxurious supper to celebrate their safe arrival and the champagne corks had already begun to pop. Their astonishment was great when a Union naval officer appeared in the saloon and curtly announced that they were all prisoners.

"The Yankees have got us, by thunder!" cried one of the passengers, a red-faced Britisher. He was one of several officers of the British army on leave and in search of adventure and fortune in the blockade-running trade.

Recounts Porter: "The captain of the steamer had been captured before, and took his present mishap as a matter of course; but one of his passengers could not be made to comprehend how one of Her Majesty's merchant vessels could be taken possession of in a friendly port while peaceable passengers were eating their supper.

" 'Look here, sir,' the Englishman exclaimed to the boarding officer, 'aren't you joking? You certainly wouldn't dare to interfere with one of Her Majesty's vessels; the Admiralty would quick send a fleet over here and dampen you fellows. This is all a joke, I know it is, and I want to go on shore at once.'

" 'You have very singular ideas of what constitutes a joke,' said the boarding officer. 'I don't think you could understand one unless it was fired at you out of a thirty-two pounder.'

" 'But,' cried the Englishman, 'how can you fire a joke out of a thirty-two pounder?'

"This remark," adds Porter, "brought down the house, and the captain of the blockade runner suggested that they had better eat supper first and discuss the joke afterward."

This seems an appropriate place to take leave of the ships and men who manned them, for they soon scattered to work out their uncertain destinies. They had done a hard and seamanlike job of smuggling for the Confederacy.

The benefits of blockade running to the Southern cause were incalculable. The business it carried to the South, the life and activity it brought, the news it told and carried away, the sympathy it communicated, the money it left behind—all these were sinews of war, without which the war must have ceased from twelve to twenty-four months earlier than it did. Blockade runners were the connecting link between the Southern Confederacy and the outer world, substantial evidence of the sympathy of other and older nations. They were of as much moral as material value; they cheered and encouraged the Southern heart.

Bibliography

ALMY, JOHN J. *Incidents of the Blockade.* (War Papers 9, Military Order of Loyal Legion.) Washington, D.C., 1892.

AMMEN, DANIEL. *The Navy in the Civil War: The Atlantic Coast.* London, 1898.

ASHE, SAMUEL A'COURT. *History of North Carolina.* Raleigh, N.C., 1925.

BIGELOW, JOHN. *France and the Confederate Navy.* New York, 1888.

BILL, ALFRED HOYT. *The Beleaguered City.* New York, 1946.

BRADLEE, FRANCES B. C. *Blockade Running During the Civil War.* Essex, Mass., 1925.

CHESNUT, MARY BOYKIN. *Diary from Dixie.* New York, 1905.

DANIEL, JOHN M. *The Richmond Examiner During the Civil War.* New York, 1868.

DAVIS, JEFFERSON. *The Rise and Fall of the Confederate Government.* Richmond, 1881.

DEROSSET, W.L., ed. *Pictorial and Historical New Hanover County & Wilmington, N.C.* Wilmington, N.C., 1938.

Dictionary of American Biography. New York, 1928-1936.

DU PONT, REAR ADMIRAL SAMUEL F. *Official Dispatches & Letters, 1861-63.* Wilmington, Del., 1883.

EISENSCHIML, OTTO, and NEWMAN, RALPH. *The American Iliad.* Indianapolis, 1947.

The Encyclopædia Britannica. 11th ed.

EVANS, ROBLEY D. *A Sailor's Log.* New York, 1901.

FREEMAN, D. S. *Lee's Lieutenants.* New York, 1942-1944.

FREMANTLE, JAMES ARTHUR LYON. *Diary.* Edited by Walter Lord. Boston, 1954.

HAGUE, PARTHENIA A. *A Blockaded Family in Alabama During the Civil War.* New York, 1888.

335

HARDEN, JOHN. *The Devil's Tramping Ground.* Chapel Hill, N.C., 1949.

HENRY, ROBERT SELPH. *The Story of the Confederacy.* Indianapolis, 1931.

HEYWARD, DUNCAN C. *Seed from Madagascar.* Chapel Hill, N.C., 1937.

HILL, DANIEL HARVEY. *Bethel to Sharpsburg.* Vols. I and II. Raleigh, N.C., 1926.

HOPLEY, CATHERINE. *Life in the South During the War.* London, 1863.

HOWARD, MCHENRY. *Recollections of a Maryland Confederate Soldier, 1861-65.* New York, 1914.

HOWELL, ANDREW J. *The Book of Wilmington.* Wilmington, N.C., 1930.

KNOX, DUDLEY W. *A History of the United States Navy.* New York, 1936.

LAMB, COLONEL WILLIAM. "The Battle of Fort Fisher," in *Battles and Leaders of the Civil War.* New York, 1884.

LEECH, MARGARET. *Reveille in Washington.* New York, 1941.

LITTLE, JOHN P. *History of Richmond.* Richmond, 1933.

MACLAY, S. E. *Reminiscences of the Old Navy.* New York and London, 1898.

MACARTNEY, C. E. *Mr. Lincoln's Admirals.* New York, 1956.

———. *Lincoln and His Cabinet.* New York, 1931.

MAFFITT, EMMA MARTIN. *The Life and Services of John Newland Maffitt.* New York and Washington, D.C., 1906.

MORGAN, JAMES MORRIS. *Recollections of a Rebel Reefer.* Boston and New York, 1917.

OATES, GENERAL WILLIAM C. (C.S.A.). *The War Between the Union and the Confederacy.* New York, 1905.

Official Records of the Union and Confederate Armies. Washington, D.C., 1860-1901.

Official Records of the Union and Confederate Navies. Washington, D.C., 1894-1922.

PORTER, ADMIRAL DAVID D. *Incidents and Anecdotes of the Civil War.* New York, 1886.

———. *The Naval History of the Civil War.* New York, 1886.

POST, CHARLES A. "A Diary on the Blockade in 1863," *U.S. Naval Institute Proceedings*, Vol. XLIV, No. 188. Annapolis, Md., 1918.

PRATT, FLETCHER. *The Navy: A History.* New York, 1938.

PRICE, MARCUS W. "Ships That Tested the Blockade of the Carolina Ports, 1861-1865," *The American Neptune*, Vol. VIII, No. 8.

——. "Ships That Tested the Blockade of the Gulf Ports, 1861-1865," *The American Neptune*, Vol. XI, No. 4.

——. "Ships That Tested the Blockade of the Georgia and East Florida Ports, 1861-1865," *The American Neptune*, Vol. XV, No. 2.

RAVENEL, MRS. ST. JULIEN. *Charleston, the Place and the People.* New York, 1906.

ROBERTS, AUGUSTUS CHARLES HOBART (Hobart-Hampden). *Never Caught.* London, 1867.

ROBINSON, WILLIAM MORRISON, JR. *The Confederate Privateers.* New Haven, 1928.

ROSS, ISHBEL. *Rebel Rose.* New York, 1954.

SCHARF, J. THOMAS. *History of the Confederate States Navy.* New York, 1887.

SCHWAB, JOHN C. *A Financial and Industrial History of the South During the Civil War.* New York, 1901.

SEMMES, RAPHAEL. *Memoirs of Service Afloat During the War Between the States.* Baltimore, 1869.

SHARPE, BILL. *Tar on My Heels.* Winston-Salem, N.C., 1946.

SIGAUD, LOUIS A. *Belle Boyd, Confederate Spy.* Richmond, 1944.

SIMKINS, F. B., and PATYON, J. W. *The Women of the Confederacy.* Richmond, 1946.

SOLEY, JAMES RUSSELL. *The Navy in the Civil War: The Blockade and the Cruisers.* London, 1898.

Southern Historical Society. *Southern Historical Papers.* Richmond.

SPRUNT, JAMES. *Tales and Traditions of the Lower Cape Fear, 1661-1896.* Wilmington, N.C., 1896.

——. *Derelicts.* Wilmington, N.C., 1920.

——. *Chronicles of the Cape Fear.* Raleigh, N.C., 1916.

TAYLOR, THOMAS E. *Running the Blockade.* New York, 1896.

VANDIVER, FRANK E., ed. *Confederate Blockade Running Through Bermuda, 1861-1865, Letters and Cargo Manifests.* Austin, Tex., 1947.

VON BORCKE, HEROS. *Memoirs of the Confederate War.* New York, 1938.

WATSON, WILLIAM. *The Adventures of a Blockade Runner, or, Trade in Time of War.* London, 1892.

WEST, RICHARD S. *Gideon Welles.* Indianapolis and New York, 1943.

WILKINSON, J. *The Narrative of a Blockade Runner*. New York, 1877.

Wilmington, N.C., City *Directory*, 1865-1866.

PERIODICALS

Charleston *Daily Courier*, 1861-1864.
Charleston *Mercury*, Nov. 16, 1864.
Frank Leslie's Weekly, 1861-1865.
Harpers Magazine, December 1870.
Harpers Weekly, 1861-1865.
Illustrated London News, 1861-1865.
New York *Herald*, Jan. 18, 1865.
New York *Illustrated News*, June 1861.
New York *Times*, 1860-1865.
New York *Tribune*, 1861-1865.
Philadelphia *Times*, Nov. 18, 1881.
Wilmington, N.C., *Daily Herald*, 1860-1862.
Wilmington, N.C., *Daily Journal*, 1861-1865.
Wilmington, N.C., *Messenger*, Jan. 18, 1880.
Wilmington, N.C., *Morning Star*, Oct. 31, 1926.

Acknowledgments

It is a pleasure to acknowledge my indebtedness to various people for assistance in the preparation of this book and to express my appreciation for their help:

To my wife, Enid, for valuable assistance in research; to Mrs. William D. MacMillam, who at the time of preliminary research work, was librarian of the Public Library, Wilmington, N.C., and who made available many rare books, newspapers, manuscripts and letters. Great assistance was also rendered by Mr. Francis James Dallett, librarian of the Athenaeum of Philadelphia, and Mrs. Isabelle Meade, assistant librarian, in supplying information on Admiral DuPont and sources of illustrative material.

Other individuals who were most helpful were: my daughter Clare Cochran Taylor and her husband Robert N. Taylor of Wrightsville Beach, N.C., for information on the Thalian Society and geographical data concerning the Cape Fear area; Mr. J. Laurence Sprunt and the late Mr. Walter Sprunt for material relating to Orton Plantation and Shandy Hall; Mr. Donald M. Hobart, vice-president and research director of The Curtis Publishing Company, a descendant of Captain Hobart-Hampden; Mr. E. N. Brandt, senior editor, *The Saturday Evening Post*, for background material on the Civil War; Mr. Bill Sharpe, publisher, *The State Magazine*, Raleigh, N.C.; Mr. E. S. Dodge, director, Peabody Museum, Salem, Mass.; Mr. Christopher Crittenden, director, North Carolina State Department of Archives and History; Mr. Milton C. Russell, Virginia State Library, Richmond, Va.; Virginia Rugheimer, librarian, Charleston Library Society; Mr. John L. Lochead, librarian, The Mariners Museum, Newport News, Va.

Also I wish to express my special thanks to the following authors and their publishers for granting me permission to quote directly from their works or to use quotations of others appearing in their books:

Mr. Alfred Hoyt Bill, author of *The Beleaguered City*, Alfred A. Knopf, Inc., New York.

Louis A. Sigaud, author of *Belle Boyd, Confederate Spy*, Dietz Press, Richmond.

Mrs. John Richie, III, of Evanston, Ill., for permission to quote from *Recollections of a Rebel Reefer*, by James Morris Morgan, Houghton-Mifflin Co., New York.

Mr. Frank H. Wardlaw, director, University of Texas Press, for permission to quote from *Blockade Running Through Bermuda, 1861-65*, edited by Frank E. Van Diver.

Ishbell Ross, author of *Rebel Rose*, Harper and Brother, New York.

R. S. West, author of *Gideon Welles*, The Bobbs-Merrill Company, Indianapolis.

Otto Eisenschiml and Ralph Newman, authors of *The American Iliad*, The Bobbs-Merrill Company, Indianapolis.

Mary Boykin Chesnut, *A Diary from Dixie*, Appleton-Century-Crofts, Inc.

Index